Story as a Way of Knowing

Kevin M. Bradt, S.J.

Sheed & Ward
Kansas City

Sheed & Ward™ is a service of The National Catholic Reporter Publishing Company.

Library of Congress Cataloguing-in-Publication Data
Bradt, Kevin M.
　　Story as a way of knowing / Kevin M. Bradt.
　　　　p.　cm.
　　Includes bibliographical references and index.
　　ISBN: 1-55612-906-8　(alk. paper)
　　　1. Storytelling—Religious aspects—Christianity.　2. Knowledge.
　　Theory of (Religion)　I. Title.
　　BT83.78.B73　1997
　　230'.01—dc21　　　　　　　　　　　　　　　　　　　96-53175
　　　　　　　　　　　　　　　　　　　　　　　　　　　　　　CIP

Published by: Sheed & Ward
　　　　　　　　115 E. Armour Blvd.
　　　　　　　　P.O. Box 419492
　　　　　　　　Kansas City, MO 64141-6492

To order, call: (800) 333-7373

Contents

Dedication

To the first storytellers in my life:
Jack, Renee, and Jackson

Acknowledgments

I WOULD FIRST LIKE TO THANK THE NEW YORK PROVINCE OF THE Society of Jesus for its generous support during my years of studies and clinical training. Thank you to the people of St. Anthony's, St. Augustine's, St. Francis de Sales, and Our Lady of the Redwoods for their love of story.

At the University of California, Berkeley, and the Graduate Theological Union, I had the privilege of being taught by master teachers: Dunbar Ogden, Rhoda Kaufman, Stan Lai, L. J. Duhl, Cynthia Winton-Henry, Margie Brown, and the late James Luguri. Other scholars taught me with their wisdom and friendship: the late Dan O'Hanlon, Frank Houdek, Georgina LaRussa, Ann Marie Hayes, Bob Lawton, J. P. Reynolds, Tony Moore, the Ambrosios, the Pascullis, the Finns, David Epston, and my colleagues at the Redwood Center Psychology Associates.

If anyone deserves a "genius" award, it is Michael Moynahan. Working with Moyna and the Berkeley Liturgical Drama Guild (BLDG) changed my life, my faith, and my imagination. Thank you to my fellow players in BLDG – Andy Utiger, Kathleen Tighe, Kay Lane, Richard Maggi, the Kosowskis, Trese Kelly, Martha Ann Kirk – and to my Loretto family who keep me sane and laughing.

Jo Milgrom was the midwife of this work. An extraordinary teacher and artist, she opened the treasures of Judaism to me. I didn't know how much I had missed the riches of the Jewish heart, mind, and soul until I found them. Thank you also to Dan Matt for his help in my study of midrash.

Finally, this book would never have been published without the enthusiastic intercession of Rose Lucey; the patience of Bob Heyer and Andy Apathy at Sheed & Ward; and the hard work, careful craftsmanship, and encouragement of my editor, Jean Blomquist.

This book is dedicated to my family. Another member of that family is Bill Cain. Being part of their story has been the greatest blessing of my life.

Grateful acknowledgment is given for copyright permissions as follows:

Excerpts from *Surplus Powerlessness: The Psychodynamics of Everyday Life and the Psychology of Individual and Social Transformation*, by Michael Lerner, copyright© 1986. Used by permission of The Institute for Labor and Mental Health.

Excerpts from the Foreword by Jerome Bruner are reprinted from *The Freudian Metaphor*, by Donald Spence. Copyright© 1987. Used by permission of W.W. Norton and Company.

Excerpts from "Writing is a Technology that Restructures Thought," by Walter Ong are reprinted from *The Written Word: Literacy in Transition*, edited by Gerd Baumann. Copyright© 1986. Used by permission of Oxford University Press.

Excerpts from *Hope Within History*, by Walter Brueggemann. ©1987 John Knox Press. Used by permission of Westminster John Knox press.

Excerpts reprinted from The Creative Word, by Walter Brueggemann, copyright© 1982 Fortress Press. Used by permission of Augsburg Fortress.

Excerpts reprinted by permission from Texts Under Negotiation, by Walter Brueggemann, copyright© 1993 Augsburg Fortress.

Excerpts from *Uncertainty: The Life and Science of Werner Heisenberg*, by David Cassidy. ©1992 by David Cassidy. Used with permission of W.H. Freeman and Company.

Excerpts from *Post-modernism and the Social Sciences: Insights, Inroads, and Intrusions*, by Pauline Rosenau, copyright© 1992 Princeton University Press. Permission is in process.

Excerpts from *Hammer on the Rock: A Short Midrash Reader*, edited by Nahum N. Glatzer, copyright© 1962 Schocken Books. Used by permission of the Glatzer family.

Excerpts from *Orality and Literacy: The Technologizing of the Word*, by Walter Ong, copyright© 1982 Methuen & Company. Permission from Methuen & Company is in process.

Excerpts from *Principles of Visual Perception*, 2d edition, by Carolyn Bloomer, copyright© 1990 Design Press. Used by permission of TAB/McGraw Hill.

Excerpts from *Back to the Sources*, edited by Barry Holtz, copyright© 1984 Summit Books. Permission from Simon & Schuster is in process.

Introduction

IN THE ROMAN CATHOLIC WORLD OF MY CHILDHOOD, I LIVED IN a world of feasts and seasons, mysteries and miracles, saints and angels, each located in elaborate stories and legends of magical realism that could be visited throughout the day via images, prayers, and rituals. Bible stories were heard at morning Mass and contemplated again at night during the family rosary. Our home in Queens was equipped with candles, icons, statues, kits for Extreme Unction, blessed palms, saints' relics, Advent wreaths, and pictures of Pope Pius XII (and for some reason, J. Edgar Hoover!) – all reminders that we dwelt in a cosmic drama across space and time in which the salvation of the world was at stake.

To this mythic sensibility, add (a) a clan of Irish relatives with a Celtic charism for storytelling; (b) two parents, gifted actors both, who coached us through family productions of Shakespeare's plays; and (c) a brother who told epic cycles of bedtime tales in which G.I. Joe and the Fighting 69th could come to the aid of Peter Pan and Tiger Lily in saving NeverNeverLand from the likes of John Wilkes Booth and the pirates of Treasure Island. In short, it would be fair to say that I grew up in a world of stories and storytellers.

But it wasn't until decades later that I became aware of how powerful and pervasive story can be in people's lives. That awareness came about, when as priest, preacher, and actor, I was completing my theological training by day, acting with the Boston Shakespeare Company by night, and preaching and presiding at worship on weekends. I began to notice something similar happening among theater audiences when I stood onstage telling the story of Romeo and Juliet as I did among parishioners when I stood in the pulpit telling the story of the Prodigal Son or the Woman at the

Well – a change in consciousness, a surrendering of defenses, a caring for the characters, a release of empathy and emotion, a creative engagement with the imagination.

Even with those who came to the rectory for counseling, I noticed how lives, relationships, problems, all were structured as stories, some that stretched back across time and culture and seemed to repeat themselves in every generation, often with the same disastrous consequences. Sadly I learned that some people could not even imagine changing the stories they were born into, no matter how much they suffered as a result. Nor did some even want to change the story. They only wanted me to hear their story and to understand.

When I had the opportunity to pursue doctoral studies, I knew I wanted to understand the power of story and how it shaped knowing, and what, if any, were the implications for our culture as a whole. How did story affect change? And why did people retain what they learned as story for years and years? What could I learn about story?

Story is arguably one of the oldest and most elemental forms of knowing. Story as a technique of knowing was eclipsed in the West, however, with the rise of "modern" scientific method in the seventeenth century. In fact, it is basically that shift in the dominance of epistemologies – from story to science – that defines the advent of the modern mind. During the last three centuries, the so-called "modern" era, story as a way of knowing was considered an inferior remnant of a "premodern" (or "nonmodern") consciousness, a "backward" kind of thinking, a primitive entertainment fit only for children, the illiterate, and the uneducated. In a postmodern age, however, ways of knowing and relating that were once dismissed as hopelessly premodern or nonmodern are enjoying something of a revival or rehabilitation, and among them, story most of all.

Story, then, is not just a frill, an illustration, a diversion, or an entertainment, as the modern scientific mindset maintained. Instead, story is much more basic. It is a way by which and through which we come to know and understand ourselves, others, the world around us, and even God. This book, then, is an exploration of story and how it structures our thought and, by extension, our lives.

Before I review what we will explore in the chapters ahead, I want to make a few brief explanatory comments on the term "storying," which I use throughout this book. By "storying" I mean the making of stories together, the thinking together in story form, and the cocreation of stories by tellers and listeners. I generally use the word "storying" rather than the more conventional "storytelling," because the latter term locates the action in the one telling. This perpetuates the mistaken notion that the listeners are merely passive recipients of the word, who do not influence, shape, or affect in any way the teller, the telling, or the tale. When I do use the term "storytelling," it is in conjunction with "storylistening" or "storyhearing" to indicate the inseparability and interaction of the two. Further, "storytelling" continues to be perceived as "child's play." When used in bibliographic searches, it calls up topics such as children's literature in primary education, juvenile literature, children's story hours in libraries, and so on. This indicates how the "modern" mind still conceives of story as something for the entertainment of children and not for the serious consideration of mature adults.

Now for a brief overview of this book. Story, I maintain, is not only a form of language but a modality, or way, of knowing that affects both what is known and the knower. Knowledge is shaped and affected by the "technologies" (e.g., spoken or written forms) it employs. We will, therefore, explore the epistemological differences among knowledge acquired through oral-aural "storying," writing, and print. Not only is the nature of knowing different in each of these respective technologies, but so is the nature, quality, and characteristics of the truth known.

In Chapter One, we will focus first on the relational dynamics and oral-aural interplay that occurs between storyteller and storylistener as they come to know the world, the self, and the other through their storying. Then we will examine how participation in storying not only implies but facilitates the restorying of self, past, present, and future. In story, both listener and teller imaginatively "leave" the constituted self to enter an alternative storyworld constructed from different hypotheses, assumptions, presuppositions, and possibilities. This imaginative journey concludes with the return to the self, but now a changed self, a self changed in and through the cocreative interaction of storying with another. This storying and restorying is what ultimately makes healing and hope possible.

Unlike the language and method of science, story does not claim to "represent" reality; instead it seeks to explore it, to consider its possible meanings and significances. This is possible in a world where reality is open, unknown, indeterminate, irreducible, where it is always "more," "other," "different," in short, mysterious. Mystery invites inquiry rather than definition, erotic participation rather than geometric proof, relationship rather than reason, pursuit rather than purchase. Therefore, we will also examine storying as that way of knowing which views reality as a coevolving mystery and a dialogue partner in the making and remaking of meaning.

The technologies of writing and print, however, encouraged other modes of knowing, modes that drastically changed the relationship between the knower and the known. Print-based technologies – from books to computers and word-processing software – were eventually dubbed "modern" and accorded normative status. Knowledge was now derived from interacting with a text, not another person. And that text was the product of one person writing in isolation in one particular moment in space and time. Texts broke loose from their original contexts and from the immediacy of interpersonal relationships. The printed word acquired a primacy and power that the spoken word never had nor could have.

Printed words endured, staying exactly the same regardless of changing circumstances. In fact, the printed word prided itself on being impervious to the flux and flow of reader and reality. Print assured stasis, continuity, stability, permanence, fixity. The truth today, yesterday, and tomorrow – always and forever the same! Print would not endure or tolerate persons "playing" with truth. Print removed truth from the conversations of people, from their speaking and listening. Truth was *in* the words, words fixed on a page, the words of a printed text. Truth was not in dialogue or the crafting and refining of knowledge, not in the amplifying and modifying of thought; the tempering and clarifying of opinions; the revising and modulating of belief. Gone was the give-and-take of storying, the constructive play of language, the exchange of ideas interacting with each other, the cocreation of shared truth and meaning. The printed text needed none of that. Nor did it need anyone to "speak" with. It simply needed to be read – silently. It was what it was: *the* truth – no longer wild, untamed, or elusive but stuffed and mounted on a wall of paper, an object to be observed and admired, not hunted or stalked, coaxed or wooed, especially now that it was "objective." With the imperialism of print as the preferred technology of "modern" knowledge, truth became identified with text, text as product, norm, and object. Truth was no longer an interpersonal process.

In Chapter Two, we will turn to Thomas Kuhn and the reevaluation of truth, texts, and knowledge that he introduced with his work on paradigms. We will consider Kuhn's own story about storying and how he came to rethink his "modern" understandings of the operations of truth and knowledge in the history of science. Kuhn personally experienced a "paradigm shift" in his own way of thinking, which then led him to propose the model of "paradigms" in understanding scientific revolutions. Kuhn's advancement of paradigms is ultimately a hermeneutical, or interpretive, move that reintroduces the relational importance between content and context, truth and perspective, product and process. In other words, Kuhn's main achievement is a reappraisal of "modern" modes of knowing and a reintroduction of elements of a narrative epistemology (i.e., story as a way of knowing) into contemporary discourse.

Chapters Three and Four will trace how epistemologies produce paradigms, paradigms shape theories, and theories influence practice. Both will focus on the changing nature of knowing and relating within different paradigms as practiced in the field of psychotherapy during the last one hundred years.

In Chapter Three, we will examine the function, purpose, and value of paradigms, together with their advantages and limitations. We will pay particular attention to the change in meaning of the word and concept *scientia* from the medieval to the modern era and to how the change in technologies affected modalities of knowing and methods of discourse and inquiry. We shall then examine the influence of modern scientific method and its offshoot, empirical positivism, on the theory and technique of Freud and the cybernetic systems thinking of family therapists mid-twentieth century.

In Chapter Four, we will examine elements of the postmodern critique, their role in the deconstruction of modern thought, and changing attitudes toward the nature of language. Postmodernism resents and condemns the misrepresentation of reality by the representational language of modern science. It prefers story instead because of story's humility and circumspection regarding truth claims about external reality. We will then consider the recovery of story in the postmodern narrative therapy of Michael White and David Epston in the 1980s. These various approaches to therapy develop from and within the context of different historical and epistemological paradigms that shape, influence, facilitate, and limit what can be said, known, and practiced. The work of White and Epston highlights the importance of narrative ways of knowing and relating in discourse and inquiry today.

Chapter Five examines the work of Walter Brueggemann and his study of story, speech, and rhetoric in the Hebrew scriptures. For Brueggemann, what is said in those scriptures is not as important as how it is said; for how it is said affects what can be thought and imagined, dared and dreamed, told and heard. Throughout his career, Brueggemann has called our attention to how story can create an alternative imagination, not only in individuals, but also within a community. If some "other" storyworld can be imagined, then the absolute ideological "totalism," to use Robert J. Lifton's term, of the dominant culture as the sole referent of reality is undermined. The overdetermining power of the status quo is destabilized and a closed future broken open with possibility. If an alternate future can be imagined, then hope can be kindled in the present and action taken now to make that future possibility a reality today. That, in turn, can recontextualize the meaning of the past and re-open questions about the judgments of history. In its ability to transform action and imagination, together with our understanding of events in the past, present, and future, story can then be viewed as a radical change agent.

In Chapter Six we continue with an examination of the roots of postmodern inquiry and understanding in the soil of the midrashic tradition of Judaism. In a world of Gentiles, a Jew was always "other," most often, *the* other – suspect, different, alien, peculiar, uncommon. This "otherness" was not a matter of mere externals; it was epistemological. Let the Greek mind (and its many descendants in the Western tradition) get all the glory for inventing logic, science, mathematics, geometry, astronomy, philosophy, rationalism, or empiricism. The Jew thought, imagined, questioned, wondered, and knew differently. When bushes burst into flame, the Jew did not think to measure the angles of the branches or the intensity of the flame's heat but removed his shoes, listened, heard, and knew that he was on holy ground. When seas parted, the Jew did not calculate the pull of the planets on the tides; she broke into song and danced her way across starfish and seashell to the safety of dry land and deliverance.

But most of all, the Jew told stories about all these things – from generation to generation. And when the Book of Stories was closed, the Jew told stories about those stories, not because the Jew couldn't master other means of knowing, but because the Jew knew that a mind all logic was like a knife all blade: it cuts the one who wields it. In Judaism, a story about a story is called a "midrash," and much of Jewish thought and law is formulated and communicated as midrash. Therefore, in Chapter Six, we will examine how and why the Jewish mind thinks, perceives, and organizes reality according to the structures of story and why this kind of intentionally non-Greek, non-Western narrative epistemology is especially appealing to postmodernists today.

In Chapter Seven, I will present several story-homilies that I have composed as, if you will, Christian midrash. They are stories about the stories from scripture used in the lectionary cycles of the Roman Catholic liturgy. I offer them here as examples of how the same narrative epistemology described throughout this work can be practiced (and literally preached) in a church of the postmodern world. Along with these story-homilies, I will provide some contextual comments to situate their telling within a place, time, and community.

In the Conclusion, I first will summarize the main points of our exploration. Then I will offer conclusions concerning this study of narrative epistemology.

This book, then, rather ironically uses the written word to draw together threads from science, psychotherapy, scripture, and homiletics that can help us recognize and reclaim the power of oral-aural storying as a way of knowing. I hope it will open your minds and imaginations to new ways of thinking and knowing about yourselves, others, the world, and your God. To close this introduction and begin our journey of reclaiming story as a way of knowing, I'd like to share a story from *Tales of the Hasidim,*[1] as recounted by Martin Buber:

> A rabbi, whose grandfather had been a disciple of the Baal Shem Tov, was asked to tell a story. "A story," he said, "must be told in such a way that it constitutes help in itself."
>
> And he told: "My grandfather was lame. Once they asked him to tell a story about his teacher. And he related how the holy Baal Shem used to hop and dance while he prayed. My grandfather rose as he spoke, and he was so swept away by his story that he himself began to hop and dance to show how the master had done it. From that hour on he was cured of his lameness."

Now that's the way to tell a story.

---

1. Martin Buber, *Tales of the Hasidim: The Early Masters* (New York: Schocken Books, 1978), v-vi.

Part One

Story as a Way of Knowing

Chapter One

From Storying to Printed Text

"TO A MAN WITH A HAMMER," AN OLD ADAGE ASSERTS, "EVERY-thing looks like a nail." How we know the world, that is, by what means, medium, or modality, determines not only what we know but also what we can know. How we communicate determines how we relate. A specific way of knowing results in a specific way of being and relating. Through my eyes, I see and know the world as image; through my ears, I hear and know the world as sound. With straightedge, the world is linear; with ruler, segmented, numerical, divisible; with compass, circular, revolving around a fixed point; with pro-tractor, spherical, comprised of inscribed arcs, angles, and degrees. Therefore, how we know – what Jacques Ellul calls the "technique" of our knowing – structures thought. Eric Havelock observes something quite similar: "Technologies of communication . . . exercise a large measure of control over the content of what is communicated."[1] Thus, how we speak determines how we think, what we can know, and what we can say. As Werner Kelber puts it, "Human consciousness is structured into thought by available forms of communica-tion. Thinking is indebted to the medium through which knowledge is acquired."[2]

As a medium of communication, story structures thought. In other words, story is not just an art form but an epistemology, a technique or way of knowing the world, the

---

1. Eric Havelock, *The Muse Learns to Write: Reflections on Oral-ity and Literacy from Antiquity to the Present* (New Haven: Yale University Press, 1986), 27.
2. Werner Kelber, *The Oral and Written Gospel: The Hermeneu-tics of Speaking and Writing in the Synoptic Tradition, Mark, Paul, and Q* (Philadelphia: Fortress Press, 1983), xv.

self, and the other. Story as way of knowing shapes our ways of interacting and relating.

Storying: Interplay between the Spoken and the Heard

The most basic and elemental mode of knowing is story as oral-aural (spoken-heard) interplay, or what I call "storying." Storying is the telling and hearing of stories as a mutually creative, interactive language-event. Storying is an action of contemporaneous interchange, happening here and now as "ongoing part of ongoing existence,"[3] in which participants – storytellers and storylisteners – come together in a relationship of reciprocal oral-aural play and imagination for the cocreative constructing, inhabiting, and exploring of shared alternative storyworlds.

Story as Literature: The Written and the Read

The mode of knowing communicated by literature is very different from that of storying. Literature is narrative preserved as a written text in fixed, final form. It is read apart from any interpersonal contexts or relationships that may have first contributed to its creation. I introduce this distinction here because storying as oral-aural interplay and story as literature utilize and express processes of human thought and consciousness that are quite different from one another. Therefore, it will be necessary to consider some of the key psychodynamic differences between orality and literacy as they affect the nature of human knowing and relating.

Walter Ong believes that "more than any other single invention, writing has transformed human consciousness."[4] Also, "the fact that we do not commonly feel the influence of writing on our thoughts shows that we have interiorized the technology of writing so deeply that without tremendous effort we cannot separate it from ourselves or even recognize its presence and influence."[5] Ong illustrates this point in his

---

3. Ibid.
4. Walter Ong, *Orality and Literacy: The Technologizing of the Word* (London: Methuen, 1982), 78.
5. Walter Ong, "Writing is a Technology that Restructures

description of functionally literate human beings as "beings whose thought processes do not grow out of simply natural powers but out of these powers as structured, directly or indirectly, by the technology of writing. Without writing, the literate mind would not and could not think as it does, not only when engaged in writing but normally even when it is composing its thoughts in oral form."[6] The literate, therefore, do not simply think and speak but think and speak in ways that are shaped and defined by a specific mode of literacy; that is, they think and speak chirographically, typographically, and now electronically.[7]

Ways of Knowing and Encounters with the Real

Each mode of story, oral-aural as well as textual, emerges in human consciousness as a very different encounter with reality. The oral-aural mode does so by forming a "critical bond"[8] among people through their interaction together in a world that is "oral, mobile, warm, personally interactive (you [need] live people to produce spoken words)."[9] Story as literature only needs a written text which "establishes what has been called 'context-free' language or 'autonomous' discourse, discourse which cannot be directly questioned or contested as oral speech can be because written discourse has been detached from its author."[10] Each, in turn, shapes and creates very different worlds of possibilities in the human imagination because of the different values and hermeneutics (methods of interpretation) they employ.

Some stories in this book, such as the Bible stories of Chapter Five and the midrash stories of Chapter Six, although originally oral-aural in their creation, development, and transmission, survive today primarily in written form

---

Thought," in *The Written Word: Literacy in Transition* (Wolfson College Lectures 1985), ed. Gerd Baumann (Oxford: Clarendon Press, 1986), 24.

6. Ong, *Orality and Literacy,* 78.
7. Ong, "Writing," 24.
8. Viv Edwards and Thomas Sienkewicz, *Oral Cultures Past and Present: Rappin' and Homer* (Oxford: Basil Blackwell, 1990), 12.
9. Ong, "Writing," 29.
10. Ong, *Orality and Literacy,* 78.

as literatures unto themselves. However, Ong reminds us that, while writing down stories assures their endurance and availability across space and time, they can only be reactivated, made present again through oral speech and sound. "The written text, for all its permanence, means nothing, is not even a text, except in relationship to the spoken word. For a text to be intelligible, to deliver its message, it must be reconverted into sound, directly or indirectly, either really in the external world or in the auditory imagination. All verbal expression, whether put into writing, print, or the computer, is ineluctably bound to sound forever."[11]

The work of such scholars as Ellul, Ong, Havelock, Milman Parry, Albert Lord, Jack Goody, Marshall McLuhan, and Ivan Illich has done much to reclaim the oral-aural dynamics of story as humankind's primary and oldest mode of communicating, thinking, knowing, and relating. Perhaps Ong articulates this best when he states that human consciousness is first oral. "It is the oral word that first illuminates consciousness with articulate language, that first divides subject and predicate and then relates them to one another, and that ties human beings to one another in society."[12]

This is true both ontogenetically (as individual human beings) and phylogenetically (as a species of social beings in community).[13] Each of us is born into a world that is at first wholly oral-aural. As fetal research has demonstrated, our first experiences of the world are oral-aural, beginning even before we are born.[14] As newborns in the delivery room, we are able to distinguish the sound of our mother's voice from other noises assaulting us. Sound guides sight as the infant's unfocused eyes track and follow that sound until a visual-oral-aural association is made.[15] Entry into the literate world follows only much later when we have developed the

---

11. Ong, "Writing," 31.
12. Ong, *Orality and Literacy,* 178-79.
13. Ibid.
14. T. Berry Brazelton and Bertrand Cramer, *The Earliest Relationship: Parents, Infants, and the Drama of Early Attachment* (Reading, MA: Addison-Wesley Publishing Company, 1990), 26, 28, 29.
15. Ibid., 53.

necessary physical, intellectual, and technological capacities and abilities to read and to write.

This natural human predisposition to orality is true in our development as a species as well. Since the emergence of *homo sapiens* between 50,000 B.C.E. and 30,000 B.C.E., most human beings have experienced the world as exclusively oral. Script was only developed fairly late, around 3500 B.C.E.[16] "The oldest script, Mesopotamian cuneiform, is less than 6,000 years old (the alphabet less than 4,000)."[17] Prior to that, all culture was orally based. Thought and knowledge of every kind was embodied, preserved, and communicated orally for millennia.

> Of all the tens of thousands of languages spoken in the course of human history only a tiny fraction . . . have ever been committed to writing to a degree sufficient to have produced a literature, and most have never been written at all. Of the 4,000 or so languages spoken today, only around 78 have a literature. . . . Those who think of the text as the paradigm of all discourse need to face the fact that only the tiniest fraction of languages have ever been written or ever will be. Most have disappeared or are fast disappearing, untouched by textuality. Hardcore textualism is snobbery, often hardly disguised.[18]

Spoken language is, therefore, primary and necessarily prior to writing. This is because all written texts "have to be related somehow, directly or indirectly, to the world of sound, the natural habitat of language, to yield their meanings. . . . Writing can never dispense with orality. . . . Oral expression can exist and mostly has existed without any writing at all, writing never exists without orality."[19]

This predisposition to oral-aural expression as primary consciousness also prompts us to think in personal, experiential, and narrative forms because they are easier to retain and remember. According to Ong, "Primary oral culture also keeps its thinking close to the human life world, personalizing things and issues, and storing knowledge in stories. Categories are unstable mnemonically. Stories you can re-

---

16. Ong, *Orality and Literacy,* 2, 83-84.
17. Ong, "Writing," 26.
18. Ibid.
19. Ong, *Orality and Literacy,* 8.

member. In its typical mindset, the oral sensibility is out to hold things together, to make and retain agglomerates, not to analyse (which means to take things apart). . . ."[20]

Does Story Exist?

There is, of course, one basic problem with the spoken story. It doesn't exist, at least, not as we define existence today. Story is not material but rather merest ephemera: air, sound, silence; the exhalation of breath whistling through contracted muscles in the throat; tongue touching teeth; and tiny conchlike bones vibrating in the ear. Unlike the printed word, typeset forever on acid-free paper in **BOLD 10 POINT PICA TYPE**, sure, certain, fixed, the oral story has no existence in or of itself but must rely on the kindness of strangers speaking and hearing its words. Once spoken, the oral story, like Prospero's "insubstantial pageant," passes out of existence, leaving "not a rack behind" (Shakespeare, *The Tempest,* 4.1.155, 156). The story over, it returns to the silence from which it came. Only an echoing in the ear and the memory of the listener remain.

> If functionally literate persons are asked to think of the word "nevertheless," they will all have present in imagination the letters of the word – vaguely perhaps, but unavoidably – in handwriting or typescript or print. If they are asked to think of the word "nevertheless" for two minutes, 120 seconds, without ever allowing any letters at all to enter their imaginations, they cannot comply. A person from a completely oral background of course has no such problem. He or she will think only of the real word, a sequence of sounds, "ne-ver-the-less." For the real word "nevertheless," the sounded word, cannot ever be present all at once, as written words deceptively seem to be. Sound exists only when it is going out of existence. By the time I get to the "the-less," the "ne-ver" is gone. To the extent that it makes all of a word appear present at once, writing falsifies.[21]

---

20. Ong, "Writing," 25.
21. Ibid., 24-25.

Thus, if you will permit me a neologism, the paradoxical mystery of storytelling is that it exists only in its own "ex-[s]piration." In other words, story achieves its own unique purpose and becomes most itself only in the action of its ceasing to exist, at least as material reality. Let me explain. The sound of the spoken story, which is its only material form, comes into existence with the exhalation or "ex-[s]piring" of breath through the vibrating vocal chords of the storyteller. And with the "ex-[s]piration" of story also comes its expiration. Sound passes out of existence into silence.

But, even then, the dynamic reality that is "storying" is still not yet born. For, unless those sounds sent by the storyteller are received by the storylistener, they are nothing but noise. That transformation from sound into story begins to happen in the still nothingness of silence that follows speech. As with so much of transformative experience, story becomes most itself only when it allows itself to pass out of its own exclusive form of material existence into something dynamic. Thus, it is in the silence in which "sound-transmitted" is transformed into "sound-received" that story is born.

> A word is an event, a happening, not a thing, as letters make it appear to be. So is thought: "This is paper" is an occurrence, an event in time. We grasp truth articulately only in events. Articulated truth has no permanence. *Full truth is deeper than articulation.* We find it hard to recognize this obvious truth, so deeply has the fixity of the written word taken possession of our consciousness.[22]

Story: Truth beyond Articulation

The ability to "say" more than what is articulated or pronounced, the ability to suggest countless possible meanings in what is *not* said is what distinguishes the oral-aural story as an epistemology and gives it its own unique purpose and distinctive identity. The truth that emerges from storying is not *in* the words, for they never exist in and of themselves as the written story does on the page. Nor is the truth of storying ever complete, exhaustive, final. Because it resists

---

22. Ibid., 25. Emphasis added.

confinement in any durable material reality, because there is no actual printed text in which it is located or contained as object, the truth of storying transcends its own articulation and exists in the space *between* teller and listener, knower and known. Neither owns it singly, individually, privately. Rather, it is held between them, shared, cocreated.

Story as Relationship

The truth of oral-aural storying is coevolved as in a relationship, and, as with any relationship, neither participant can make decisions about it independently or unilaterally without destroying the mutuality of meaning and trust that sustains it. As long as each respects the conditions of this knowing-as-relationship, this truth will continue to yield more and more of itself; there will always be more to know, to hear, to say, to discern, to consider. As with husband and wife, lover and beloved, friend and companion, the truth of story grows or contracts, deepens or surfaces, *with* the relationship of teller and listener. It cannot be separated or abstracted from the relationship. If either teller or listener breaks off this relationship, the "critical bond" of interacting through storying miscarries and ceases, and the particular telling of *this* story to *this* listener at *this* time in *this* context is left forever uncompleted and stillborn. In effect, the story is not heard; the story is not told.

Storying as an epistemology or way of knowing, thus, exists as an interpersonal transaction within a relationship that is constantly being reconfigured, changed, and recontextualized by the exchange of the "story-spoken" and the "story-heard," the meaning meant and the meaning interpreted. This particular process of communication also structures consciousness interpersonally in a way quite different from writing and print.

Knowledge as Relational

Those involved in the act of oral-aural storying are not only sharing the denotative content or digital communication conveyed by words and language, but are also doing so in a live, immediate, simultaneous, face-to-face meeting. The relational information or analogical communication conveyed in this way affects and changes what is spoken and what is heard moment by moment.[23] Words printed on a page never change, no matter how they are mumbled, mangled, or mouthed. But "textless" words, those spoken, change with every hesitation, pause, breath, and sigh.

In the interdependent transaction of storying, what is really being exchanged is the gift of "knowledge-as-personal-presence": knowledge that is living, dynamic, and changing with the relationship between knower and known. In other words, "storied" knowledge is supremely and essentially relational. The relationship of teller and listener affects each act of storying and shapes the context of the knowing as well as the content of what is known.

Attending: Alternate Values of Knowing

In storying, as with any erotic endeavor, from sexuality to prayer, from mysticism to art, mere physical "attendance" is not enough. Those present must instead "attend" to what is happening: attention must be paid. Forgotten repertoires of "attending skills" from that time before the "modern" mind objectified the world must be remembered and reinvoked. From the exile imposed upon them by the rule of science, such epistemological attitudes as respect and reverence; wonder, awe, astonishment; devotion, honor, fidelity; adoration, worship, thanksgiving must be summoned home to the realms of knowing. They must be gathered back from their banishment among what Michel Foucault calls the "subjugated knowledges"[24] of "premodern" history and "primitive" cultures. Agency and availability must be practiced by both participants in knowing together: for how one receives in storying directly affects what the other can give and how one gives directly affects what the other can receive.

---

23. Paul Watzlawick, Janet Beavin Bavelas, and Don Jackson, *Pragmatics of Human Communication: A Study of Interactional Patterns, Pathologies, and Paradoxes* (New York: W. W. Norton, 1967), 60-67.

24. Michel Foucault, *Power/Knowledge: Selected Interviews and Other Writings* (New York: Pantheon Books, 1980), 82-84.

In this way, teller and listener, giver and receiver, are both actively participating in mutual exchange and self-disclosure through their reciprocal experience and cocreative undertaking of storying together. They need each other to achieve what they could not do by themselves: to give and to receive in their telling and listening to one another.

Storying, thus, unites teller and listener together in an event of shared experience, experience that is different but complementary. Together they create a story *between* them, but they do so as teller and listener, and, therefore, with different purposes, tasks, and obligations. Thus, while both are engaged in the unfolding of a single reality between them in which both partake, contribute, and interact, this same single reality does not reveal itself singly or identically to listener and teller. Instead this single reality, created not by the one or the other but by both parties together, is perceived multiply, that is, in different ways according to the attunement, mode, and acuity of the different senses – sound, hearing – mediating that reality.

Here again, we see what is distinctive about storying as epistemology. Knowledge that comes in and through the action of storying is mediated as a holographic whole: that is, it is formed by the dynamic interacting of parts together and reveals itself from multiple perspectives and dimensions through multiple modalities simultaneously. Any attempt to isolate, analyze, or separate out any of the individual operations of this contemporaneous contextual event of knowing would destroy the singleness and unity of the experience; it is, by its very nature and constitution, intrinsically multimodal and must be grasped as such. Forms of knowing that operate according to formal analytic, abstract, and contextless categories, when applied to the interactional dynamics of storying, completely distort and destroy what they would study.[25] As with most forced conversions, the violence and methods used often maim what they would remake, kill what they would cure, thus losing what they would save.

---

25. These modes of thought can be applied with great benefit to story, but only *after* story has passed from existence as an event of personal presence and interaction into that of a discrete fixed object of study with material form and shape, as in a text.

> Oral cultures of course have no dictionaries and few
> semantic discrepancies. The meaning of each word is
> controlled by . . . the real-life situations in which the
> word is used here and now. The oral mind is uninter-
> ested in definitions. Words acquire their meanings
> only from their always insistent actual habitat, which
> is not, as in a dictionary, simply other words, but
> includes also gestures, vocal inflections, facial expres-
> sions, and the entire human, existential setting in
> which the real, spoken word always occur. Word
> meanings come continuously out of the present. . . .[26]

Thus, the oral-aural story cannot exist without both the
engagement and participation of teller and listener together.
But each must serve it differently, namely, in the ways they
have been called: that is, one by telling, the other by listening.

Storying: Mutual Revelation of the Self

But something else always happens in the process of storying, something inherent in the way story structures consciousness. In serving the story in their own different but
complementary ways, by their mutual listening and telling,
the speaker and hearer of stories are also serving one another. For, as they discover in the practice of storying together, what is being told and heard are not just elements of
the narrative plot but parts or aspects of themselves that
were previously unknown, parts of themselves not heard or
told before *this* encounter with the story and each other.

By actually lending their own bodies and senses to
become the physical substance and matter of the story as it
is sounded and heard in the world, the teller and the listener
become part (and partners) of the story and each other.
Together, they form the medium of the story, a single medium comprised of the interconnection and transference of
the differentiating energies between them. Together, they
are the story's sole and unique embodiment in *this* moment;
there is no other. As the story comes through them into
existence, it comes through not just their mouths and ears
but through their whole "bodies-of-experience" as well, firing

---

26. Ong, *Orality and Literacy,* 47.

neurons and synapses where memories are housed. As the story passes through them, physically changing them (and their brains) in the process, the story also accumulates unique resonances from their lives and experience. Story and experience thus mix together and commingle in the storying process and leave indelible traces with each other, so that neither story nor experience can be known again without memories and associations of the other.

Story as a form of knowing, then, "thickens" with each telling and listening. Why? Because each telling and listening of a story now also includes all previous tellings and hearings as well. Content is shaped by context; and the content of each new act of storying is comprised of the contexts of all previous tellings.

Creating New Storyworlds

Each act of storying creates a "brave new storyworld" that enfolds all previous tellings and tellers, listenings and listeners within it. The reception and passing on of story changes all of them, both the stories themselves and those who tell and listen to them. In the world of story, such change is not perceived either as defect or loss but as the enhancement of being that comes with aging, use, and wear in nature, just as wrinkles etch character in faces, washings soften cloth, and handling darkens leather. Each enactment enriches what embodies it. Thus, the story itself changes, together with those who enact and embody it in their tellings and hearings. They become part of each other: the story in its tellers and listeners; the tellers and listeners in the story.

Storying affects what it signifies. Through the act of storying, two separate and distinct persons, each with his or her life-story, are brought together into a new relationship with each other, with themselves, and with their own lives. Two life-stories interpenetrate each other and create a third: namely, the life-story of two now joined in a single act of collaboration and creation. This new story of relationship not only includes both teller and listener in a jointly shared, if differently perceived, world; it also recontextualizes all their own previous self-narrations and experience. This inevitable "supercollision" of personal life-stories and storyworlds in the act of storying together creates something new and wholly different. Storying produces a third entity in the ex-[s]piring of separate differentiating subjectivities and creates a different whole, an alternative storyworld, where a new quantum reality is born, one that can only exist in the joint intersubjectivity of all participants. Now, in the act of imagining the story together, storytellers and storylisteners are also imagining themselves anew.

The imagining of story, thus, overflows into the reimagining of self, the world, and others. This change occurs because the story event activates the imagination, which, as we are discovering, is more Einsteinian than Newtonian: that is, it is driven to fracture all laws that would confine it, be they rules of logic, gravity, space, time, or noncontradiction. In the imagination, all is relative, bent, curved, dynamic, and fluid. In the imagination, time, unlike a river, flows forward and backward, into the future as well as the past. "In a sense, we go 'back to the future.'"[27] Storying, thus, makes possible new reconfigurings, "punctuations,"[28] and interpretations of past experience. Meanings that were previously closed are now reopened and reassessed. By such "re-visioning" of past history, new possible outcomes in the future can now be imagined. New futures are the stuff of hope, and, hope, "the thing with feathers – /that perches in the soul – /and sings the tune without the words/ – and never stops – at all,"[29] is what can transform the present.

Story and the Restorying of Self

In the telling and the listening of story and self, what is also unfolding is a reconfiguring, reconstructing, or "restorying" of the elements of the lives of tellers and listeners, both as individuals and as persons-in-relationship. They are telling themselves and hearing themselves, telling their lives and hearing their lives, in ways they could never have done

27. Richard Jensen, *Thinking in Story: Preaching in a Post-literate Age* (Lima, OH: C. S. S. Publishing Co., 1993), 9.
28. Watzlawick, Bavelas, and Jackson, *Pragmatics,* 54-59.
29. " 'Hope' is the thing with feathers," in *The Complete Poems of Emily Dickinson,* ed. Thomas H. Johnson (Boston: Little, Brown and Company, 1960), 116.

before, when still alone, single, and individual. Nor could the private, silent reading of the story's text in print produce anything approaching the relational interaction that story's epistemology demands.

Now, because of the interactive relationship created in the act of storying, one is involved in a new way, not just with one's own story but with that of another. And this yields yet still another perspective on the self, namely, being related with one's own story *through* the story of another. This kind of interactive storying involves the interweaving of mutuality and difference, alterity and complementarity, and enables teller and listener to imagine freshly together and to wonder what might happen next – both in the story of their making and their shared lives as well. If there were no one to story with, all this potential and possibility would collapse in upon itself, unpollinated, sterile, fruitless, unborn, unrealized: an egg, a seed but not the life they could release together.

Thus, the interactive, reciprocal, and collaborative conditions and relationships that storying demands not only change the nature and content of the truth that can be known; they also transform and change the lives and identities of those who participate in narrative knowing.

The Indeterminacy of Story. The world is changed by story in much the same way as Werner Heisenberg expressed his principle of indeterminacy. Actual reality does not exist in any absolute, objective way, apart from knower. Actual reality can only exist as the result of a particular interaction between knower and known in which both, knower and known, are changed as a result of their interacting. And this interaction, like the oral-aural interaction of storying, is unique and unrepeatable: the very act of an observer observing phenomena affects, influences, and therefore changes what is observed.[30]

Storying, like science, therefore, "makes" or constructs reality in much the same way every act of knowing, investigating, or observing shapes, influences, and transforms what is known. In a world of binary thought that demands to know whether reality is *either* wave *or* particle, story

---

30. Fred Alan Wolf, *Taking the Quantum Leap: The New Physics for Nonscientists* (San Francisco: Harper & Row, 1981), 115

provides the answer with "Yes. Of course. Why ever not? You see it's like this. Once upon a time . . ."

However, there is one important difference between story and science. Story, unlike science, doesn't claim to speak any truth – except a fictive one. Its truth claims are, at best, tentative, humble, analogous. That is because storying is an evanescent, perishable, insubstantial action, passing in and out of existence. Because storying is "an essentially dynamic oral event," characterized primarily by change, the truth it mediates will always be highly unreliable. Thus, the world of truth that story creates will always be "changeable and kinetic rather than static,"[31] always variant, inexact. No one intrinsic meaning can inhere within a spoken story always and everywhere in any absolute or universal way. Whatever meaning is conveyed in storying, therefore, will always have to be context-specific, that is, specific to the actual conditions of the telling and to the experience and knowledge of its creators and participants, its listeners and tellers.

The Humility of Story. For story can only speak in the here and now, in this present moment, in this place, among these people, in this telling, in this context, once and only. Tell the exact same story a moment later to the same people and an entirely different story may very well be heard, for ". . . no two oral performances by a single artist are ever the same."[32] E. M. Forster observed this when he commented that a "pause in the wrong place, an intonation misunderstood and a whole conversation [may go] awry."[33] Meaning, significance, and impact may be very similar from telling to telling, but they will never be identical. "In spoken form the word is repeated and transformed every time it is used." In written form, the word can be frozen, made "static, invariable, or even 'petrified'. . . . Once written, the word can only with difficulty be changed."[34]

With storying, however, truth refuses to be pinned down, reduced, or equated with any particular form or for-

31. Edwards and Sienkewicz, *Oral Cultures,* 2, 12.
32. Ibid., 167.
33. E. M. Forster, *Passage to India,* quoted in Ibid., 193.
34. Edwards and Sienkewicz, *Oral Cultures,* 2.

mula or text. That is because there is always more truth: "Full truth is deeper than articulation."[35]

Technology as Taxidermy: Transcribing, tape recording, or videotaping the spoken story preserves it but in much the same way that taxidermy operates: it must first kill and mutilate what it would save. "[Albert] Lord has noted that the mere presence of a collector creates circumstances abnormal for the performer, and even the use of video or recording equipment may cause both performer and audience, distracted by the equipment, to behave differently than they would in a more natural context. Inevitably, the observer has a distorted view of what is taking place."[36]

Thus, in a world that still trusts its truth only if it exists as "hard" data complete with some form of "*object*-ive" proof, the oral-aural story does not even qualify as "existent" because it is literally "no-*thing*." But perhaps it is not story but the "myth of matter" with its pre-limiting expectations and procrustean models of "truth" and "reality" that should be suspect.

Question: "What is the shortest distance between two points?" Answer: "A story."[37] How ironic that it is stories, and not objects or things, that seem perfectly at home in a quantum universe where "matter does not exist with certainty at definite places, but rather shows 'tendencies to exist . . .'"[38] Like the subatomic particles that comprise all matter, stories come in and out of existence, appearing and disappearing in disjointed, discontinuous ways, jumping from place to place, "seemingly without effort and without bothering to go between the two places."[39] Thus, stories like elementary particles of reality are never exactly what or where you expect them to be. And that is why any consideration of storying as a way of knowing seems too dangerous to "modern" systemizations of knowledge which, for too long,

35. Ong, "Writing," 25.
36. Albert Lord, "Homer and Other Epic Poetry," in A. J. Wace and F. H. Stubbings, *A Companion to Homer* (New York: Macmillan, 1963), 193.
37. Quotation from lecture by Anthony de Mello at Christ the King Retreat House, Syracuse, NY (August, 1983).
38. Fritjof Capra, *The Turning Point* (New York: Simon and Schuster, 1982), 80.
39. Wolf, *Quantum Leap*, 3.

have prided themselves on identifying and defining reality itself in their own images.

The oral-aural story thus quite literally may be perceived as the ultimate antimatter of "modern" epistemological efforts in science and philosophy to reduce all existence to matter, object, thing. Like all oral traditions, story forms the negative white spaces around and between the fixed black letters of the texts of modernity and calls our attention to what is *not* on the page: truths and ways of knowing and relating that have been suppressed and devalued, even removed from consciousness, by the prevailing empirical models of science, truth, and reality. With every story spoken and heard, a counterstory or countermodel of reality is also implied, or, to paraphrase Borges: "A story which does not contain its counterstory is considered incomplete."[40]

Perhaps, then, it is not what is fixed, permanent, or enduring in our world or knowledge that alone deserves the appellation "real." Perhaps quantifiable, material substance and form, observed, measured, and recorded, is not the only way to arrive at truth. Perhaps rather it is in the mutually interactive personal relationship *between* the knower and the known, the observer and the observed, the storyteller and the storylistener, where we can find a different way to think, know, and relate about what we call truth and reality. This is what I mean by storying as epistemology.

40. The original quote is "A book which does not contain its counterbook is considered incomplete." Jorge Luis Borges, "Tlon, Uqbar, Orbis, Tertius," in *Labyrinths,* (New York: New Directions, 1964), quoted in Brazelton and Cramer, *Earliest Relationship,* 130.

The Challenge of Literacy

Storying as a way of knowing, as a structuring of human consciousness and perception, was changed forever with the development of writing. Ong sees the various forms of writing, such as script, print, computer, as "all the same because . . . [they] are all ways of technologizing the word." In fact, Ong believes that of all these technologies, it is writing that is the "most drastic" because it "initiated what printing and electronics only continued, the physical reduction of dynamic sound to quiescent space, the separation of the word from the living present, where alone real, spoken words exist."[41]

This technologizing of the word has drastically altered and restructured our more "natural human mental processes"[42] of thought that originally occurred in the oral-aural exchange of storying. It would take another whole book to explore adequately the restructuring of oral-aural consciousness occasioned by these technologies. But, since the value of something is often best appreciated only after it has been lost or misplaced, let me simply summarize some of the major points made by Ong in his writing on this topic. Please keep in mind that what Ong says about writing is also a commentary by implication on the oral-aural psychodynamics of storying.

Writing and the Externalization of Mind

Ong, referring to the comments of Socrates on writing in Plato's *Phaedrus,* observes that the philosopher saw writing as an intrusion into the "early human lifeworld" because it pretended "to establish outside the mind what in reality can only be in the mind. Writing is simply a thing, something to be manipulated, something inhuman, artificial, a manufactured product."[43] Socrates complained that a written or printed text was unengaged, "passive," "unresponsive." A text cannot enter into debate or dialogue, answer questions or ask them; it cannot challenge or change its opinion, explain itself, elucidate, or expand its meaning. All it can do

---

41. Ong, "Writing," 28, 30.
42. Ibid., 23.
43. Ibid., 27.

is repeat itself in the exact same words over and over again. Socrates also contended that texts destroyed memory and enfeebled the mind: "Those who use writing will become forgetful, relying on an external source for what they lack in internal resources. Writing weakens the mind."[44]

Ong builds on these observations of Socrates. He states that once words have been translated from dynamic, vibrating, changing sounds to the "rigid visual fixity" of text, the words are "reduced to space," "frozen and in a sense dead." The spatialization of language, the move from interior sound to exterior text, produces what Ong calls the most telling effects of writing on oral-aural consciousness: separation and distancing. "Writing is diaeretic. It divides and distances, and it divides and distances all sorts of things in all sorts of ways."[45] Ong then discusses what and how writing separates and divides.

Division and Separation. "Writing separates the known from the knower. It promotes 'objectivity.'"[46] By being removed from the context of the interactive personal relationship created by speaking and listening, the words of a text are radically depersonalized and altered, "neutered" if you will. Knowledge ceases to be dialogic and becomes a monologue instead. With the loss of the interpersonal relationship of speaker and hearer, the action of knowing is no longer a shared, collaborative, cocreative activity based on participation and rapport. Now, only one half of the conversation responsible for the coevolution of narrative knowing is written down, recorded, and preserved, namely, that which is spoken. How what is spoken is heard and received by the listener is lost from the written text.

I mention this last point to emphasize how texts change "knowing," an interactive dialogic activity, to "knowledge," an impersonal denatured object that one possesses. As Ong puts it, "Between knower and known writing interposes a visible and tangible object, the text. The objectivity of the text helps impose objectivity on what the text refers to. Eventually writing will create a state of mind in which knowledge itself can be thought of as an object, distinct from

---

44. Ibid., 27-28.
45. Ibid., 31, 36.
46. Ibid., 37.

the knower. This state of mind, however, is most fully realized only when print intensifies the object-like character of
the text." The problem here, which Ong points out, is that
knowledge is and must always be personal: "the physical text
is not itself knowledge" but must always be interpreted and
made personal.[47]

"Writing separates interpretation from data," Ong continues. The written text is fixed as "a visual given, a datum,
separate from any utterer or hearer or reader." In a sense,
the text is dumb, mute; it has no voice to give the words any
kind of life or energy, color or shading, rise or fall. In
oral-aural cultures, words cannot help but carry interpretation with them in the way they are sounded and heard.
"Writing distances the word from sound, reducing oral-aural
evanescence to the seeming quiescence of visual space."[48]

There is also a loss of immediacy in writing. According
to Ong, "Writing distances the source of communication (the
writer) from the recipient (the reader), both in time and
space." One of the essentials of storying and all oral-aural
communication is that speaker and hearer "are necessarily
present to one another." But "writing distances the word
from the plenum of existence."[49] Imagine a Royal Shakespeare production of *King Lear*; now imagine the audience
hunched over their Folger texts, reading word for word,
never looking up at the stage or actors. Now imagine how
much the audience has missed in the way of experience,
knowledge, and relationship. The context of the spoken word
is the world of existence, sound as well as silence, the verbal
as well as the nonverbal. But in the act of reading the whole
human organism, even its posture, literally folds in on itself
as it struggles to delimit and "disable," if you will, all the
other operations of the sensorium other than vision. And
even that sense must be strictly confined to a narrow point
on a page.

Writing, then, emphasizes exactness over interaction.
Deprived of the plenum of existence with its "holistic context
made up mostly of nonverbal elements, writing enforces
verbal precision." The oral-aural word relies on the media-

---

47. Ibid., 38.
48. Ibid., 38-39.
49. Ibid.

tion, assistance, and modulation of communities: the community of the senses, together with the community of associations, memories, and meaning, shared within a community of people. Deprived of such interaction, the printed text is narrowly confined to a world where "the entire immediate context of every word is only other words, and words alone must help other words convey whatever meaning is called for. Hence texts force words to bear more weight, to develop more and more precisely 'defined' – that is 'bordered' or contrastive meanings. Eventually, words used in texts come to be defined in dictionaries, which present the meaning of words in terms of other words." Perhaps we should not be surprised then that texts tend to overcompensate for their experiential impairment with increasingly exclusive epistemological claims of truth and certainty. Ong says, "In oral utterance, the context always includes much more than words, so that less of the total, precise meaning conveyed by words need rest in the words themselves. Thus in a primary oral culture, where all verbalization is oral, utterances are always given their greater precision by nonverbal elements, which form the infrastructure of the oral utterance, giving it its fuller, situational meaning. Not so much depends on the words themselves."[50]

Thus, while texts become increasingly restrictive, logocentric, and self-referential, the oral-aural world of storying is constantly mediating its contextual meanings through the changing lived human experience of its participants.

"Writing separates past from present," Ong says. Writing, like most forms of preservation, fixes in time and space what would otherwise change, evolve, develop, and eventually perish. "By freezing verbalization," writing separates meaning and expression from their historical, as well as social and cultural, contexts, and, in so doing, distorts and destroys what it originally sought to preserve. In oral-aural cultures, each story of the past is continually being revised, updated, and transformed in the experience of the present – either implicitly or explicitly – with each new telling, with each new hearing.[51]

---

50. Ibid., 38-40.
51. Ibid., 40.

Because the languages of oral-aural cultures are *not* fixed, frozen, or preserved, meaning can coevolve, develop, and expand with experience. In a sense, the "dictionary" for an oral-aural people is the whole plenum of existence, that is, their shared world of interaction and communication. And with each new act of storying, this oral-aural "dictionary" is updated and revised and made contemporary. Thus, while the words of the ancient stories may not change, the meaning of the stories are always absolutely current, immediate, and apropos to the situation of those listening.

Bureaucracy, Power, and Control. Writing also encourages administrative, bureaucratic, and managerial styles of relationship based on supervision and power. "'Administration' is unknown in oral cultures, where leaders interact non-abstractly with the rest of society in tight-knit, often rhetorically controlled, configurations. . . . administration comes into being with the development of written documentation and scribal expertise."[52] In a bureaucracy, the human lifeworld of experience is slowly transported from the wide expanses of the plenum of existence and corralled into the flattened dimensions of linear print and rectangular paper. What is wild and untamed in the world of experience must be broken and domesticated, made docile and manageable.

To accomplish this, power must be delegated to a supervisory class of people who will oversee these procedures and decide how to translate human experience into languages, categories, and codes that are simple and convenient for purposes of recordkeeping, surveillance, and evaluation. By developing rules, quotas, printed forms, spreadsheets, statistics, carbon paper, copying machines, filing cabinets, databases, a whole new technology is established for knowing, experiencing, and relating to self, other, and the world.

The irony, of course, is that, in time, the world on paper becomes even more important and of greater concern than the world of human experience, so much so that if no record of an event, meeting, or encounter can be produced, then, in the world of bureaucracy, it could never have happened – no matter how many people *say* it did. If it's not *written* down somewhere, it doesn't exist; if there are no permanent records of people in a bureaucracy, they never existed – until

---

52. Ibid.

records can be generated for them. Only when a person exists on paper can a bureaucracy acknowledge that such a person may actually exist in life.

Writing and the Abstraction of Thought. Writing separates thought from "socially effective discourse," logic from rhetoric, thus isolating and disconnecting the processes of cognitive activity from those of expression and communication. Thought, removed from the contextualization of use and experience, quickly grows abstract, generalized, and impersonal. As Ong says, "The invention of logic, it seems, is tied . . . to the completely vocalic phonetic alphabet and the intensive analytic activity which such an alphabet demands of its inventors and subsequently encourages in all sorts of noetic fields."[53]

Truth, Facts, and the Exile of Wisdom

"Writing separates academic learning (*mathesis* and *mathema*) from wisdom (*sophia*)," Ong maintains. Abstract thought combined with logic tends to produce elaborate and highly organized structures and systems of knowledge which are capable of yielding absolutely clear, concise answers, definitions, and certitudes, such as those found in mathematics and geometry. The only problem is that such abstract, analytical knowledge often exists apart from any reference to "actual use or . . . integration into the human lifeworld."[54]

Wisdom, on the other hand, is a form of knowing that is essentially personal, relational, and experiential. Wisdom demands dialogue, debate, interaction, disagreement, mistakes, learning by apprenticeship, and, most important of all, the adaptation and tempering of knowledge to specific human purposes, values, and contexts. Wisdom does not exist in and for itself but to serve the needs of those who study or invoke it. Thus, wisdom does not prize such intellectual virtues as correctness, exactitude, or repeatability the way printed texts do. Its knowing is simply of a different, not inferior, kind from that of abstract, analytical logic.

---

53. Ibid., 40-41.
54. Ibid., 41.

Writing and Language: Elites and Outlaws. In addition to exiling wisdom for the sake of precision, exactitude, and facts, writing divides society according to what Ong calls a "special kind of diglossia," which splits "verbal communication between a 'high' language completely controlled by writing even though also widely spoken (Learned Latin in the European Middle Ages) and a 'low' language or 'low' languages controlled by speech to the exclusion of writing."[55] While "diglossia" may conjure the rarefied, arcane, and esoteric reaches of knowledge where even linguists fear to tread, nothing could be more political or have more immediate practical consequences. For here we face all the covert structures of class, power, gender, race, and other potentially divisive categories as they are immediately conveyed by the literacy and illiteracy of peoples as well as by the sound of their speech, dialects, and accents. Those schooled in language and literacy from books and texts have, until most recently, been among an elite few in history, mostly rich, powerful men of leisure and class who did not have to labor or work but who could spend their time perfecting the speech and ideas of the powerful, the successful, the dominant.

Ong confines his discussion of "high" language to historical issues of gender, noting that high language is "not only a written language but also a sex-linked language . . . used only by males (with exceptions so few as to be negligible)." But Ong could have well expanded his comments to explore how whole groups of the poor, marginal, and disenfranchised have been systematically subjugated and kept in inferior social conditions by the languages they have been permitted to learn and speak ("the low, vernacular languages") and those absolutely forbidden to them (the high text-based languages).[56] Despite contemporary literacy campaigns in the world today, it was not too long ago that our most "advanced," progressive, and liberal of civilizations considered teaching reading and writing to be a capital crime punishable by death – but only for certain populations within a society. Two examples of this are the outlawing of all schooling and education among the Irish

---

55. Ibid.
56. Ibid., 42.

Catholics under British rule[57] and the torture, maiming, and murder of African-American slaves in the United States who attempted to learn or teach reading and writing.[58]

Along with efforts to control who could read and write came efforts to control how the language itself was conveyed in written form. Writing tends to standardize language according to rules of grammar, thus eliminating difference and variety for the sake of regularity and conformity. In the process, the rich expressionism of regional and local speech is diluted and lost, resulting in a certain leveling of communication and flattening of experience.

Division and Distance within the Mind. In addition to dividing elements within a society, writing also creates separations or divisions within the mind and between being and time. "Writing," according to Ong, "divides and distances more evidently and effectively as its form becomes more abstract, which is to say more removed from the sound world into the space world of sight." Certain languages, such as Chinese and Japanese, however, use ideograms or pictographs for characters and, thus, "involve the right cerebral hemisphere of the brain more than do writing and reading

---

57. "Ireland provides a vivid example of the intended uses of instruction rooted in literacy to remold a people: in language, culture, morality, and religious beliefs." Harvey Graff, *The Legacies of Literacy: Continuities and Contradictions in Western Culture and Society* (Bloomington, IN: Indiana University Press, 1987), 248.

58. "Penalties for literacy included whipping, loss of fingers, branding, and sale or segregation." Ibid., 362. Contrast that sentence with the following excerpt from Gary Paulsen, *Nightjohn* (New York: Delacorte Press, 1993), 73-74: "'It is against the *law* for you to read. To know any letters. To know any counting is *wrong*. Punishment, according to the *law,* is removal of an extremity.' . . . The toe came off clean, jumped away from the chisel and fell in the dirt. Blood squirting out, all over the block. . . . 'Other foot.' [The master] spit and wiped the chisel off on the stump." Professor Graff speaks the language of the academic. Novelist Paulsen speaks the language of story. One language provides distance; the other immediacy. Here is an example of how language affects our knowing and how the mode of our knowing affects our relationship to that which is known.

the alphabet, which involve the left hemisphere more. The right hemisphere normally implements totalizing, intuitive, less abstractive or less analytic processes; the left hemisphere is more analytic – and more involved in the alphabet." Ong locates the historical roots of "formal logic, modern science, and ultimately the computer" in the alphabet because it is, by nature, "the most analytic of writing systems, dissolving all sound as such into spatial equivalents, in principle, if never completely in fact."[59]

Finally, "the most momentous of all its diaretic effects in the deep history of thought is the effect of writing when it separates being from time."[60] Here Ong cites Havelock's important work[61] on how philosophy as a mode of thought "depends on writing because all elaborate, linear, so-called 'logical' explanation depends on writing." Ong goes on to say, "The elaborate, intricate, seemingly endless but exact cause-effect sequences required by what we call philosophy and by extended scientific thinking are unknown among oral peoples, including the early Greeks before their development of the first vocalic alphabet."[62]

The kind of thinking supported and encouraged in the study of philosophy "requires the coinage of a large number of abstract nouns"[63] and replacing narrative verbs of action, doing, and happening with intransitive or copulative[64] verb forms of "to be." As Ong puts it, "Oral speech and thought narrativizes experience and the environment, whereas philosophy, which comes into being slowly after writing, is

---

59. Ong, "Writing," 42-43.
60. Ibid.
61. Eric Havelock, "The Linguistic Task of the Presocratics, Part One: Ionian Science in Search of an Abstract Vocabulary," in *Language and Thought in Early Greek Philosophy*, ed. K. Robb (La Salle, IL: Hegeler Institute, Monist Library of Philosophy, 1983), 7-82, cited in Ibid., 43.
62. Ong, "Writing," 43.
63. Ibid., 44.
64. Havelock notes in "The Linguistic Task of the Presocratics" (20), that such verbs state "permanent relationships between conceptual terms systematically." In fact, the secondary meaning of the verb "copulate" is "to fuse permanently." I mention this to draw attention to the aspects of equivalency and permanency implied in such verb forms. (*Webster's Seventh New Collegiate Dictionary,* s. v. "copulate").

radically anti-narrative. Plato did not want storytelling poets in his republic.[65]

Writing Stasis Replaces Story Kinesis. In writing, stasis replaces the interactive dance and commotion of kinesis; permanence supplants the "live" but transient encounter in the here and now; the abstract impugns the particular and concrete; the general supersedes the individual; the eternal and timeless is preferred to simple presence. Thus, as being replaces becoming and concepts subvert stories, knowing, experiencing, and relating move from the personal to the "apersonal" to the impersonal. "The mobile oral world has been supplanted by the quiescent text, and Plato's immutable ideas have been provided with their action-free, seemingly timeless chirographic launching pad."[66]

In the movement to the stasis of writing from the kinesis of storying, we see the narrowing of existence into categories. Ong observes the differences between orality and literacy by comparing the simple Russian illiterates of Alexander Luria's research[67] with the storytelling Greeks of Homeric times. According to Ong, both groups found thinking situationally, functionally, contextually far more natural and obvious than abstract thought. "Oral cultures tend to use concepts in situational, operational frames of reference that are minimally abstract in the sense that they remain close to the living human lifeworld. . . . [T]he epithet *amymon* applied by Homer to Aegisthus . . . means not 'blameless,' a tidy abstraction with which literates have translated the term, but 'beautiful-in-the-way-a-warrior-ready-to-fight-is-beautiful.'"[68]

In experiments involving the grouping and classification of objects, Luria[69] found that the literate (even those most recently so) could no longer think in anything but abstract categorical terms. In fact, when confronted with the

---

65. Ong, "Writing," 44.
66. Ibid.
67. Alexander Luria, *Cognitive Development: Its Cultural and Social Foundations,* ed. Michael Cole, trans. Martin Lopez-Morillas and Lynn Solotaroff (Cambridge, MA: Harvard University Press, 1976). Luria's research was conducted in Uzbekistan in 1931.
68. Ong, *Orality and Literacy,* 49.
69. Luria, *Cognitive Development,* 74.

different groupings and classifications made by illiterate subjects in the study, even those just barely literate could no longer think in such situational or operational terms as they (most probably) had before they could read. Further, they also insisted that their newly acquired abstract categorical mode of thought was *the* single correct way of thinking.

Thus, in learning to read and to think even somewhat analytically, the literate had also developed a single view of the world based on dualistic categories of mutually exclusive opposites, such as "correct"/"incorrect," "right"/"wrong," "one/none." Literacy had so seduced them into the syllogistic world of formal logic and reasoning that they could no longer consider or imagine other alternate possibilities.

Print, Literacy, and the Modern World

The invention of Gutenberg's printing press in 1450 separated "knower from known more spectacularly than writing" ever did. The printing press "affected the development of modern capitalism, implemented western European exploration of the globe, changed family life and politics, diffused knowledge as never before, made universal literacy a serious objective, made possible the rise of modern sciences, and otherwise altered social and intellectual life."[70]

Texts and technology interposed themselves as objects of observation and communication between nature and the direct personal experience of the world. They not only separated knower from the known *physically* but also increased "the *psychological* separation between the self and the object of its knowledge."[71] The advent of these techniques of knowing were unconsciously redefining not only what was known but also what could be known with the result that a whole new world was gradually being constructed: the "modern" world complete with entirely new "modern" ways of thinking, experiencing, and relating.

This "modern" world preferred reading and writing to speaking and listening; facts, information, and proofs to sto-

---

70. Ong, "Writing," 45; Ong, *Orality and Literacy,* 117-18.
71. Ong, "Writing," 47.

ries; texts that were portable, private, individual objects to the communal interactive work of storying with others. It wanted nothing more than the ready accessibility of "truth-in-a-book," "truth-on-a-page," truth, in short, as external, manipulable object. The "modern" world needed truth that would always be there, forever, exactly the same, sure, clear, certain, visible, repeatable, unchanging, constant, indisputable.

Products of a newer technology are often perceived to be more credible, authoritative, and reliable than products of an earlier technology. This was especially true with the printing press; it gave whatever appeared in print the popular presumption of truth whether it was true or not. As Ong puts it, "If a book states an untruth, ten thousand printed refutations will do nothing to the printed text: the untruth is there for ever. . . . Texts are essentially contumacious."[72] Whatever was printed, therefore, acquired an importance, a permanence, a larger significance and influence, and, thus, seemed to be true or at least to suggest truth, simply because it was printed. How often one hears students say: "But I read it in a book (newspaper, etc.), so it must be true."

The Imperialism of Print

As more and more books were printed, their texts possessed power; knowledge of them gave power. Those who owned books or texts had privileged access to the truth and the power such access brings. Those who read texts told others what the texts said, what they meant, what they commanded. However, it would be more accurate to state that those who read texts told others what *they said* the texts said, meant, and commanded. Each "reading"[73] of a text,

---

72. Ong, "Writing," 27.
73. The word "reading" is used here according to its secondary and tertiary meanings in *Webster's Seventh New Collegiate Dictionary*: "a particular version," "a particular interpretation or performance." Actors are known for being able to give the exact same words of a text, say a passage from Shakespeare, many different "readings," which can entirely change and transform not only the meaning of the words but also, as a result, the function of the passage in the overall plot of the play. Compare Laurence Olivier's defiantly triumphal "reading" of *Henry V* during World War II and the recent darker "reading" of the

therefore, also contained an implied interpretation of that text.[74] Each reader chose (sometimes consciously, more often unconsciously) *one* particular way to communicate the text from among many other possible readings. But because all the other possible readings and interpretations of the same text could not be sounded simultaneously, they could not be heard. And because they were not heard, they did not exist. Thus, the choice of a particular "reading" or interpretation of a text not only affected how the text was heard and understood by those who could not read for themselves; it also determined which *version* of a text was heard and promulgated and which potential or alternate versions were not heard or permitted into consciousness and were, therefore, effectively suppressed.[75]

Those who could not read, therefore, had to rely on those who could to tell them what the text said, meant, commanded. Since they themselves could not distinguish

---

same play by Kenneth Branagh.

74. Texts derive their meanings not only from themselves and the many possible "readings" they contain but also from the other texts they are juxtaposed with in contextual dialogue. John Donahue argues that the parable of the Good Samaritan (Luke 10:25-37) and the "parabolic narrative" of Martha and Mary (Luke 10:38-42) are not independent story units that just happen to lie next to each other on the pages of Luke. Instead, Donahue insists both stories must be read together – intertextually – as two different aspects of a single commentary on the meaning of true discipleship (Luke 10:1-24). *The Gospel in Parable: Metaphor, Narrative, and Theology in the Synoptic Gospels* (Philadelphia: Fortress Press, 1988), 136-38.

75. The suppression of stories from the conversation of texts distorts all texts and the tradition to which they belong. Martha Ann Kirk notes this in her study of how the systematic exclusion of Hebrew and Christian scriptures about women from the oral-aural canon of biblical texts spoken at Catholic worship has left the faithful – both women *and* men – with a tradition that is literally "mute" and "dumb" regarding the place and role of women in God's plan of salvation and liberation. The tongue of God's self-revelation in the mothers, wives, daughters, and sisters of Israel and the church has been cut out, and with that, history and tradition has been silenced. *Celebrations of Biblical Women's Stories: Tears, Milk, and Honey* (Kansas City: Sheed & Ward, 1987), 75-77, 80.

between the actual words of the text and the interpretation given to them, they, more often than not, complied with what they had been *told* the text said. The authority of a text, thus, came to be transferred to those who owned the books and could control the reading (and writing) of the texts. In this way, the literate came to exercise power over the illiterate by influencing what could (and could not be) told in the texts. This, in turn, affected how the large illiterate masses thought, acted, even hoped. The illiterate based their behavior on what they *believed* the text to be saying as they heard it sounded and shaped in the mouths of the literate. The fundamental failure to discriminate between text and interpretation affected all parts of society, giving increasing power to the literate, the rich, the powerful, and the educated, while making the illiterate further dependent upon them and their "readings" of reality.

Text as Truth. Because of this shift from orality to literacy, coming to know the truth was ceasing to be a narrative activity, a making, a processing, a pooling of memories and life experience, an invoking of old traditions in new contexts. Knowledge no longer needed to be translated interactively into the collaborative wisdom of a community, a region, or people for it to have meaning, application, validity. Now truth adhered to the texts themselves as objects from outside the community that came from the cities and centers of power where the texts were produced. But truth unmoored from context and relationship becomes a commodity: cold, impersonal, dead, absolute. Coming to know the truth was no longer a shared endeavor of mutual discussion, discernment, and participation, the "interplay of minds."[76] Instead, texts were slowly leeching the collective power and authority of a community and concentrating it in the hands of an elite and powerful few, who were as distanced and separated from the community as the printed uniform words on the page were from the community's native experience.

---

76. Marshall McLuhan, *Gutenberg Galaxy: The Making of Typographic Man* (Toronto: Univerity of Toronto Press, 1962), 23.

Thus, knowledge from texts as well as the mastery and management of that knowledge conferred privilege and made truth into personal property that had to be protected, defended, and guarded by those who possessed it against those who did not. This was accomplished, in large part, by restricting literacy and education, controlling access to books and periodicals, as well as censorship of the press. As mentioned above, the new technology of print itself also carried great weight, conveying greater truth and value to what was written over that which was spoken. In short, print was preferred. It simply told you what was true, what to think, what to believe. Because it reported "facts," how could it be denied? Print, together with the world it was making, was simply irresistible.

The Disenfranchisement of Storying. After Gutenberg, oral-aural storying, that most ancient, interpersonal, but alas "inexact" technique of knowing, seemed embarrassingly crude compared to print's linear precision, dependable efficiency, and uniform organization and presentation of knowledge. Orally-based thought and expression was now considered, as Ong puts it, "primitive," "savage," "inferior," "coarse," or "despicable." "The terms are somewhat like the term 'illiterate': they identify an earlier state of affairs negatively, by noting a lack or deficiency."[77]

Among the poor, the disenfranchised, the dispossessed, and all those without access to education and literacy, oral-aural storying persisted[78] but as a devalued currency. It was categorized as a product of the "illiterate." Because "'illiteracy' came to be synonymous with stupidity,"[79] oral-aural stories were considered "beneath scholarly attention."[80] Edwards and Sienkewicz sum up this thinking: "Only those who

---

77. Ong, *Orality and Literacy,* 174-175.
78. It was not until the Brothers Grimm that many of the stories of the "folk" were put into print and then only after they had been bowdlerized. Jack Zipes, *The Brothers Grimm: From Enchanted Forests to the Modern World* (New York: Routledge, Chapman, and Hall, 1988); Maria Tartar, *The Hard Facts of the Grimms' Fairy Tales* (Princeton: Princeton University Press, 1987).
79. Edwards and Sienkewicz, *Oral Cultures,* 5.
80. Ong, *Orality and Literacy,* 8.

can read and write are considered educated, just as only the lettered word has been considered worthy of the name 'literature.' "[81] Only *written* stories, therefore, were considered "literature" and suitable for serious study. Oral stories, on the other hand, were considered "crude, formless, unstructured,"[82] "prelogical or . . . illogical,"[83] incapable of creating "intricate structures of verbal expressions."[84]

In fact, after the rapid dissemination of print technology throughout Europe, storying was relegated to the realms of children and "primitives,"[85] and literally, "made fun" of. Story as form and practice of real knowledge was discredited, perhaps all the more so because the very pleasure, playfulness, and emotional engagement it aroused was now seen as suspect. According to Lee Bolman and Terrence Deal, "Stories are often seen as the medium used by those who have nothing factual to offer . . . . Such stories are often viewed as a source of entertainment rather than of truth."[86]

Real knowledge in this new "modern" world had to be serious, sober, and rational, the product of the pure intellect, uncontaminated by seductive emotions or wanton, uncontrollable feelings. "Modern" knowledge was too important to be played with or enjoyed; now knowledge had to remake the world, move commerce, advance business, improve science, determine profits, assign losses, predict the rise and fall of markets, rationalize political claims, justify the annexation of lands and the subjugation of peoples.

Oral-aural storying increasingly became a relic of an old way of being, knowing, and relating. It belonged to a "medieval" or "premodern" world and consciousness that was quickly fading into distant memory. Story had become an antique in the attic of a discarded past, a quaint outdated

---

81. Edwards and Sienkewicz, *Oral Cultures,* 5.
82. Albert Bates Lord, *Epic Singers and Oral Tradition* (Ithaca, NY: Cornell University Press, 1991), 30.
83. Ong, *Orality and Literacy,* 57.
84. Lord, *Epic Singers,* 30.
85. Ariel Dorfman, *The Empire's Old Clothes: What the Lone Ranger, Babar, and Other Innocent Heroes Do to Our Minds* (New York: Pantheon Books, 1983), 8.
86. Lee G. Bolman and Terrence E. Deal, *Reframing Organizations: Artistry, Choice, and Leadership* (San Francisco: Jossey-Bass Publishers, 1991), 256-57.

instrument for the amusement and entertainment of the innocent and "undeveloped": children, the childlike, the native, the peasant, the poor, the powerless, the disenfranchised, the marginal, the illiterate, the nonwhite, the non-European, the nonmale, the non-Christian, and all those who "didn't know better," who were not quite full citizens in the new "modern" typographic world.

> Literacy is imperious. It tends to arrogate to itself supreme power by taking itself as normative for human expression and thought. This is particularly true in high-technology cultures, which are built on literacy of necessity and which encourage the impression that literacy is an always to be expected and even natural state of affairs. The term "illiterate" itself suggests that persons belonging to the class it designates are deviants, defined by something they lack, namely literacy. Moreover, in high-technology cultures . . . literacy is regarded as . . . unquestionably normative and normal.[87]

Text as Normative. The normativeness of literacy and print and the corresponding discrediting of oral-aural story has continued to exist as an intellectual bias down to our own time. Thus, while some scholars have studied forms of oral-aural storying, such as the great epics of Homer, most have done so from a purely *literary* point of view. "A symptom of this distortion of the oral by the written word is the tendency of observers to judge the importance of various elements of [oral] performance from a literary perspective. Thus commentators often highlight plot over elaborate descriptive passages and other elements not essential to the main story line."[88]

In fact, for years scholars had concluded that Homer's epics were far too "skillful" poetically to be mere oral creations; thus, he obviously *had* to have composed them originally as written texts.[89] Ironically, the very oral characteristics that distinguished such epics – such as digression, elaboration, repetition, exaggeration, ritual invective, and formulaic passages – were held in "very low esteem" as "uncouth and distasteful," "disjointed or unfinished,"

---

87. Ong, "Writing," 23.
88. Edwards and Sienkewicz, *Oral Cultures,* 2-3.
89. Ong, *Orality and Literacy,* 57.

"flowery or obsequious" because, from a literary point of view, they were considered redundant for failing to advance the plot. Redundant? Yes – but essential. These oral devices "could be compared to the stylized and repeated patterns of waves and spirals often used in weaving or on a geometric Greek vase." The Greek vase was considered a great work of art *because* of, not *in spite* of, its "redundant" geometric patterns. Unfortunately, in the world of letters, oral stories were not viewed with the same regard. "When the literate tool of analysis is applied to an oral context, a disequilibrium is created between the medium and the message."[90]

This belittling of storying and its dismissal from the realms of discourse reveals the profound bias against oral-aural consciousness that has existed even down to our own day with few exceptions.

The Subversiveness of Storying

But perhaps there is another reason why oral-aural storying either had to be dismissed as the discourse of the crude, the ignorant, the infantile, and the simple or else "translated" into a text-based literature before it could receive "serious" attention from scholars. Any recovery of storying as a valid epistemology, a valid way of knowing, would pose a real threat to the "modern" models of objective truth, scientific knowledge, and settled reality that still dominate our world culture today.

That is because storying challenges the objectivity, control, and permanence that print technology brought to "modern" consciousness as illusory. By its very nature, oral-aural storying resists all attempts to freeze its truth in fixed space and time. Consistency, stability, precision, uniformity are empty categories and of no interest to those who story. Instead, change, emendation, plurality, expansion, and revision form the very essence of storying. By its very nature, storying defies all those attempts at control and standardization that printed texts and "modern" technology sought to impose on the flux of nature and experience.

---

90. Edwards and Sienkewicz, *Oral Cultures*, 217, 3, 147, 217, 148, 147.

Recently, the absolute normative nature of "modern" consciousness, hurried into existence by the printed word and mechanistic technology of that period, has begun to be reexamined and critiqued.

> The very term "modernity" has been given a significance both normative and distortive by the myth of progress which has crucially shaped Western thought since the Enlightenment. It is a normative significance because modernity is understood as intrinsically superior to whatever preceded it – the opposite of being modern is being backward, and it is difficult to entertain the notion that backwardness may have something to say for itself. And, *ipso facto,* it is a distortive significance because such a perspective makes it very hard to see modernity for what it is – *a historical phenomenon,* in principle like any other, with an empirically discernible beginning and set of causes, and therefore with a predictable end.[91]

This reevaluation of "modern" forms of thought which Berger urges is increasingly called the "postmodern" critique today. It should be viewed as "not an attack, but rather an effort to perceive clearly and to weigh the human costs"[92] that resulted from absolutizing all things "modern" as definitive norm and enduring (ahistorical) standard, while relegating all other "premodern" and "nonmodern" ways of knowing, thinking, and relating, such as story, to a "backward" inferior status of thought. In fact, in many ways, it is the reemergence of story as a legitimate mode of consciousness, more than anything else, that has made the postmodern critique possible.

---

91. Peter Berger, "Toward a Critique of Modernity," in *Religion and the Sociology of Knowledge: Modernization and Pluralism in Christian Thought and Structure,* ed. Barbara Hargrove (New York: Edward Mellen Press, 1984), 335. Emphasis in original.
92. Ibid., 336.

Chapter Two

Thinking in Story

PERHAPS NO ONE HAS DONE MORE TO CREATE A BRIDGE FROM the modern world into a postmodern one, both in academic circles as well as the popular imagination, than Thomas Kuhn, the historian and philosopher of science. Kuhn himself states quite explicitly that his seminal work on paradigms and scientific revolutions derives from discovering an alternative reading of the texts of science. This basic hermeneutical move, namely, the awareness of the interactivity and interdependence of content and context, truth and perspective, product and process is the very heart of recovering story as narrative mode of thought or epistemology. In fact, the categories of "modern" and "postmodern" that I use throughout this work derive basically from Kuhn's contribution of paradigms to the history of science. In this chapter, we will consider how Kuhn came to conceive of paradigms as possible alternate readings of a contextual reality. By pursuing the mind's eye of Kuhn's initial insight, I suggest that we arrive at a "storying" brain.

Learning How to Read "Possible Worlds"

The recovery of story as a structuring of consciousness reclaims the imagination as an essential component of conceptualizing, knowing, and relating. It allows for simultaneous alternative interpretations of reality or what Jerome Bruner calls "possible worlds": "we ask of a proposition not whether it is true or false, but in what kind of possible world it would be true."[1] This completely transforms the "modern" concept

---

1. Jerome Bruner, *Actual Minds, Possible Worlds* (Cambridge,

of truth and reality as singular, linear in evolution, logical in development. If there can only be one possible conclusion or answer, what Donald Spence calls "the axiom of the singular solution,"[2] then it must be a solution that corresponds to objective truth and reality. If objective, then it must necessarily be absolute, thus, falsifying all other views, opinions, or interpretations.

By recontextualizing "modernity" as "a historical phenomenon,"[3] Kuhn relativized the Enlightenment myth of progress along with the normative absolute claims of modern science and history. In this way, Kuhn turned the "modern" view of the world, the self, and the other into just one possible interpretation of reality among others instead of *the only one*. This insight is the foundation of the postmodern critique occurring today.

A Story about the Reading of Stories

Let us now turn to Kuhn's own account of how he rediscovered the importance of story as mode of thought in the doing, reading, and studying of science. In essence, it provides a story about the reading of stories.

In 1947, Thomas Kuhn, then a young doctoral student in physics, was asked to prepare a set of lectures on seventeenth-century mechanics. Initially he saw his task as an eminently simple one: recounting the indisputable "facts" of the past "with literary grace in approximate chronological order." Since Kuhn felt it necessary to "discover what the predecessors of Galileo and Newton had known about the subject," he turned to the works of the Greeks as his starting point. But there was just one problem: Aristotle. Kuhn had always had immense respect for Aristotle, especially for his abilities as both an acute observer and natural scientist. But, when it came to his theories and definition of motion, Aristotle had been "simply wrong." Kuhn writes, "How could his characteristic talents have failed him so when applied to

---

    MA: Harvard University Press, 1986), 45.

2. Donald Spence, *The Freudian Metaphor*, with a foreword by Jerome Bruner (New York: W. W. Norton & Company, 1987), 57.

3. Berger, "Critique of Modernity," 335.

motion? How could he have said about it so many apparently absurd things. . . . The more I read, the more puzzled I became. Aristotle could, of course, have been wrong – I had no doubt that he was – but was it conceivable that his errors had been so blatant?"[4]

Young student Kuhn had read Descartes and his contemporaries; he knew how they had ridiculed Aristotle "by quoting his definition of motion in Latin, declining to translate on the ground that the definition makes equally little sense in French." But, he kept asking himself, if Aristotle's definition of motion had been so ridiculously absurd and so obviously wrong, how had it "made sense for centuries before, probably at one time to Descartes himself"?[5] Why had generations upon generations of intelligent scholars taken it so seriously, believing it to be true?

Reading Texts and Reading Worlds

Then, in an "decisive" moment that quite literally changed his life, Kuhn reports that "all at once [I] perceived the connected rudiments of an alternate reading of the texts with which I had been struggling." "For the first time," he was able to enter wholly and imaginatively into the contextual world of Aristotle, "where qualities were primary," and material bodies or substances were not. Once he learned that the content of Aristotle's world was interdependent with Aristotle's perspective and historical context, he found that Aristotle's conclusions proceeded quite logically and elegantly from his original premises, in much the same way that any good story does. Kuhn writes, "Much apparent absurdity vanished. I did not become an Aristotelian physicist as a result, but I had to some extent learned to think like one. Thereafter I had few problems understanding why Aristotle had said what he did about motion or why his statements had been taken so seriously."[6]

---

4. Thomas Kuhn, *The Essential Tension: Selected Studies in Scientific Tradition and Change* (Chicago: University of Chicago Press, 1977), x-xi.
5. Ibid., xiii.
6. Ibid., xii, xi, xii.

In this way, Kuhn learned how to put on a "different thinking cap" and to appreciate the strange and alien world of fourth-century B.C.E. Greece with its categories, concepts, and terminologies so different from his own. He had approached the texts of Aristotle "posed in a Newtonian vocabulary."[7] But when the answers he had demanded were not forthcoming in the exact same Newtonian language, there were only two conclusions he could draw: either Aristotle had been hopelessly wrong, as he had first thought, or he, the student, had to learn how to change his ways of conceptualizing and thinking. Fortunately, Kuhn chose the latter, as his subsequent career as an eminent philosopher and historian of science attests.

Gestalt Switch: The Rabbit or the Duck?

It is of particular interest to me that Kuhn writes that his discovery of an alternate reading of Aristotle's classic text reminded him of a "Gestalt switch." By staring at the "well-known Gestalt diagram of the duck and rabbit," specifically the shifting relationship between ground and figure,[8] Kuhn became aware of how the exact same arrangement of lines in external space could change appearance in his mind, presenting him with "two equally good alternatives"[9] of reality, namely, the duck and the rabbit.

Although Kuhn locates his insight here in an analogy from the sense world of sight and perception, his insight is still essentially hermeneutic or narrative in substance. Reality is not only read and interpreted according to such determining factors as context and perspective; the reality that is known is created through the fictive participation and interaction of the mind. In other words, reality is not *in* the lines of the diagram. It exists rather in the dialogue between mind and perception. The mind chooses, organizes, structures, and gives meaning and value to what it perceives. From this interaction, the mind constructs the possibility of

---

7. Ibid., xiii, xi.
8. Ibid., xiii, 6-7.
9. Carolyn Bloomer, *Principles of Visual Perception*, 2d ed. (New York: Design Press, 1990), 53.

alternative worlds. This is directly opposed to a philosophy of mind based on the purely objective nature of reality.

The objective nature of reality was a favored position of advocates of the "modern" mind. To apprehend the world all that was necessary was to perceive reality correctly, that is, objectively, as it was in itself, independent of any "contaminating" subjective elements. Knowledge of the truth was to be pure, absolute, singular, whole, and exclusive. Postmodernists, however, encouraged by the findings of quantum physics and recent cognitive research on brain/body/mind studies, today hold that the apprehension of reality occurs within the dialogical interaction of subject and object as they "story" or cocreate an operative or paradigmatic version of the world together. According to this postmodern interpretation, the mind is actively involved in constructing what it perceives from what it already has perceived in the past, what it expects to perceive in the future, as well as from the contextual circumstances and perspective of its actual perceiving here and now.

By referring to the Gestalt switch between the image of duck and rabbit, Kuhn, therefore, is expressing in visual terms the same basic hermeneutical principle mentioned above as the essential element of a narrative epistemology, namely, the interactivity and interdependence of content and context, truth and perspective, product and process. Let us look at this briefly.

Postmodern Lessons from an Optical Illusion

In a Gestalt diagram or optical illusion, the mind sees a reality that first appears single and simple. It then literally changes before the eyes as ground and figure shift their relationship to each other in the eyes of the observer. Note that nothing is changing in the lines on the paper. The change is occurring entirely within the mind of the observer. A second image or alternative reality now appears where once the first image was. The mind, accustomed to seeing and imagining the possibility of only one reality at a time, now is forced to contain two alternative images, two different interpretations or constructions of reality. It finds the simultaneous coinherence of contradictory alternative images disquieting and, therefore, tries to determine which of the two is the real, one, true, objective image that is "actually" before its eyes at this particular moment in space and time.

What the "modern" mind, preconditioned to a single view of nature, forgets is that neither image that appears, neither the duck nor the rabbit, is *more* real than the other. But minds conditioned in most "modern" Western cultures, especially since the development of linear perspective, think that "a figure suggests meaning, while a ground seems relatively meaningless." Therefore, it is not uncommon for Western minds to ascribe more reality to figure than to ground; in fact, to perceive the figure as *the* real image, that is, the *one* correct, right, true image. Bloomer writes, "In Western cultures, figure ('positive') has always been accorded major importance, while ground ('negative') has been defined as all factors that can be eliminated without affecting meaning."[10] Therefore, a mind and eye trained in Western ways of seeing will perceive the image manifesting as figure to be "positive," that is, more weighted, preferred, important, meaningful, and, if only unconsciously, more real, correct, true, and dominant. Whichever image has receded to the background of vision will be "negative," accorded less reality, truth, power, or force.

Here again we see how the principle of relational interactivity and interdependence, so important to postmodern narrative conceptions of perception and thought, has been lacking in the development of modern consciousness. The "modern" Western mind, trained in dualistic, either/or categories of thought failed to appreciate that figure and ground do not exist in themselves as discrete entities, separate and apart from each other but only in relation to each other. Without background, there would be no figure; without figure, there would be no background. "Figure and ground are inextricably bound together: the form of one creates the form of the other."[11]

10. Ibid., 51, 54.
11. Ibid., 55.

The Eye of the Beholder

For our purposes then, the most important thing to remember is that neither image in and of itself enjoys any existential priority over the other; neither possesses a *more* intrinsically real or objective existence. Which aspect appears first as figure and which recedes into the background depends wholly on *how* the one looking perceives, organizes, and contextualizes them. The framing, then, of the particular arrangement of figure and ground, the contextualization of their relationship, depends in large measure upon the perspective of the viewer and the structures of her consciousness, including the cultural canons by which her eye has been trained to see. "Figure/ground relationships do not exist in the outside world; they are created by the mind. A figure in one situation becomes the ground in another. . . . A thing becomes a figure when you pay attention to it; at that particular moment, all else dissolves into a background."[12]

It cannot be stressed enough that this differentiation occurs in the observer, not in the images or objects being viewed. The alternating appearance of duck or rabbit to Kuhn resulted from the shifting of his focus, not from any ontological change in reality. "The way humans perceive a stimulus depends on the perceptual context within which the stimulus is embedded. The same visual stimulus will be perceived differently in different visual situations."[13]

As Kuhn became aware of how his Newtonian perspective unnecessarily disqualified Aristotle's contributions, he learned how to read Aristotle from that philosopher's own historical context and to read Newton within his seventeenth-century context. In this way, Kuhn found he could read and learn from both Aristotle *and* Newton without having to jettison one or the other.

Seeing through Cultural Prisms

So far our discussion has tended to describe the question of perceptual context in historical terms (past, present, "pre-,"

---

12. Ibid., 52.
13. Ibid., 58.

"post-"). But I would not want to imply that there is one and only one perspective for each historical period in time. It would be too easy to conclude from this that reality must, after all, be singular at any one moment or that models of reality can only succeed one another but not coexist simultaneously. Therefore, let us turn now to a consideration of contemporaneous cultural perspectives and their role in structuring consciousness and our perceptions of reality.

As the postmodern critique argues, perceptual context is not simply what is "out there" in external reality, the various squiggles, lines, curves, and frame of a Gestalt diagram. Perceptual context also refers to the interior structures of consciousness – if you will, the optic – by which and through which reality is seen by an observer. Thus, within alternate non-Western, nonmodern cultural canons, the perceptual context of figure and ground and their relationship may seem utterly foreign. As a result, what is seen, the "visual stimulus" mentioned above, or the manifestation and expression of reality will actually appear quite different. As Kuhn was learning through the medium of Gestalt diagrams, reality was not necessarily exactly the same in all places for all times.

In fact, there are many non-Western cultural traditions that do emphasize that figure and ground "cannot exist without the other." Thus, in these cultures, the ground has as much importance and interest as the figure does: "Oriental art has always placed great value on the use of 'empty' space to represent meaningful parts of a picture."[14] As Ananda Coomaraswamy puts it,

> In Western art, the picture is generally conceived as seen in a frame or through a window, and so brought toward the spectator; but the Oriental image really exists only in our own mind and heart and is thence projected or reflected onto space. The Western presentation is designed as if seen from a fixed point of view, and must be optically plausible; Chinese landscape is typically represented as seen from more than one point of view, or in any case from a conventional, not a "real," point of view, and here it is not plausibility but intelligibility that is essential.[15]

14. Bloomer, *Visual Perception*, 54, 55.
15. Ananda Coomaraswamy, *The Transformation of Nature in Art* (New York: Dover Publications, 1934), 29-30.

What we see, therefore, is not necessarily "what is actually out there" but depends in large part on how we have been trained to see and interact with what is being observed: that is, on what our eyes have been taught to prefer, to expect, to anticipate. What we look for and identify as real and meaningful and what we ignore and dismiss as meaningless is, thus, more a function of our education, formation, training, and cultural conditioning than an intrinsic property of what is being seen.

Further, what we see depends on how our eyes have been taught to arrange, relate, order, prioritize, and structure parts to the whole of whatever it is that appears in our visual field. Thus, it should not surprise us that late seventeenth-century Europeans accustomed to seeing reality through the eyes of a Rembrandt, Vermeer, Rubens, or Poussin might easily mistake the vast empty spaces of a Japanese landscape of the Ukiyo-e school from the exact same period "as pieces of the picture that have been torn away."[16]

Aristotle and *Newton? Duck* and *Rabbit?*

Returning to Kuhn and his "reading" of Gestalt diagrams, we can now appreciate how his looking through the eyes of Newton at Aristotle left Kuhn in a dilemma, caught between what he thought were two mutually exclusive alternatives. Only one could be right; the other then had to be wrong. How could he entertain both simultaneously?

In the Gestalt diagram of the rabbit and the duck, Kuhn's mind at any one instant could perceive only one image as figure. That figure was ascribed meaning and importance, while the other image receded into the background of Kuhn's attention and valuing. But as Kuhn's focus shifted, the image-as-figure dissolved and gave way to the other contradictory image as it moved from ground to figure in Kuhn's view. Kuhn's mind was plunged into an experience of "an overall ambiguity" as his brain was "unable to decide which meaning is preferable."[17] For minds conditioned by late Western canons of "modern" thought, meaning is singu-

---

16. Bloomer, *Visual Perception*, 55.
17. Ibid., 53, 54.

lar: only one meaning can exist at a time. Ambiguities, therefore, are defects to be clarified, resolved, and removed at all costs; they are to be eliminated.

But the experience of a Gestalt diagram or an optical illusion proposes two different meanings simultaneously. The fun of an optical illusion is the result of an excitement mixed with a certain uneasiness and anxiety as the mind tries to "freeze" a vacillating reality, to "fix" it permanently into a single customary form comprised of dominant figure and receding background. The mind challenges itself to resolve conclusively the hopelessly shifting, changing, indeterminate, ambiguous appearance of reality before it. When, according to the single set of categories it is operating under, the mind fails in its attempt, the mind creates a special classification for this anomaly (optical "illusion") and then calls this phenomenon an exception to the rule. This normalizes the anomaly, but, because the mind is still troubled by such an exception to its preconditions for reality, it assigns it to the marginal realms of inferior "inconsequential" knowledge, together with the play of children, their stories and games. By thus trivializing such alternative knowledge, the mind can further distance itself from this "deviant" version of reality.

Ironically, optical illusions, like contemporaneous variant versions of the same story, have often been treated this way, not because they actually disturb the "normal" routine operations of the eye, but because they instead disturb our *ideas* about the operations of the eye. That is, they actually force us to question our assumptions about perception, knowledge, and reality itself. In fact, optical illusions force us to face a new, very different, and actually, in some ways, more accurate or fuller understanding of what human cognition is and how it works.

Binocular Vision: Two into One

One of the things that evolution and the passage of geologic time has made us forget is that disparity, difference, and ambiguity are at the heart of every waking moment of our existence as embodied, sensate creatures. For the human organism to survive over countless millennia of evolution, its brain has had to develop ways of coordinating its systemic functioning with its process of perception – a process that bombards it every second with ten thousand different exteroceptive and proprioceptive sensations, all raw, discordant, unrefined, chaotic, contradictory, and confusing. The brain cannot just admit all these sensations into consciousness as if they were all "real," "objective," and equally deserving of full attention. The brain, therefore, has to be engaged every second in drastic selection processes deciding which sensory perceptions should be admitted to consciousness as approximations of "reality" and which should be screened out, ignored, or suppressed. Of course, as we saw above, the criteria for this operation depends on which mental constructs the mind has been trained or conditioned to judge as "real." If the mind does not perform this vital process of detecting, filtering, and amplifying sensation, the brain would be overwhelmed and could not function properly.

But the mind is not just selecting perceptions; it is also organizing and interrelating them into patterns, shapes, coherent wholes. In other words, the mind is constructing models, approximations, or versions of what it is experiencing, according to the particular structures of consciousness. If the mind has been structured to perceive according to "modern" techniques of knowing, that is, as merely the passive recipient of patterns of a single reality, then it will seize upon one version of reality and equate it with truth and objective existence itself. If, however, the mind has been trained to be aware that its construal of reality is interdependent with the particular conditions of its perceiving, then it will see its version of reality as one possible interpretation among other alternative possibilities or, as Bruner has put it, one "possible world" among other possible worlds.[18]

Kuhn's fundamental insight in his analogy about Gestalt diagrams and alternative perceptions or interpretations of the texts of science and history is, thus, applicable to the constructive, interpretive, if you will, *fictive* operations of the mind and the structures of consciousness. But, since Kuhn chose to express this in vocabulary that was visual, let us continue to consider the operations of human sight and its implications for our purposes.

---

18. Bruner, *Actual Minds*, 45.

Although we have so adapted our seeing to be unaware
of the fact, human vision is, nevertheless, binocular. That
means that the human visual system is constantly providing
the brain with *two* distinct images in two different visual
fields from two different perspectives. In order to survive,
the human organism has had to perceive *one* single image
from these disparate images. In fact, the response of the
nervous system to the changing coordinates and variables in
the external world of stimulation and sensation had to be so
synchronous that eye and hand could work interactively as
one reflex in a three-dimensional universe. Bloomer writes,
"The brain processes the two retinal images in such a way
that we normally experience them in a single image (through
image fusion). The visual fields are slightly different (a
condition termed *binocular disparity*). . . ." Admittedly, the
differences between the two separate images and visual
fields are slight but they are real nevertheless: "human
beings are extremely sensitive to even slight binocular disparities." Any impairment in image fusion can result in
double vision which, despite comic representations in the
popular media, can be a frightening ordeal resulting in
dizziness, lack of balance, falling, nausea, fainting, and
unconsciousness, as the brain shuts down from an experience of profound disorientation and confusion. Bloomer comments: "Fortunately, image fusion is usually easy and
completely unconscious. But interestingly, the mind does not
give equal weight to the images from each eye."[19]

Due to brain lateralization, the retinal image from one
eye will always be stronger and dominate the other. Despite
the protocols of modernity with its notion of reality as singular, disparity is an inevitable, inescapable, and permanent part of biology and human perception. Thus, it is
important to note that human perception does not "give" us
either a view of reality as single or a single view of reality.
Instead, what is seen is really a version of reality that results
from the interaction of a human subject with the shifting,
changing, multiple pluralities and vagaries of reality in such
a way as to make a kind of coherent sense out of what is most
divergent and discrepant in experience. In other words, the

---

19. Bloomer, *Visual Perception*, 50, 51, 50.

mind is rendering or interpreting a version of reality *as if* it were singular.

Once again, I make this distinction to emphasize the interactive, constructive, fictive nature of the mind as it relates to the reality it seeks to know and understand. Thus, the mind is not replicating reality so much as interpreting it, crafting a provisional narrative version of it. The human mind then can be described as a "storying" mind.

Returning to the analogy of sight, we are aware that the normal adaptation and transformation of visual disparity into a single image can be further disturbed by specific clinical experiments designated to frustrate mental closure. Bloomer writes, "Bizarre effects can occur when the image shown to each eye is markedly different. As the brain attempts to form a solid, single image, it may alternately accept and reject parts of each eye's image. . . . With patterns or pictures, different parts of the images phase in and out, combining and recombining in various and constantly changing ways. This phenomenon is called *retinal* or *binocular rivalry*."[20] Different images in each eye, thus, clash, conflict, and vie with one another as the mind seeks to normalize the disparity and to close upon one single image of reality as certain and sure. When it cannot, the mind becomes extremely disturbed and anxious.

The Hunger for Closure

In its long struggle to survive in a hostile environment, the human organism has, more often than not, been profoundly disquieted and confused by experiences of ambiguity and indeterminacy and has, therefore, sought closure in all its encounters with the external world. Over the seventy million years that the different aspects of the perceptual system have been developing in mammals, the brain has needed to transform whatever is disparate, discontinuous, chaotic, and contradictory in its experience into some kind of coherent, stable continuity. In this way, the human mind has grown accustomed to assigning a single meaning and significance to whatever it senses, so that it can prepare the human organism to execute the appropriate response and reaction.

---

20. Ibid., 50-51.

Closure thus allows the mind to identify and classify "a stimulus in such a way that the observer feels free to move on to something else. Depending on the importance of the stimulus, closure is usually accompanied by feelings of relief."[21] Closure does provide relief from ambiguity and hurries us along to our next transaction. But while closure is important for human activity, it must be remembered that closure primarily serves an operational function for our species and so is provisional and not finally absolute.

In other words, closure is not the only epistemological task we are called upon to perform as humans. In fact, perhaps our most important vocation as human beings is not closure but "the art of unknowing,"[22] that is, remaining open to "possible worlds" with their multiple interpretations of reality; entertaining an alternative imagination with all its possibilities; the nurturing and deepening of our sense of wonder, awe, and "abiding astonishment;"[23] and profound reverence for all of creation and existence as intrinsically mysterious and numinous, finally elusive of simple explanations, singular definitions, or univocal descriptions.

Reality as Interactive

Knowing is fine, but sometimes not-knowing, "unknowing," is better. Stephen Kurtz talks of the great "fear of unknowing that has pervaded the Western mind," especially since the Scientific Revolution and the Enlightenment with their "compulsion to make sense." He goes on to say that "knowing, understood as a state of mind, is a condition of reasoned assuredness: a state of closure that structures further experience. Unknowing, by contrast, is a state of openness that does not foreclose experience through predetermined struc-

---

21. Ibid., 20, 14-15.
22. Stephen Kurtz, *The Art of Unknowing: Dimensions of Openness in Analytic Therapy* (Northvale, NJ: Jason Aronson, 1989), 7-8.
23. Walter Brueggemann, *Abiding Astonishment: Psalms, Modernity, and the Making of History* (Louisville, KY: Westminister/John Knox Press, 1991). The title of Brueggemann's book is taken from a phrase in Martin Buber, *Moses* (Atlantic Highlands, NJ: Humanities Press International, 1946), 75-76.

ture." Kurtz, of course, is not arguing for gross ignorance or a form of epistemological agnosticism. Together with an increasing number of writers, he is proposing a rediscovery of alternative structures of consciousness in which the "unity of the observer and observed" is preserved, not divided. "When excitement or terror are expunged [from knowing], all that remains is the minor pleasure of fixing 'Q.E.D.' after the proof."[24]

In other words, the Cartesian split of subject from object – the agent from her experience of nature, the individual from his communal identity, the mind from body, the reason from emotion and affect – is not intrinsic to the human condition or inherently normative. Rather it is one form of structuring consciousness that resulted from "a historical phenomenon," namely, the ideas, assumptions, and cultural circumstances of the "modern" era. "The hubris in the scientific project lies especially in the wish to substitute knowledge for nature. . . . The I is reduced to a knower and reality to the knowable." Hence, the particular structuring of "modern" consciousness is not eternal or absolute but just one form among others.[25]

Morris Berman writes similarly of reclaiming a "participatory consciousness," which he associates with premodern and nonmodern cultures.

> The view of nature which predominated in the West down to the eve of the Scientific Revolution was that of an enchanted world. Rocks, trees, rivers, and clouds were all seen as wondrous, alive, and human beings felt at home in this environment. The cosmos, in short, was a place of *belonging*. A member of this cosmos was not an alienated observer of it but a direct participant in its drama. His personal destiny was bound up with its destiny, and this relationship gave meaning to his life.[26]

Ironically, it was the discoveries of quantum theory and subatomic physics in the early part of this century that led

---

24. Kurtz, *The Art of Unknowing,* 5, 4, 245, 216, 5.
25. Berger, "Critique of Modernity," 335; Kurtz, *Art of Unknowing,* 218-19.
26. Morris Berman, *The Reenchantment of the World* (New York: Bantam Books, 1984), 10, 2. Emphasis in original.

to the conclusion that reality was not quite as objective, closed, or determined as previously thought.[27] "Objective reality" was no longer thought to exist "out there," pristine, intact, only waiting to be found, passively observed, and dutifully acknowledged by a subject. The accumulating body of research by such scientists as Heisenberg, Einstein, Bohr, Schroedinger, and Planck began to revolutionize not only science but all conventional theories of truth, knowledge, and reality as well. "Quantum physics cracked the metaphorical pane of glass that had been assumed to separate the detached observer from the observed world; we are, we found, unavoidably entangled in that which we study."[28]

In his principle of uncertainty, Heisenberg concluded that reality moves from potential to actuality only with the observation of a subject.[29] But that same act of observation which actualizes reality must also necessarily delimit it, thus, changing and influencing the outcome. To be real is to be specific and limited. As Ian Barbour puts it, "Observing consists in extracting from the existing probability distribution one of the many *possibilities* it contains. The influence of the observer, in this view, does not consist in disturbing a previously precise though unknown value, but in forcing one of the many existing potentialities to be actualized."[30]

Thus, the primary canon of the modern mind is refuted: the object cannot be known absolutely or purely in and of itself apart from an observer. This is because the mere presence of a subject profoundly affects the object observed. At the same time, the object cannot be observed without the presence of the subject. According to Wolf, "To observe is to disturb, for observation breaks the wholeness of nature." Thus, the very acts of observation and measurement, once thought to be, as Barbour puts it, "pure," "neutral," indifferent, and benign, were now seen as influencing the outcome

---

27. Wolf, *Quantum Leap*, 117-24.
28. Timothy Ferris, *Coming of Age in the Milky Way* (New York: Doubleday, 1988), 367.
29. David C. Cassidy, *Uncertainty: The Life and Science of Werner Heisenberg* (New York: W. H. Freeman and Company, 1992), 233-35.
30. Ian Barbour, *Religion in an Age of Science: The Gifford Lectures 1989-1991*, vol. 1 (San Francisco: Harper, 1990), 103. Emphasis in original.

of *what* was observed and measured. "Perceptions of the world," Leonard Shlain writes, "are observer-dependent." The knower shapes and affects what is known, if only by delimiting it through observation, while what is known shapes and affects what the subject looks for next and eventually comes to see and know.[31]

Thus, to return to Kuhn, the solution to his dilemma – the duck or the rabbit? Aristotle or Newton? – did not lie with either of the two options available but required him to include a third party, namely, himself as the observer influencing the outcome of what he was trying to perceive. Kuhn had to move from an assessment of the contents or product of truth to a critical examination of the process, context, and perspective of his knowing.

Modernist Concepts of Reality

During the last three hundred years or so of what we have been calling the "modern" age, it was generally assumed that reality was singular and simple; that all we had to do to perceive reality was to open our eyes and let it flood in upon the palimpsest of our consciousness as it patiently waited to record "what is out there" on our passive brain. With such an accurate "impression" of external reality in our inner minds, all we had to do was to conform our lives, ourselves, our actions and operations, as well as our modes of thinking, to what was "given" to us from such an objective, impartial, and confident observation of nature. As Roger Lowe puts it, "This form of thought insists that knowledge can be founded upon, or grounded in, absolute truth. It assumes that knowledge is 'about' something external to the knower, and can present itself objectively to the knower." This "form of thought" is what Lowe identifies as "modernism" or Enlightenment or Western thought.[32]

---

31. Wolf, *Quantum Leap,* 61; Ian Barbour, *Myths, Models, and Paradigms: A Comparative Study in Science and Religion* (New York: Harper, 1974), 113, 105; Leonard Shlain, *Art and Physics: Parallel Visions in Space, Time, and Light* (New York: William Morrow and Company, 1991), 132.
32. Roger Lowe, "Postmodern Themes and Therapeutic Practices: Notes Towards the Definition of 'Family Therapy': Part 2." *Dulwich Centre Newsletter* 3 (1991): 43.

According to "modernism," "truth," "fact," "certitude," and "reality" were presumed to be objective, existing in some external plane, independent and apart from any conditions that may compromise the neutrality of the knower. It was the subject's job, aided by scientific method and more and more refined technology, to eliminate all confusion, contamination, competing distractions, individual biases, or miscalculations from the pursuit of knowledge. The object of knowledge was absolute truth – truth pure, whole, direct, entire. Everything else was to be excluded: self, history, race, culture, values, meaning, politics, language, context, perspective.

But today we are coming to realize how inadequate, indeed misleading, such descriptions of the human mind are: "Perhaps the greatest myth of Western civilization is the spectator view of knowledge – the notion that it is possible to stand aside from our perceptual and conceptual tools and see what is really out there."[33]

The Constructive Brain

In the late twentieth century, the cognitive sciences are helping us to appreciate that what has been presented to us as a one-way reality is more an interactive thoroughfare that we are building as we travel it. After almost three hundred years of "modern" science's obsession with the externality of what is "out there" and an exclusive focus on the object, science itself has had to turn its attention to how the subject contributes to the "construction" of reality and knowledge. For even the eye, that purportedly guileless window on reality, is never innocent; it is always interpreting and thus making, assembling, inventing, designing what it sees.[34] According to neurobiologist Semir Zeki of the University of London, "interpretation is an inextricable part of sensation. To obtain its knowledge of what is visible, the brain cannot therefore merely analyze the images presented to the retina; it must actively construct a visual world."[35]

---

33. Lawrence Hedges, *Interpreting the Countertransference* (Northvale, NJ: Jason Aronson, 1992), 60.
34. Bloomer, *Visual Perception*, 43.
35. Semir Zeki, "The Visual Image in Mind and Brain," *Scientific American*, 267, no. 3 (September 1992): 69.

In the optical illusion "Kaniza's triangle," a triangle is *suggested* by incomplete lines but not actually present. Referring to this famous optical illusion, Zeki states that "the brain creates lines where there are none." The brain fills in what is missing, supplies coherence where it is absent. Thus, the subject is always actively contributing to and influencing *what* is known, simply by choosing what to observe and what to ignore, what to imply, what to include and what to exclude from awareness. "In short," Bloomer says, "perception is the process by which a person actively constructs reality."[36]

As neuroscientists today continue to refine their own empirical research into the brain and the workings of the mind, they are finding that the object of their study is even more mysterious and puzzling than they could ever have imagined and that it does not behave as they had once expected.

The Mind as More than a Computer

Only a few years ago it was common to think of the brain primarily in terms of computer systems, but today it is understood that the brain is not just passively recording empirical data (or "facts") being "entered" into its memory banks by nature. Instead, the brain is a highly complex system that already includes prior constructs of cultural and social order, meaning, and language that are essential to the constitution of reality. "It is," according to Bloom and Lazerson, "this collection of information that the brain interprets to make the mental constructs that is our perception of our world at any given moment."[37] As the bicameral brain is both perceiving, excluding, and integrating experience according to the dominant modalities of each hemisphere and its tripartite structure, it is actually constructing versions of "reality" from a holographic assembly of sensations, thoughts, memories, associations, and perceptions as they interact with one another.

The brain's constructive role in the processing of integrative thought, perception, and sensation and its immense

---

36. Zeki, "Visual Image," 76; Bloomer, *Visual Perception*, 43.
37. Floyd Bloom and Arlyne Lazerson, *Brain, Mind and Behavior*, 2d ed. (New York: W. H. Freeman and Company, 1988), 92.

abilities for interactive creativity, interpretive organization, and synthetic originality are being acknowledged by experimental neuroscientists such as Francis Crick and C. Koch. They encourage their fellow researchers to push on in their empirical work but caution them not to hold on too tightly to any one particular model of epistemology but to "recall the modifications of scientific thinking forced on us by quantum mechanics."[38]

Learning How to Read "Possible Worlds"

Kuhn's discovery of an alternate way to read the texts of Aristotle led him to view knowledge in a wholly new imaginative way, one very different from the way he had been taught. He had learned that conceptual frameworks, prevailing models of mind and reality, and criteria of interpretation radically affected content and meaning. As a result of his reflections, Kuhn observed that knowledge was not a simple matter of accumulation, the result of "indisputable facts" being added together. Nor was knowledge a single body of objective truths that unfolded through time in continuous linear progression or naturally evolving stages. Kuhn comments, "What my reading of Aristotle seemed therefore to disclose was a global sort of change in the way men viewed nature and applied language to it, one that could not properly be described as constituted by additions to knowledge or by the mere piecemeal correction of mistakes."[39]

Now, thanks to Kuhn's awareness of the possibility of alternative interpretations of texts, Aristotle did not have to be "absurd" for Newton to be "true." Nor did Aristotle's views have to be reduced to mistakes needing either to be corrected or else discarded from "the existing stockpile of scientific knowledge."[40] Instead both Aristotle *and* Newton could speak truly about motion as long as their contributions were viewed from their different perspectives, namely, their specific historical and cultural contexts. Instead of canonizing one reading of nature as *the* truth, Kuhn understood that

---

38. Francis Crick and C. Koch, "The Problem of Consciousness," *Scientific American*, 267, no. 3 (September 1992): 156, 153.
39. Kuhn, *Essential Tension*, x, xiii.
40. Ibid., 226.

different perspectives could generate different realities and epistemological traditions with each generating a different set of questions, answers, procedures, and results. "These are the traditions which the historian describes under such rubrics as 'Ptolemaic astronomy' (or 'Copernican'), 'Aristotelian dynamics' (or 'Newtonian'), 'corpuscular optics' (or 'wave optics'), and so on."[41] Now Kuhn realized that the value and meaning of even the most empirical and quantitative data would have to be plotted within interpretive grids that adjusted for the refractive effects of history, context, perspective, and culture. With alternate readings of the texts of history and science, Kuhn saw that truth could be multiple, various, and plural, changing dynamically with each new reading and reader of text and tradition.

---

41. Thomas Kuhn, *The Structure of Scientific Revolutions* (Chicago: University of Chicago Press, 1962), 10.

Part Two

Ways of Knowing in Psychotherapy

Chapter Three

Rejecting Story: Modern Psychotherapy

EPISTEMOLOGIES PRODUCE PARADIGMS, PARADIGMS SHAPE theory, and theory influences practice. This is another way of stating our main thesis: how we know, the modalities and techniques of our knowing, not only affect what we know but actually construct the versions of reality known. Those models or versions of reality, or "worlds," define our presuppositions, assumptions, expectations, and the limits of our thinking. And our thinking, in turn, affects how we act and behave toward ourselves and others. In this chapter, we will look at how epistemology, paradigms, theory, and practice interact and relate in the field of psychotherapy.

Kuhn's discovery that "there are many ways to read a text"[1] led years later to his writing the landmark book, *The Structure of Scientific Revolutions*. The book continues to be acclaimed as "a classic of modern scientific research,"[2] but Kuhn's own description of that critical moment in his education is very telling for our purposes: it was "the discovery of a new way to read a set of texts."[3] This discovery literally changed Kuhn's life and led him to forsake his career as a scientist for that of an historian. He spent the rest of his life pursuing the many hermeneutical implications of his discovery concerning the importance of perspective and context in the reading and interpretation of texts.[4]

---

1. Kuhn, *Essential Tension*, xii.
2. Hans Küng and David Tracy, eds., *Paradigm Change in Theology: A Symposium for the Future* (New York: Crossroad, 1989), 7.
3. Kuhn, *Essential Tension*, xii.
4. Ibid., x-xii.

63

Kuhn's contribution of "an alternative reading" of the texts of history and science enabled scholars in many fields "to understand more deeply and comprehensively the problems of growth in knowledge. . . ."[5] By locating both the contents and processes of inquiry within specific historical and cultural contexts, scholars could move beyond deadlocked debates about the eternal truth or falsity of competing texts as explanations of reality and examine instead the meaning of the texts by locating them within their appropriate contexts. Now instead of needing to defend one tradition against another as definitive, final, and exhaustive of all truth and knowledge, scholars could instead expand their investigations to an exploration of how various traditions evolve and develop and either continue to renew themselves or stall, stagnate, and die out.

The Power of Paradigms

Kuhn undertook a study of how new modalities of thought and inquiry had overturned and replaced old ones throughout the history of science. He called these moments of radical change in thinking about thinking "scientific revolutions."

Kuhn used the term "paradigm" to refer to those models, patterns, traditions of thought, or descriptions of reality that had achieved such overwhelming consensus within a given community or culture as to become acceptable as a functional substitute for reality itself.[6] In classical Greek, the word "paradigm" literally meant "to show side by side." Today in English, it means "an example or pattern." It comes from the same Greek root that also gives us the English word "diction," meaning "verbal description" or "choice or words especially with regard to correctness, clearness, or effectiveness" (*Webster's Seventh New Collegiate Dictionary,* s.v. "paradigm" and "diction"). Kuhn used the term to imply "an entire constellation of beliefs, values, techniques . . . shared by the members of a given community,"[7] a "disciplinary matrix," "model," or "exemplar"[8] that enables the construc-

---

5. Ibid., 7.
6. Kuhn, *Scientific Revolutions,* viii.
7. Ibid., 175.

tion and positing of a worldview, complete with rules and sets of assumptions, for the testing of truth and the study of reality. As such, a paradigm presets the limits, structures, forms, and conditions for all valid thought, language, and speculation about the nature of reality within a specific context of history and culture. "In science the shared assumptions and the categories themselves, explicit and implicit, have been termed a *paradigm* by Thomas Kuhn. The paradigm is the shared conception of what is possible, the boundaries of acceptable inquiry, the limiting cases. It forms the framework for deciding whether ideas are acceptable or whether something is 'fact' or not."[9] Use of the word "paradigm" has extended far beyond the field of science since Kuhn first used it. Today scholars in many diverse fields use it to denote *"interpretative models, explanatory models, models for understanding"*[10] that can effectively interrelate, connect, and interpret data.

A paradigm thus acts as a template to preselect and screen suitable data, to organize data according to the acceptable categories of the model, and finally to test and verify the data. By establishing certain common presuppositions, assumptions, and axioms as normative, a paradigm simplifies and facilitates communication within a culture and strengthens social cohesion. By providing a common logic, language, and grammar for different disciplines, a paradigm also enables several researchers

> to explore jointly one well-delimited area of inquiry and to coordinate (more often, it must be admitted, to dispute) and compare their efforts. A shared paradigm allows them to communicate about an area in a specialized language and set of assumptions. . . .
>
> A successful paradigm, or successful set of assumptions about the world, enables any group, in this case a scientific one, to agree on problems and priorities; they can select problems amenable to solution.[11]

As stated by Ornstein above, paradigms determine "what is possible, the boundaries of acceptable inquiry, the

---

8. Kuhn, *Essential Tension*, 297.
9. Robert Ornstein, *The Psychology of Consciousness*, 2d rev. ed. (New York: Penguin Books, 1986), 59.
10. Küng, *Paradigm Change*, 7. Emphasis in original.
11. Ornstein, *Psychology of Consciousness*, 59.

limiting cases." Thus, "whether ideas are acceptable or whether something is 'fact' or not" depends on whether they can be reconciled with a paradigm's "shared assumptions and categories themselves." If they cannot, they will "be rejected as meaningless or irrelevant," as James Burke so succinctly puts it.[12]

What is important to remember, however, is that truth and inquiry operate symbiotically within a given "paradigm" or cultural tradition used to structure reality. "The structure therefore sets the values, bestows meaning, determines the morals, ethics, aims, limitations and purposes of life. It imposes on the external world the contemporary version of reality. The answer therefore to the question, 'Which truth does science seek?' can only be, 'The truth defined by the contemporary structure.'"[13] Accordingly, a paradigm will always "discover" as self-evident, objective, and impartial those parameters, structures, and relationships that it "finds" to be most in agreement with its own view of nature, and, therefore, most operative and determinative of its functioning.

Limits of Paradigms

While a paradigm may guarantee stability of knowledge, language, and categories of inquiry across diverse communities of independent researchers, it does so at a cost: namely, by becoming insensitive to new, discordant, or anomalous information. The result, Ornstein maintains, is that "scientists working under a successful paradigm may begin to lose sight of any possibilities beyond their own particular set of assumptions." In its most benign form, this can lead to what Ornstein calls a dangerous "parochialism" in which alternate views or opinions are not rigorously explored but simply dismissed as irrelevant or incorrect.[14] According to Burke, "At every level of its operation, from the cosmos to the laboratory bench, the structure controls observation and investigation. Each stage of research is carried out in re-

---

12. Ibid.; James Burke, *The Day the Universe Changed* (Boston: Little, Brown and Company, 1985), 309.
13. Ibid., 309-10.
14. Ornstein, *Psychology of Consciousness*, 60.

sponse to a prediction based on a hypothesis about what the result will be. Failure to obtain that result is usually dismissed as experiment failure."[15]

Here the principle of entropy enters. Questioning or changing the model is resisted at all costs, even when it is obvious how incorrect or misleading the model has become. "Every attempt is made to accommodate anomalies by a minor adjustment to the mechanism of the structure, as was the case with Ptolemy's epicycles or Descartes' vortices."[16] A rigid intellectual fundamentalism sets in and familiarity and reliability are preferred to truth's disturbance of the universe. In this way, by becoming self-referential, the model or paradigm becomes self-perpetuating, thus frustrating any inquiry into or critique of its own validity.

But a paradigm can also be turned to malignant uses, namely, when it is turned from a means to an end, that is, from a heuristic model *of* reality to a substitute *for* reality itself. Then all distinctions between model and reality are lost as the two become coextensive and wholly identified with each other. The result is that the model, which was to aid inquiry into the elusive and mysterious *plenum* of reality, supplants and replaces it entirely. The representation becomes the reality. The icon becomes the idol. As the model replaces *all* reality, it becomes preemptive and exhaustive; nothing outside the model can exist. And since all reality is fully disclosed within the model, no other models need exist nor should exist. Any further inquiry then becomes not only superfluous and wasteful but even suspect. The usurpation of reality by the model not only precludes and invalidates all other alternate models; it construes even the consideration of an alternative model as threat.

Masakuni Kitazawa once stated that to know the postmodern it is necessary to know its referent, the modern.[17] But to understand either the postmodern or the modern, it is necessary to understand the "premodern," what historians refer to as the "medieval" world. Therefore, let us turn now

---

15. Burke, *The Day the Universe Changed*, 328.
16. Ibid.
17. Masakuni Kitazawa, "Myth, Performance, and Politics," *The Drama Review 36* (Fall 1992): 160.

to a brief examination of how paradigms as systems of minds shape and affect the process of inquiry.

Meaning and Connection in the Medieval World

The medieval world is perhaps the best example of a paradigm. It synthesized all reality into one grand unified cosmological system known as the Great Chain of Being,[18] "one of the major conceptions of Occidental thought."[19] According to the Great Chain of Being, all creation, both material and immaterial, formed a single interrelated system of expanding spheres revolving in uniform circular motion around earth's fixed point. Within each of these spheres of being, all existence was organized hierarchically, thus, connecting everything into a single interlinked chain of being "from the lowest being – stones, grains of sand, and the like – through the plants and the animals to man and beyond man to the angels and finally to God at the apex of the great chain of being."[20]

Accordingly, the earth was literally the fixed point at the center of all the spheres of the universe. Everything else, the sun, the moon, the stars, and all the other planets, revolved around the earth in uniform circular motion. Since reason was the highest of faculties, man as "rational animal," was the crowning achievement of all terrestrial creation, the center of the world, "a little less than the gods . . . with all creation under his feet" (Psalm 8). As Huston Smith puts it, "Virtually without question all life and nature were assumed to be under the surveillance of a personal God

---

18. This paradigm was based on Aristotelian philosophy and Ptolemaic astronomy, preserved by Arab scholars in the East and reclaimed by European scholastic philosophers and theologians in the twelfth century. David Lindberg, *The Beginnings of Western Science: The European Scientific Tradition in Philosophical, Religious, and Institutional Context, 600 B.C. to A.D. 1450* (Chicago: University of Chicago Press, 1992), 244-254.

19. Arthur Lovejoy, *The Great Chain of Being: A Study of the History of an Idea*, The William James Lectures 1933 (Cambridge, MA: Harvard University Press, 1936), 20.

20. Charles Van Doren, *A History of Knowledge: Past, Present, and Future* (New York: Ballantine Books, 1991), 229.

whose intentions toward man were perfect and whose power to implement these intentions was unlimited."[21]

In this world, *scientia*[22] was the Latin word to describe *all* human knowledge, from the speculation of philosophy and mathematics to the crafts of carpentry and poetry. Knowledge too was organized like a great chain in interlocking hierarchies from the macrocosmic to the microcosmic: from theology to botany, from astronomy to anatomy, from literature to love.

The "elegance," "beauty," and comprehensiveness of this medieval synthesis is undeniable. While many scientists today still hope for a "grand unified theory" to explain everything that is and has been, the medievals already had one. That it had little to do with empirical reality concerned them not at all. Empirical observation or measurement was the stuff of "applied" science, "fit only for execution by menials or slaves." Theology, the queen of the sciences, and her handmaiden, philosophy, were "pure" sciences dealing in ideas, intuition, and revelation "and were thus – as the empirical sciences never can be – apodictically certain."[23]

Thus, in a way that is all but impossible for us to comprehend today, what was most ontologically real, sure, and certain for our medieval predecessors were those truths (*"scientia"*) so perfect and pure that could never be demonstrated adequately to the senses. Those eternal truths, known or deduced from what was revealed or implied in the scriptures and subsequently developed in the ongoing teaching of the Church, served as axiomatic first principles for all other knowledge. Whatever contradicted them could neither exist nor be true, except hypothetically for the sake of argument.

The Copernican/Galilean-Cartesian Revolution. What then caused the shift from the medieval world paradigm to the modern one? Most conventional histories answer the Copernican[24] or Galilean-Cartesian Revolution.[25] Medieval

---

21. Huston Smith, *Beyond the Post-Modern Mind*, 2d ed. (Wheaton, IL: The Theosophical Publishing House, 1989) 4.

22. P. B. Medawar notes that *scientia* in this period of history meant knowledge that is "hard won," disciplined, systematic, serious as opposed to simple hearsay and opinion. *Limits of Science* (New York, Oxford University Press, 1987), 3.

technology and the invention of such instruments as the telescope, microscope, thermometer, barometer, printing press, vacuum pump, pocket watch, pendulum clock with minute-hands, calculator, slide rule, hydraulic press, etc., allowed for the replication of empirical studies, the standardization of measurement, and the comparative testing and evaluation of results in quantitative terms.

By using such increasingly precise instrumentation and other empirical methods of observation, people such as da Vinci, Bacon, Copernicus, Kepler, Galileo, Newton, Pascal, Huygens, Leibnitz, Descartes, and Locke began to develop standardized norms and methods for empirical research in a way not possible before. Such developments as the differential calculus; the laws of gravity, physics, and mechanics; binary numbers; and statistics led to ever more precision and accuracy in measurement.

By 1597, the invention of the crank had converted the rotary motion of water wheels into the linear movement of rod engines; and these, in turn, powered sawmills with metal blades. With their push-pull action powering larger and larger mills and machines, these early rod engines foreshadowed an apotheosis of technology that would eventually result in that massive social upheaval known as the Industrial Revolution. Jacques Ellul describes the psychological fallout that resulted from this absorption in technology: "Technique is the translation into action of man's concern to master things by means of reason, to account for what is subconscious, make quantitative what is qualitative, make clear and precise the outlines of nature, take hold of chaos and put order into it."[26]

By the end of the seventeenth century, *scientia* no longer meant "the knowledge that anyone has or may have." "Science," now in the vernacular, came to acquire two very specialized meanings: the process of organized empirical inquiry or "scientific method" and the body of knowledge

---

23. Ibid., 8, 9.
24. Thomas Kuhn, *The Copernican Revolution: Planetary Astronomy in the Development of Western Thought* (Cambridge, MA: Harvard University Press, 1957), 229-31.
25. Van Doren, *History of Knowledge*, 211.
26. Jacques Ellul, *The Technological Society* (New York: Vintage Books, 1964), 43.

acquired as a result of that methodology.[27] The development of technology and modern scientific method elevated empirical knowledge among the ranks and orders of all other forms of knowing and eventually absolutized it. What could be measured, quantified, compared, explained, demonstrated, or proven moved to the foreground of reality.

The explosion of these new technologies and the rise of scientific method imposed serious disjunctions between the empirical evidence of the senses and the unquestioned premises and assumptions on which the medieval world had been founded. Some "scientists" in this age, like Copernicus, Kepler, and Brahe, began to ask themselves what *might* the universe look like *if* the new data were correct. They began to conceive possible alternative models of the universe that proceeded from other first principles, premises, and assumptions. As long as their thoughts were considered merely speculative, no one balked. However, when Galileo dared to go beyond mere hypothesis, trouble began. "He insisted that what he could prove mathematically and by means of his observations was *true*. . . ."[28] It was this epistemological move, from hypothesis to assertion of fact, from theory to truth claim, that put Galileo in direct conflict with both the sacred and secular powers, already struggling futilely to hold a quickly disintegrating worldview together. Galileo was condemned by church, government, and science because he stubbornly preferred the evidence of his own untrustworthy senses to the unquestionable assertions of revealed knowledge that guaranteed its truthfulness by its transcendence of the senses entirely.

Newton's "Modern" World. In 1642, Galileo died and Newton was born. As the child came of age, so did what is called today the "modern mind."[29] Newton spoke a language different from his predecessors, based on a language of his own inventing, the differential and integral calculus, which he developed from his own synthesis of mathematics, observation, measurement, and experiment. "Perhaps no other single gift to science has ever been more valued."[30] With the invention of the differential and integral calculus, Newton

27. Van Doren, *History of Knowledge*, 184.
28. Ibid., 202.
29. Smith, *Beyond the Post-Modern Mind*, 4.
30. Van Doren, *History of Knowledge*, 206.

"not only summed up the universe in four simple algebraic formulas, but he also accounted for hitherto unexplained phenomena, made accurate predictions, clarified the relation between theory and experiment, and even sorted out the role of God in the whole system."[31] Using this language, Newton postulated laws of physics, mechanics, and motion that ushered in a whole new paradigm in the history of human knowledge. "Indeed, it was Newton's astounding achievement to synthesize Descartes's mechanistic philosophy, Kepler's laws of planetary motion, and Galileo's laws of terrestrial motion in one comprehensive theory."[32]

Newton's model conceived the universe as a giant machine or clock set in perfect motion by a Creator who guaranteed the smooth and orderly running of the cosmos by such universal laws as gravity, necessity, deductive reasoning, and cause and effect. Of course, this model also presupposed that everything within that universe, including the human person, was also a machine and operated according to pre-established mechanistic principles.

Newton's laws and methodology followed from four basic assumptions: (1) Things move and act in a continuous manner. (2) Things act for reasons based on prior causes; therefore, all action is determined and predictable. (3) All action can be analyzed and broken down into component parts. (4) The observer observes and never disturbs.[33] "The proof," Van Doren writes, "could be found in the fact that mechanical principles were true. The proof that they were true was that they worked. The circularity of the reasoning, which was itself mechanical, merely confirmed the conclusion."[34]

As we have seen, paradigms have a way of organizing knowledge across diverse disciplines and the Newtonian worldview was no exception. It affected everything – from technology to theology, from economics to education, from politics to child-rearing.

---

31. Berman, *Reenchantment*, 29.
32. Richard Tarnas, *The Passion of the Western Mind: Understanding the Ideas that Have Shaped Our World View* (New York: Ballantine, 1991), 269.
33. Wolf, *Quantum Leap*, 56.
34. Van Doren, *History of Knowledge*, 217.

By the time of Newton's death in 1727, the educated European had a conception of the cosmos, and of the nature of "right thinking," which was entirely different from that of his counterpart of a century before. He now regarded the earth as revolving around the sun, not the reverse; believed that all phenomena were constituted of atoms, or corpuscles, in motion and susceptible to mathematical description; and saw the solar system as a vast machine, held together by the forces of gravity.[35]

This view even affected how men and women thought of themselves and their own humanity. Newtonian mechanics not only transformed such simple machines as levers, wedges, wheels, axles, pulleys, and screws into complex machines driving other machines; it also transformed the human person – body, mind, and soul – into one more machine. The world had changed, thanks to Newton, its "hero."[36] In the retrospective of history, the dawning of that new world would be called by various names: the Scientific Revolution; the Age of Reason; the Enlightenment; the Machine Age; the Industrial Revolution; the Rise of Capitalism; the Age of Democracy (or Revolution, Empiricism, etc.). Embracing all of these, however, is the "modern" world.

In the modern world, individuals now possessed within themselves the saving means of their own liberation and deliverance through the grace of critical reason, empirical observation, and scientific knowledge. Thanks to epistemological certainty, objectivity, experimental predictability, and technical innovation, nature could be controlled and subdued – but at a cost.[37]

> The gloriously romantic universe of Dante and Milton, that set no bounds to the imagination of man as it played over space and time, had now been swept away. Space was identified with the realm of geometry, time with the continuity of number. The world that people had thought themselves living in – a world rich with color and sound, redolent with fragrance, filled with gladness, love and beauty, speaking everywhere of purposive harmony and creative ideals – was crowded now into minute corners in the brains of

---

35. Berman, *Reenchantment*, 28-29.
36. Ibid., 29.
37. Tarnas, *Western Mind*, 282-83.

scattered organic beings. The really important world outside was a world hard, cold, colorless, silent and dead; a world of quantity, a world of mathematically computable motions in mechanical regularity. The world of qualities as immediately perceived by man became just a curious and quite minor effect of that infinite machine beyond.[38]

The world had become "an impersonal phenomenon, governed by regular laws, and understandable in exclusively physical and mathematical terms." The sustaining actions of God in creation were now seen as "the result of innate mechanical regularities generated by nature without higher purpose." The "good life" was synonymous with secular fulfillment. "Science replaced religion as preeminent intellectual authority, as definer, judge, and guardian of the cultural world view." Now independence, autonomy, freedom, self-expression, and individual determination was the human vocation. Tarnas writes, "The modern world order was not a transcendent and pervasive unitary order informing both inner mind and outer world, in which recognition of the one necessarily signified knowledge of the other. Rather, the two realms, subjective mind and objective world, were now fundamentally distinct and operated on different principles."[39]

The elaborate interlocking hierarchies, systems, and networks of the medieval world with their symbolic correspondences between every level and realm of creation – human, divine, terrestrial, celestial – were brushed aside. All that existed now were "straightforwardly material entities . . . having no special relation either to human existence per se or to any divine reality." Spirit was reduced to mind and mind to matter. "The world was now neutral, opaque, and material, and therefore no dialogue with nature was possible. . . ."[40]

Newton's methods and conclusions were, however, celebrated as "the triumph of the modern mind." Newton had

---

38. E. A. Burtt, *The Metaphysical Foundations of Modern Science* (Garden City: Doubleday Anchor, 1955), 238-39, quoted in Jerome Langford, *Galileo, Science, and the Church*, 3rd ed., (Ann Arbor, MI: The University of Michigan Press, 1992), 169-170.
39. Tarnas, *Western Mind*, 285-87.
40. Ibid., 287-88, 296.

revealed "the paradigm of scientific practice" and in the process "revealed the true nature of reality."[41] The scientific laws and empirical principles that emerged with Newton's synthesis dominated all areas of learning and knowledge from his day to the present.[42] Richard Osborne points out that Newton's "picture of the mechanical universe, so precise in detail, so apparently perfect, was not challenged until Einstein, and still dominates the popular imagination."[43]

Positivism: The Exclusivity of the Empirical

During the nineteenth and early twentieth century, as Donald Schon points out, the extension of empiricism and scientific method into all arenas of inquiry was accelerated by the rise of positivism and its institutionalization in most universities and professional schools. This philosophy of knowledge held that "empirical science was not just a form of knowledge but the only source of positive knowledge of the world." Any other method of inquiry was considered "mysticism, superstition, and . . . pseudoknowledge." Further, scientific knowledge and method was also to be used to control social, political, and moral problems through the use of technology. According to Peter Gay, "Positivism was not an organized school of thought so much as a pervasive attitude toward man, nature, and styles of inquiry. Its votaries hoped to import the program of the natural sciences, their findings and methods, into the investigation of all human thought and action, both private and public."[44]

The positivists, however, were unwittingly applying an "objective metaphor to the world and thus committing the very crime they were attacking."[45] By focusing solely and exclusively on the object *in se* in complete "untainted" isola-

---

41. Ibid., 270.
42. Van Doren, *History of Knowledge*, 210.
43. Richard Osborne, *Philosophy for Beginners* (New York: Writers and Readers Publishing, 1991), 68.
44. Donald Schon, *The Reflective Practitioner: How Professionals Think in Action* (New York: Basic Books, 1983), 34-35, 32; Peter Gay, *Freud: A Life for Our Time* (New York: W. W. Norton & Company, 1988), 34.
45. Spence, *Freudian Metaphor*, 3.

tion from environment or context, the positivists naively discounted any influence of the observer on the individual object. Thus, by using an objectivist lens to view reality, they naturally found objects everywhere, including the human subjects they studied. This trapped them inside a self-validating model and blinded them to their predicament. Thus, rejecting the myths of religion as superstition, they unquestioningly created their own.

This empirical-positivist philosophy of science and knowledge was especially dominant in Austria and Germany in the late nineteenth century when the field of psychotherapy was coming into its own.[46] It thoroughly informed and influenced the development of classical psychiatry and "orthodox" psychoanalysis from Freud's day to our own.[47]

Freud and His Scientific Training

Freud and his contemporaries were trained, according to Gay, as rigorous empirical, "natural" scientists throughout their studies of medicine, neurology, and psychiatry. Their education and clinical training under such famous scientists and doctors as Wundt, Brucke, Helmholtz, Meynert, and Charcot emphasized endless laboratory experiments on living subjects, both animal and human. This method concentrated on precise systematic measuring, observing, recording, and analysis of isolated "uncontaminated" data with finer and finer instrumentation. This method of rigorous experimental science sought the ideals of objectivity, impartiality, "*reductionism, causal explanation*, and *prediction*."[48]

As Freud and his colleagues embarked on their practices as psychotherapists, they developed their own personal theories and techniques for individual treatment. Their predominant epistemological model, however, remained a positivistic one borrowed from the physical sciences, deterministic causality, experimental design and research,

---

46. Schon, *Reflective Practitioner*, 32, 34-35.
47. Wolf, *Quantum Leap*, 45.
48. Gay, *Freud*, 24-37; Jerome Bruner, *Acts of Meaning* (Cambridge, MA: Harvard University Press, 1990), xiii. Emphasis in original.

intrapsychic psychology, and the radical individualistic philosophy of the Enlightenment.[49]

Like many of the psychologists of his day, Freud believed that only empirical knowledge should be considered scientific and worthy of study, since it alone could be considered universal, objective, and free of bias. It was his ambition to understand the necessary universal workings of the human mind in the same way Newton had comprehended the laws of the physical universe. It was his belief that even what was most irrational, unconscious, or disturbed in human activity, be that mental or physical, followed definite mechanical rules of operation regulating the hydraulic flow of energy within the human organism. According to Van Doren, "He was a mechanist and a determinist. He sought the explanation of the mind's working in the body, believing that the health or the illness of the mind was dependent on a balance, or imbalance, of physical forces. . . . [H]e continued to believe that the human being is more than anything else a machine."[50]

Psychoanalysis: Bias-Free and Objective?

Freud believed that his own approach to psychotherapy, namely, psychoanalysis, was an empirical and bias-free method. When he referred to psychoanalysis as "an impartial instrument, like the infinitesimal calculus," he did so in the belief that his theories were as compelling, necessary, objective, and neutral as Newton's mathematical proofs.[51] In this way, as Bruner puts it, "psychoanalysis invoked positivism to legitimize its claim to being a deterministic science that dealt in causality."[52]

Freud's theory and technique took their shape from the epistemological die in which they had been cast. Thus, the dissection of the human psyche followed methods and procedures similar to the dissection of animal carcasses, lab specimens, or human cadavers. Gay writes, "Freud the zoologist studying the gonads of eels, Freud the physiologist studying

49. Ibid., 31-32; Spence, *Freudian Metaphor*, 154.
50. Van Doren, *History of Knowledge*, 282.
51. Spence, *Freudian Metaphor*, 43.
52. Jerome Bruner, foreword to *Freudian Metaphor* by Spence, xi.

the nerve cells of crayfish, Freud the psychologist studying the emotions of humans, engaged in a single enterprise."[53]

Freud, ever the empiricist, also believed that the whole of reality, be that physical or psychological, could be understood only by a carefully detailed analysis of its individual component parts in isolation. The analysis and interpretation of this data would then yield the scientific truths or natural laws that drove the operations of the whole. Therefore, basic units under analysis should be completely isolated in the laboratory from any contaminating influences of the surrounding or original environment. All forms of personal subjectivity in the observer were to be suppressed ruthlessly and rigid distance and objectivity maintained at all times. Whatever part was flawed could then be discovered, corrected, reinserted into the whole of which it was a part, and the reassembled whole then returned to its original environment, ready to withstand any further disturbances or irregularities in its surroundings.

Freud's Scientific Method: Psychoanalysis

Freud the scientist applied this empirical method in psychotherapy as well. Individuals in psychoanalysis were to be seen and studied in complete isolation from any contaminating influences, such as family of origin, spouse, or children, as if they were being observed in the sterile environment of the laboratory or operating room. Psychoanalysis, like surgery, would then discover and isolate where the "abnormality" or neurosis was within the drive system of the patient, analyze the flaw or injury to its component parts, correct it through talking, free association, transference, or other techniques, and then return the cured patient to his or her original environment, ready to resume a "normal" life in a "normal" way.

All during this operation the analyst was to sit out of sight of the client, silent, opaque, skillfully and minutely observing everything about the patient – not just content but gestures, tone of voice, affect, resistance, punctuality, and dress. "Countertransference," that is, any emotion or feeling toward the client on the part of the analyst, was to be consid-

---

53. Gay, *Freud*, 36.

ered "an insidious obstruction to the analyst's benevolent neutrality." For Freud, this countertransference was a bias that had no place in psychoanalysis. It had to be mastered and eliminated. For the analyst had to maintain his role as skilled observer and impassive empiricist "to carry through the operation as correctly and effectively as possible."[54]

According to Bruner, positivism's claim to perfect objectivity in science and knowledge is "viewed with austere suspicion in today's intellectual world." And he extends this critique to Freud and psychoanalysis: "In a deep sense, the difficulties of contemporary psychoanalysis inhere precisely in its claim to being a 'science' in the positivistic sense of the term and by avoiding the thorny issues of interpretation and hermeneutics. By trying to live up to such a claim, it achieves the ironic outcome of being not only questionable science, but an incorrigible form of interpretation as well."[55]

Freud had adopted a mechanistic approach similar to Newton's in his determination to make psychotherapy an "objective science," one completely impartial and free of all bias. But by failing to distinguish experimental science as just one model of knowledge among many others, Freud was unaware of his own *a priori* objectivist and positivist biases.

The Shift to Systemic Thought

Toward the middle of the twentieth century, an epistemological shift from linear to nonlinear ways of thinking began to occur across several diverse fields of study.

> At midcentury the social sciences became more social: the study of small groups flourished, animals were observed in their natural environments instead of in the zoo or laboratory, psychological experiments were seen as social situations in experimenter-bias studies, businesses began to be thought of as complex systems, mental hospitals were studied as total institutions, and ecology developed as a special field, with man and other creatures looked upon as inseparable from their environments.[56]

---

54. Ibid., 254.
55. Bruner, foreword to *Freudian Metaphor* by Spence, x, xv.
56. Jay Haley, ed., *Changing Families: A Family Therapy Reader*

Convergencies of theories in other fields, such as functionalism in anthropology,[57] Bertalanffy's General Systems Theory in biology,[58] and Alan Turing's computer theory in mathematics,[59] also signaled that a new general way of thinking about thinking was beginning to emerge across the sciences. Norbert Wiener also used this new epistemology to develop cybernetics, "the study of control processes in systems, especially analysis of the flow of information in closed systems."[60] He then merged technology and theory during World War II to design cybernetic weapon systems.[61] This new conceptual shift in epistemology was eventually dubbed "systems theory."[62] Systems could now be found everywhere from brain to thermostat, from family to biosphere, from marriage to organizations.

Changing Views of Interaction and Causality

Systems theory and cybernetics studied the pattern of relationships *among* the parts instead of focusing on the substance of parts in isolation from other parts. Interaction was now key. In fact, one definition of system, Davidson states, was "any entity maintained by the mutual interaction of its parts, from atom to cosmos. . . ." In this new epistemology, two plus two no longer equals four but something much greater, "more than the aggregate of its parts."[63]

Now in the meeting of mind and matter there was an additional, if unquantifiable, factor that had to be accounted for, namely, the interactive relationship occurring *between* knower and known. This systemic interaction made knowing and reality dynamic, and it was that dynamic which made

---

(New York: Gruen and Stratton, 1971), 1, quoted in Nichols and Schwartz, *Family Therapy*, 97.

57. Nichols and Schwartz, *Family Therapy*, 97.
58. Mark Davidson, *Uncommon Sense: The Life and Thought of Ludwig von Bertalanffy.* (Los Angeles: Jeremy P. Tarcher, 1983), 21-44.
59. Van Doren, *History of Knowledge*, 348-50.
60. Nichols and Schwartz, *Family Therapy*, 589.
61. Ibid., 106.
62. Ibid., 96.
63. Davidson, *Uncommon Sense,* 26; Nichols and Schwartz, *Family Therapy*, 101.

the whole greater than the mere sum of its parts. Now the mind no longer genuflected in resigned obeisance to the decrees of a preexistent reality but engaged in a relationship of cocreation, mutual interdependence, and reciprocal communication with what it observed.

Central to systems thinking was "the shift from *linear* to *circular* causality."[64] As the linear working of the mechanical clock had once served as the dominant model of thought in Newton's universe, now the non-linear self-regulating interactive systems circuitry of computers[65] replaced it. Now such cybernetic concepts as systemic feedback, adaptation to change, self-correction, self-organization, homeostasis or self-maintenance, had to be studied to understand the flow of information between sender and receiver.[66]

The Rise of Family Therapy

Systems thinking also recontextualized the practice of psychotherapy and led to a completely new theoretical and technical approach called family therapy. As it developed, family therapy created its own very distinctive theories, techniques, and modalities, which it hoped would shake psychotherapy's narrow dependency on the "positivist, empiricist, rational-logical model of modern science."[67] Family therapists "rejected the intrapsychic role theory and psychoanalytic concepts . . . learned in training and focused instead on the dynamics of interchange between persons."[68] They saw systems theory not just as another treatment *method*, but as an entirely "new way of conceptualizing human problems."[69]

---

64. Ibid., 108. Emphasis in original.
65. Watzlawick, Bavelas, and Jackson, *Pragmatics*, 126-128.
66. H. A. Guttman, "Systems Theory, Cybernetics, and Epistemology," in *Handbook of Family Therapy*, eds. A. S. Gurman and D. P. Kniskern (New York: Brunner/Mazel, 1991), 41.
67. Pauline Rosenau, *Post-modernism and the Social Sciences: Insights, Inroads, and Intrusions* (Princeton: Princeton University Press, 1992), 9.
68. Nichols and Schwartz, *Family Therapy*, 40.
69. Paul Watzlawick and John Weakland, eds., *The Interactional View: Studies at the Mental Research Institute, Palo Alto, 1965-1974* (New York: W. W. Norton & Company, 1977), xii.

While Freud and most mental health professionals treated individuals in strict isolation from the contaminating influence of environment, family, and other variables, now family therapists invited clients and their families to attend sessions *together*, sometimes including several generations of a family in treatment. They no longer concentrated their attention on the "pathology" of the one individual in the family that had been labeled as the "identified patient." Instead they observed all family members and studied family structure, interaction, behavior, and process. They conceived "pathology" not in any one individual but in the operations of the whole family system. "The family *is* a system in that a change in one part of the system is followed by compensatory change in other parts of the system."[70]

Like a computer, families seemed to function according to rigid but unwritten rules of circular causality. Nichols and Schwartz write, "Using the concept of *circularity*, family therapists changed the way we think of psychopathology, from something caused by events in the past or inside the person, to something that is a part of ongoing, circular causal sequences of behavior. Johnny is withdrawn and shy because father overprotects; father overprotects because Johnny is so withdrawn and shy."[71]

Each action of each member of a family seemed to be both the cause and the effect of every other member's behavior. Through their interactions and relating, members of a family were always influencing, affecting, directing, and regulating one another. Together the family members seemed to operate more as one single organic system than as a group of individuals. Underneath all their various and diverse behaviors and interactions, the family members seemed to have one single aim and purpose: the maintenance of the family's homeostatic functioning. This homeostasis or self-regulation resisted all change, thus preserving and continuing the family as a closed system. This "systems" model of epistemology eventually generated new theories and techniques that revolutionized and reshaped the field of psychotherapy for the next forty years.

---

70. Haley, *Changing Families*, 288. Emphasis in original.
71. Nichols and Schwartz, *Family Therapy*, 125. Emphasis in original.

The Limits of Family Systems Therapy. Today, however, voices critical of "systems thinking" in family therapy have begun to be heard among practitioners themselves.[72] These voices willingly admit that systems thinking has contributed important insights into the structure, functioning, and dynamics of family interactions. But little attention has been paid to the relationship between the family system and the therapist(s) interacting with it. Thus, while clinicians have applied a thoroughgoing systems model to family dynamics and structure, they have unwittingly retained an empiricist epistemology regarding their own clinical observations and research.

This is because family therapists and researchers still have, until recently, seen themselves as impartial, "objective" observers studying family systems from outside. In this way, they sought to uncover from their "external" omniscient vantage point what was "really" happening among the members of the family. The subjects might have been human rather than animal, but the empirical laboratory model of nineteenth century scientific research still obtained throughout the field in subtle ways.

What the first generation of family therapists and researchers had failed to remember regarding their own work was what might be called the basic assumption of postmodernism, that is, Heisenberg's principle of uncertainty: the act of observing changes what is observed and measured. These therapists needed to carry the systems model of epistemology one step further and become aware that they too were within a system of interactive relationships which shaped their findings and actively influenced the observed behavior of their subjects. That system was the therapeutic relationship itself existing *between* families and therapists.

---

72. Lynn Hoffman, "Constructing Realities: An Art of Lenses," *Family Process*, 29, no. 1 (1990): 1-12; Michael Nichols, *The Self in the System: Expanding the Limits of Family Therapy* (New York: Brunner/Mazel, 1987); Michael White and David Epston, *Narrative Means to Therapeutic Ends* (New York: W. W. Norton & Company, 1990); Harlene Anderson and Harold Goolishian, "Supervision as Collaborative Conversation: Questions and Reflections," in H. Brandau, ed., *Von der Supervision zur systemischen Vision* (Salzburg: Otto Muller Verlag, 1990).

This meant that the actual clinical conditions of observing the family seriously affected or "disturbed"[73] the family's behavior and interactions and therefore distorted the therapist's findings. Thus, such things as whether the family was observed by a single therapist or a team, in person or behind one-way mirrors, with all family members present or some absent, actually changed and influenced the behavior of the family being observed. And that behavior in turn influenced what the observers saw. As a result, the "real" family could never be seen. Nor could the observation or analysis of the family and its dynamics ever be called "objective" or "neutral."

The Question of Norms. Throughout the first generation of family therapy, a second empiricist fallacy skewed both the theory and practice of clinicians in the field, namely, their failure to question their own preconceptions and assumptions about what they considered "normal" family functioning. As "professionals" outside the family, they used all sorts of strategic techniques and interventions to change families. But change requires norms of some kind. If family therapists were to be "experts" in "correcting" or "repairing" dysfunctional families, then they had to have some preconceived ideas – explicit or implicit – about what constituted "normal" or "healthy" behavior and interaction in the first place.

It is only now, from emerging cross-cultural perspectives and hermeneutic models of epistemology, that it can be seen that the values informing American family life in the 1950s and early 1960s affected family therapy as well. Those values derived from powerful political, economic, and cultural forces that dominated society during that era and achieved unspoken normative status. During this same period, television moved into the American home and became a member of the extended family. Along with other media of the day, it represented, without question or comment, the unchallenged values of the dominant white suburban middle-class culture as normative. Biases of all kinds against race, gender, and class were subliminally reinforced beyond awareness and thus excluded from debate or analysis. Many of these same unexpressed values and biases also affected early family therapy.

---

73. Wolf, *Quantum Leap*, 61.

In a sense, where the family therapists failed was in their inability to move to an epistemological level and context from which they could reflect on the assumptions of their own model and engage in some intelligent self-evaluation and critique. They would have to question the cultural values and biases that had shaped their implicit therapeutic norms. In other words, if they were going to follow a cybernetic or systems epistemology, then they should have done so more thoroughly. They should have at least looked at their norms and values from a systemic, interactive, contextual perspective, one that asked where those beliefs had come from, what forces or structures had influenced them, and what structures, views, ideas, and behavior, they, in turn, maintained.

This would have led them to considering how norms and values are culturally conditioned. Then, further questions would have to be asked. What relationship existed between sociocultural norms and economic values within American families? What ends did they serve? Who benefited from these particular norms and values? Who suffered? Who was included in or excluded from the mainstream of society by these values? What sociopolitical structures of hierarchy and power were maintained by such standards and criteria? By failing to ask these questions or to reflect on their own epistemology, family therapists repeated the essentialist thinking of the empiricists and unconsciously preserved their own residual beliefs as if they existed in some objective reality beyond space, time, critique, or context.

The Nonnormative Approach. Some family therapists thought they had resolved this issue by claiming that they had a "nonnormative" approach to family functioning. Don Jackson wrote a now-famous essay describing normality as a myth.[74] In fact, a hallmark of family therapy became its "nonnormative" stance: "By nonnormative, we mean that we use no criteria to judge the health or normality of an individual or family. As therapists, we do not regard any particular way of functioning, relating or living as a problem if the client is not expressing discontent with it."[75]

---

74. Don Jackson, "The Myth of Normality," *Medical Opinion and Review*, 3 (1967): 28-33.
75. Richard Fisch, Review of *Problem-solving Therapy*, by Jay Haley, in *Family Process* 17 (1978): 107.

But this is reminiscent of skeptics who doubt all assertions of categorical truth – except their own. They fail to see how their own skepticism follows from a dogmatic pronouncement that nothing is certain. In similar fashion, most family therapists failed to see how their own insistence on being "nonnormative" was itself a proposal of a norm. However sincere the attempt to be nonnormative might have been among such practitioners, wishing didn't make it so. The desire to be value-free didn't resolve the question of values. If anything, those who disclaimed norms all together rendered their own unconscious values inaccessible from any critique and thus preserved them all the more rigidly and covertly.

According to Nichols and Schwartz, this has been one of the most serious complaints leveled at the field by feminist critics.[76] How does a therapist maintain a "nonnormative" stance with families where battering, incest, rape, and other abuse occur? Therapists following the logic of a nonnormative position would not have even considered these to be problems as long as "the client is not expressing discontent."[77]

The nonnormative stance was also often invoked by therapists who claimed to be "culturally blind." But researchers in cross-cultural counseling find that those who make such claims often "respond according to their own conditioned values, assumptions, and perspectives of reality without regard for other views. What is needed for counselors is for them to become 'culturally aware,' to act on the basis of a critical analysis and understanding of their own conditioning, the conditioning of their clients, and the sociopolitical system of which they are both a part."[78]

Omnipresent Norms, Values, and Culture

Each and every epistemological model, as we have seen above, contains norms and values that are necessarily implied by its own paradigm. An epistemology that models

---

76. Nichols and Schwartz, *Family Therapy*, 147-50.
77. Fisch, Review of *Problem-solving Therapy*, 107.
78. Derald Sue and David Sue, *Counseling the Culturally Different: Theory and Practice*, 2d ed., (New York: John Wiley & Sons, 1990), 138.

itself on cybernetics and systems circuitry is necessarily going to view everything it comprehends as a computer, including families. And since computers are self-operating, self-regulating machines that function according to their own internal systemic rules, it is also very easy to view families as isolated self-contained systems outside of all contexts. "By viewing the family out of context, family therapists locate family dysfunction entirely within interpersonal relationships in the family, ignore broader patterns of dysfunction occurring across families, and fail to notice the relationship between social context and family dysfunction."[79]

Thus, by not questioning the norms and values intrinsic to their epistemological model, family therapists failed to reflect on how their prior beliefs shaped and defined their own theories and techniques. Like the positivists before them, they presumed that their ideas were simply self-evident and, therefore, value-free.

From a postmodern perspective, therefore, Freudian analysis or psychotherapeutic practices based on systems exist within the same world of "modernism" and are really more alike than different from each other. That is because both approaches to therapy derived from mechanistic epistemology. Bruner argues that any psychology based on a computational or cybernetic model is ultimately as mechanistic and reductionist as the empiricism of nineteenth century scientism. The computer may be far more sophisticated than Newton's clock and operate according to space-age circuitry and rules, but it is finally just another result-oriented machine that uses functionality as its norm. As a result, all questions of personal values, assumptions, preconceptions, as well as the meaning of one's life, hopes, desires, actions, and experience must be suppressed, because such subjectivity has no place in modernism's scientific method. Instead only functioning is considered. "Computing became the model of mind, and in place of the concept of meaning there emerged the concept of computability."[80]

---

79. J. M. Avis, "Deepening Awareness: A Private Study Guide to Feminism and Family Therapy," in L. Braverman, ed., *Women, Feminism, and Family Therapy* (New York: Haworth Press: 1988), 17.

80. Bruner, *Acts of Meaning*, 6.

Chapter Four

Reclaiming Story: Postmodern Psychotherapy

TODAY SYSTEMIC THERAPISTS ARE THEMSELVES BECOMING increasingly aware of some of the theoretical limitations of family therapy. They are concerned with the overtechnicalization of theory and technique, the increasing literalization of computer metaphor and mechanism in systems thinking, and an ever-narrowing of perspective.[1] As long as the operational functioning of a family system remains the dominant norm of therapy, then the personal subjectivities involved in the interaction between therapist and family will continue to be subordinated to a subtle modern form of objectivism.[2] External norms and definitions of "correct," "optimal" systemic functioning will continue to take priority over the actual people in the session.

These self-critical voices within family therapy are some of the first to question the adequacy of "systems thinking" for psychotherapeutic use and to suggest the need for a more meaning-oriented, nonmechanistic epistemology from which to proceed. Thus, the question that arises from their colloquies and musings is this: could there be another epistemological model that contains within its own form and structure an intrinsic resistance to being confused or identified with reality? This, as we shall see, is the goal of those

---

1. Hoffman, "Constructing Realities"; Michael Nichols, *The Self in the System: Expanding the Limits of Family Therapy* (New York: Brunner/Mazel, 1987); White and Epston, *Narrative Means*; Anderson and Goolishian, "Supervision as Collaborative Conversation."
2. Nichols, *Self in the System,* 23.

newer approaches to psychotherapy, dubbed postmodern, that are beginning to be articulated in the field.

Postmodernism as Critique of the Modern

The current questioning of epistemology and method in psychotherapy is significant because it originates in the larger context of the shift from "modern" forms of discourse to "postmodern" ones.[3] Tarnas writes, "The postmodern intellectual situation is profoundly complex and ambiguous — perhaps that is its very essence. What is called postmodern varies considerably according to context, but in its most general and widespread form, the postmodern mind may be viewed as an open-ended, indeterminate set of attitudes that has been shaped by a great diversity of intellectual and cultural currents. . . ."[4]

The term "postmodernism" is used today as a corrective to the categorical claims of science and the "modern" mind as the sole arbiters of all objective truth and reality. "Modernism is assumed to have had its genesis in the Enlightenment and the term is used interchangeably with Enlightenment or Western thought. This form of thought insists that knowledge can be founded upon, or grounded in, absolute truth. It assumes that knowledge is 'about' something external to the knower, and can present itself objectively to the knower."[5]

In trying to counter the "irrationality," essentialism, and hierarchy of the medieval worldview,[6] modern science overreached itself and eventually became as dogmatic and authoritarian in its claims as its predecessor, the Church, had been. Modern science claimed for itself a new kind of infallible authority: "objectivity." Now science could so guarantee truth and certitude that its methods were overapplied

---

3. W. T. Anderson, *Reality Isn't What It Used to Be: Theatrical Politics, Ready-to-Wear Religion, Global Myths, Primitive Chic, and Other Wonders of the Postmodern World* (San Francisco: HarperCollins, 1990), 6; Rosenau, *Post-modernism and the Social Sciences*, 5-8; Lowe, "Postmodern Themes," 43.
4. Tarnas, *Western Mind,* 395.
5. Lowe, "Postmodern Themes," 43.
6. Rosenau, *Post-modernism and the Social Sciences,* 5.

beyond the confines of its own discipline to nonscientific fields as well. The result was an extreme form of "scientism" that claimed only its methods could be used validly and effectively in the pursuit of knowledge. As Rosenau puts it, "Modern science established its reputation on objectivity, rigorous procedures of inquiry, the material rather than the metaphysical. Science, in turn, came to claim its own monopoly of truth. Its authority expanded and superseded that held by its more irrational and arbitrary antecedents."[7]

By discovering "objective truth," science and its handmaid, technology, were supposed to release humans from their fears and superstitions, cure disease, and usher in a utopian age of unmatched progress and achievement. Instead science rewarded modernism's search for ultimate reality and truth with mixed blessings. Rosenau articulates some of them: "As we in the West approach the end of the twentieth century, the 'modern' record – world wars, the rise of Nazism, concentration camps (in both East and West), genocide, world-wide depression, Hiroshima, Vietnam, Cambodia, the Persian Gulf, and a widening gap between rich and poor – makes any belief in the idea of progress or faith in the future seem questionable." One could also add to this list the eugenic experiments of the Nazi doctors, Chernobyl, holes in the ozone layer, and global warming. As a result of the legacy modern science has left the world, Rosenau goes on to say that postmodernism today "reacts to uncritical confidence in modern science and smugness about objective knowledge. . . . Post-modernists are uneasy with their more conventional colleagues' uncritical acceptance of philosophical foundationalism, the Enlightenment heritage, and the methodological suppositions of modern science."[8]

Elements of the Postmodern

Quantum Physics. The irony in all this, of course, is that if anything led to the overthrow of "modern" science as the prevailing "system of mind" in our time, it was "modern" science itself as it sought to grasp the objective nature of absolute reality in finer and finer detail, even down to the

---

7. Ibid., 9.
8. Ibid., 5, 9.

subatomic level of existence. Much to its surprise, it instead found that the very particles of reality were changing with every observation and attempt at measurement.

> [Werner] Heisenberg discovered an extension of [Wolfgang Pauli's] dark point: not one or the other variable is uncontrolled, but *both* are uncontrolled in a reciprocal way. A fundamental imprecision in the measurements of conjugate atomic variables is required by nature, no matter how precise the researcher's instruments. . . .
>
> . . . In the very act of measuring the properties of a quantum object at any given moment, the physicist selects one of the possibilities for that property. At the same time, he or she introduces a new range of possibilities for the result of any future measurement of that property, but without a causal determination of which possibility will actually be observed. The very act of measuring the position of an electron disturbs its velocity, because light is required to "see" the electron. The future course of the electron's motion, its sequence of positions in space, cannot be predicted with certainty, because its present position and velocity are not known with absolute certainty.[9]

The scientists of this century found that the very particles of reality were changing with every observation and attempt at measurement. Fritjof Capra writes, "At the subatomic level, matter does not exist with certainty at definite places, but rather shows 'tendencies to exist'. . . [S]ubatomic particles have no meaning as isolated entities but can be understood only as interconnections, or correlations, between various processes of observation and measurement."[10]

Perspective and Context. Ludwig von Bertalanffy, the prominent organic biologist and polymath, was one of the first people to understand the broader epistemological implications of quantum physics and to apply them in a more general way to other areas of knowledge and research beyond physics. He emphasized the importance of perspective and context in all acts of observation, inquiry, and investigation. Nichols and Schwartz write, "Bertalanffy coined the

---

9. Cassidy, *Uncertainty,* 233-235.
10. Fritjof Capra, *The Turning Point* (New York: Simon and Schuster, 1982), 80.

term 'perspectivism' to characterize his belief that while reality exists, the reality one *knows* can never be fully objective because their view of it is filtered through their particular perspective. To a man with a hammer, everything looks like a nail. To a physicist, a table is a collection of electrons; a chemist sees the same table as organic compound; the biologist sees a set of wood cells; and the art historian sees a baroque object."[11]

What the table is, therefore, is not obvious in itself nor predetermined by any inherent structure. Rather it depends on which observers are looking, from where, and how they are seeing.[12] Nor is one view of it more objectively accurate, right, correct, or complete than another. Each view can be valid, given the specific perspective of the observer, the context of the viewing, and the relationship between knower and known. What a table means, represents, symbolizes, and how it will function, therefore, depends on the perceiving, interpreting, and resulting knowing of the knower. What one sees, therefore, is affected by what one is looking for. And what one is looking for is determined by what one has seen and known already and can imagine.

Any knowledge of the "real" is, therefore, at best partial, limited as it is by perspective and context, and thus always open to greater clarification and enlightenment from the inclusion of other alternative perspectives. Davidson writes, "Bertalanffy also recognized that the act of observation has an effect on the phenomena being observed. This strengthened his perspectivist conviction that one should be humble about one's observations and theories, rather than believing that they are the absolute truth. This keeps one's mind open to valuable new ideas."[13]

Constructivism. The "perspectivism" of Bertalanffy discussed above is also very similar to the methodological approach known today as "constructivism."[14] Constructivism

---

11. Nichols and Schwartz, *Family Therapy,* 105.
12. Bertalanffy developed this insight to create General Systems Theory (GST). GST is "a holistic way of thinking based on an awareness of the behavior of systems in general." Davidson, *Uncommon Sense,* 224.
13. Ibid.
14. Hoffman, "Constructing Realities," 2-3.

advances the thesis that there is no one, singular, unique aboriginal reality "out there" enjoying absolute ontological privilege to the exclusion of the perceiver or which "preexists and is independent of human mental activity and human symbolic language. . . ."[15] Bruner writes, "Indeed, as the philosopher, Nelson Goodman, once put it we know now that facts are not found, but made. Or, as W. V. Quine states it, physics turns out to be ninety-five percent speculation and five percent observation. And it is sometimes puzzling what status to give the latter."[16]

From this perspective, we can say that fact is fictive, the product of a complex mutually interactive process between the internal and external experience of a subject that must always include an artful selection, ordering, interpretation, and transformation of raw sensory data into a universe of meaning. "But the decision about what is essential and what is irrelevant apparently varies from individual to individual and seems to be determined by criteria which are largely outside individual awareness. . . . [R]eality is what we make it or, in Hamlet's words, '. . . there is nothing either good or bad, but thinking makes it so.'"[17] The assumptions, presuppositions, and expectations of the observer are now seen as major interactive elements that have to be factored into any analysis and interpretation of the data.

What we call reality, therefore, is not some kind of primordial substance or prime matter but a mutually interactive process, one in which we participate in a creative and active way with what we observe or know. What we bring to our encounter with creation determines what we see and find there. As Bruner puts it, "What we call the world is a product of some mind whose symbolic procedures construct the world. . . . The world of appearance, the very world we live in, is 'created' by mind."[18]

And what we see, find, and create changes us and how we see the world. In other words, we experience what we have created and what we have created determines what we experience. Just as we are constantly constructing a world from the phenomena we observe, we are in turn being de-

15. Bruner, *Actual Minds*, 95.
16. Bruner, foreword to *Freudian Metaphor* by Spence, ix-x.
17. Watzlawick, Bavelas, and Jackson, *Pragmatics*, 95
18. Bruner, *Actual Minds*, 95-96.

fined by our definitions of that world and the categories with which we credit it. Davidson, citing unpublished lecture notes by von Bertalanffy, writes, "There are no facts flying around in nature as if they are butterflies that you put into a nice orderly collection. Our cognition is not a mirroring of ultimate reality but rather is an active process, in which we create models of the world. These models direct what we actually see, what we consider as fact."[19]

Just as "the act of observation has an effect on the phenomena being observed,"[20] so too are we shaped, influenced, and affected by the "realities" we construct and permit ourselves to see. Each past encounter with the world, each past construction of reality leaves us predisposed to certain expectations, assumptions, and preconceptions about the nature of reality and these in turn determine what new realities we can admit to consciousness in the future. But the worlds we make are not constructed *ab ovo* but, Bruner writes, from "other worlds, created by others, which we have taken as given. We do not operate on some sort of aboriginal reality independent of our own minds or the minds of those who precede or accompany us."[21]

The ramifications of this are truly "revolutionary" in the paradigmatic sense that Kuhn meant. The whole project of modern science, to know reality as directly, immediately, and objectively as possible, independent of any "contaminating" influences of a subject, concludes in paradox. The presence and interaction of a knower with the known is necessary to activate reality, but that same presence also disturbs and changes what is known.

Thus, assertions about the nature of reality no longer can be made with the same kind of absolute certainty or predictability as before. Knowledge of reality must be more forthcoming about its inherent limitations and concede that it is finally always relative, discontinuous, uncertain, indeterminate, containing potential complementarities and possibilities yet to be explored. Bruner writes, "In our times – after Einstein's relativity, Bohr's complementarity, and the riddles of discontinuity in quantum theory – even physics

19. Davidson, *Uncommon Sense*, 214.
20. Nichols and Schwartz, *Family Therapy*, 105.
21. Bruner, *Actual Minds*, 95-96.

has acceded to the uncertainty that is inherent in the concept of nature. It is not at all clear how one should characterize what is 'real' in nature and what is a construct in the mind of the physicist. Nature itself has become a construct, its 'facts' subject to the perspective of the theory that drives the search for them."[22] Now nothing ever can be quite as clear, simple, or distinct as Descartes had once presumed.

It is precisely here where reality ceases to be simple, single, univocal, or objective that the trajectory of the "modern" system of mind destabilizes and "all that is solid melts in air."[23] In its place, postmodernism takes shape with its project to critique the excesses, distortions, biases, and over-statements of modern science and philosophy and to offer a reevaluation of their influence and effects on the methods and categories of contemporary thought. To develop this alternative critical perspective, postmodernism chooses methods that are radically different from the canons of modern science. Where "modernism" sought "to isolate elements, specify relationships, and formulate a synthesis, post-modernists do the opposite. They offer indeterminacy rather than determinism, diversity rather than unity, difference rather than synthesis, complexity rather than simplification. They look to the unique rather than to the general, to intertextual relations rather than causality, and to the unrepeatable rather than the re-occurring, the habitual, or the routine."[24]

Reality to the postmodern mind is various, multiple, ambiguous, highly subjective, dependent on one's point of view and perspective. Hence, for any conversation about nature and reality in the postmodern world to be intelligible, it must include context and perspective as part of its parameters.

Knowledge as Constructed. To many, postmodernism seems a rude, bastard child born of questionable academic parentage from the political and social chaos and upheaval of the last thirty years. But its intellectual lineage finds historical roots that actually go back to Giambattista Vico and the

---

22. Bruner, foreword to *Freudian Metaphor* by Spence, ix-x.
23. Marshall Berman, *All That is Solid Melts Into Air* (New York: Penguin Books, 1988), 15.
24. Rosenau, *Post-modernism and the Social Sciences*, 8.

hermeneutical tradition in the early eighteenth century.[25] According to Anderson, where Vico's more scientific and rationalist contemporaries believed "that truth meant objective, permanent, superhuman validity," he subscribed to the belief "*verum factum*," that truth is made. "As God's truth is what God comes to know as he creates and assembles it, so human truth is what man comes to know as he builds it, shaping it by his actions."[26]

As the bicameral brain perceives, excludes, amplifies, and integrates experience according to the dominant modalities of each hemisphere and its tripartite structure, it is actually constructing versions of "reality." The brain is not just recording what is "out there." It is instead creating within itself an analogous version of what it interprets as being "out there."

Knowledge and Language

To the recovery of the hermeneutical tradition of Vico and the more recent discoveries of the constructive, fictive, and interpretive processes of the brain, the role of language in the "making" of knowledge must also be added as another concern of the postmodern critique.

Language "renders" reality.[27] It "actualizes" or instantiates what is merely possible. "Language is viewed as *mediating* or even *constituting* reality, rather than *reflecting* or *representing* reality."[28] Knowledge needs language to be known. Language incarnates knowledge; it shapes and reveals it. Language personalizes knowledge the way body manifests spirit to the world. For knowledge to exist at all, to be "real," it requires the enfleshment and mediation of language.

But the very same process of "languaging" that makes knowledge actual and real also limits it.[29] Language defines and describes, but these same operations that make knowl-

---

25. Ibid., 12-14; Anderson, *Reality Isn't*, 67.
26. Anderson, *Reality Isn't*, 67.
27. Jay Efran, Michael Lukens, and Robert Lukens, *Language, Structure, and Change: Frameworks of Meaning in Psychotherapy* (New York: W. W. Norton & Company, 1990), 30.
28. Lowe, "Postmodern Themes," 43. Emphasis in original.
29. Efran, Lukens, and Lukens, *Language*, 29.

edge real, actual, and available also require its limiting, confining, reducing, modifying, specifying. Therefore, while language is a necessary vehicle for mediating knowledge, it is also, at best, a partial and imperfect one. Thus, paradoxically, like the effect of observation and measurement in the study of quantum physics, language conceals *and* reveals reality, renders *and* restrains knowledge at the same time. But without language, there would be no knowledge. We can say then that language does communicate knowledge. But the modality of language also determines the modality of knowledge.

Representational Language. Language that seeks to represent or reflect reality "concretizes, finalizes, and excludes complexity."[30] It speaks with literal precision; words are treated as "expressions of nature,"[31] "as if they [are] the events they refer to."[32] De Gramont continues, "A word is taken literally when it is taken to be the state or entity it refers to, as when the expression 'I am an American' is taken to be a literal expression of identity, as opposed to an expression of affiliation. When reified in this manner, an identity is something that is literally possessed; i.e., that one might fight over, or feel proud of, or ashamed of."[33]

Language as representational system fixes meaning to specific settings but it also can confine it there. As de Gramont puts it, "[M]eanings that initially go with words will be . . . literal in their inability to refer beyond those settings." Rosenau adds, "Representation takes for granted the referential status of words, images, meaning, and symbols; it assumes that each constitutes a fixed system of meaning and that everybody understands them more or less the same way."

The use of language as representation yielded both a modern physics and metaphysics in which objects were said to exist in and of themselves, independent of all interactive processes of observation, inquiry, and measurement. They

---

30. Rosenau, *Post-modernism and the Social Sciences*, 94.
31. David Tracy, *Plurality and Ambiguity* (San Francisco: Harper & Row, 1987), 36.
32. Patrick de Gramont, *Language and the Distortion of Meaning* (New York: New York University Press, 1990), 90.
33. de Gramont, *Language and the Distortion of Meaning*, 94.

could be known directly, immediately, fully, and accurately as they "really" were. Rosenau continues:

> [Representation] assumes the ability to reproduce and duplicate external reality. Objects are supposed to refer directly to things outside themselves that can be represented. In other words, representation implies that things exist independently in the real world. . . . Attempting to represent an exterior world also affirms reality as knowledge, as universal, as truth. . . .
>
> . . . An "external object of nature is conveyed to the inner subject or mind through the agency of 'representatives' of sense or 'ideas.'" . . . Within the framework of representation there is a separate subject and object; the subject as researcher seeks to represent and the object of inquiry is represented. Because of its claim of objectivity, representation leads to a "compulsion to judge accuracy or correctness."[34]

The introduction of such concepts as relativity, uncertainty, and complementarity by the quantum physicists in the early part of this century completely changed our ideas about the nature, description, and language of reality. "As Bohr would soon emphasize more explicitly, we can never know nature as it really is; we can know it only as it appears to us as we become part of the experiment itself." Just as instrumentation and measurement were no longer understood to be "inert," "passive," or "neutral" media, so too language was understood to affect, shape, even create, what it expressed. As Heisenberg wrote in a letter to Pauli (dated 23 February 1927), "the solution can now, I believe, be expressed pregnantly by the statement: the path only comes into existence through this, that we observe it." Cassidy comments, "What [Heisenberg] seemed to be saying is that not only is it fruitless and senseless to inquire about reality beyond our observations, but as far as we are concerned, there really is no more to reality than what we can observe of it. In a sense we create reality ourselves by becoming a part of it through the disturbance of our measuring instruments."[35]

---

34. Ibid., 93; Rosenau, *Post-modernism and the Social Sciences*, 96-97.
35. Cassidy, *Uncertainty*, 235-36.

Just as reality no longer existed apart from an observing or measuring subject, neither did it exist apart from the language used to express it. Language no longer merely represented reality passively; it actively created, shaped, and defined how reality was perceived and understood in the human mind.

Language in the Postmodern Age. Thus, language in the postmodern age isn't what it used to be either. "Language has no direct relationship to the real world; it is, rather, only symbolic. Representation, then, is inadequate in all its various forms because images of the world are language dependent and cannot be exchanged between people with any degree of certainty. All representation is mediated by language that makes it 'linguistically reflective' rather than reality related." Like the child who pointed out that the Emperor was not wearing the splendid clothes His Royal Majesty thought he was, postmodernism takes delight in exposing how representational language, in fact, misrepresents reality.

> These post-modernists argue that in the absence of truth one must welcome multiple interpretations, whereas representation assumes something out there is true or valid enough to be re-presented. Modern representation assumes "meaning or truth preceded and determined the representations that communicated it." Post-modernists argue it is the other way around; representations create the "truth" they supposedly reflect.
> . . . Post-modernists believe that representation encourages generalization, and in so doing it focuses on identity and fails to appreciate the importance of difference. Representation takes a "resemblance between things" and ascribes "complete congruence, denying difference." It emphasizes the sameness of the original and the represented. It assumes homogeneity, implying equivalence and identity of interest.[36]

Postmodernists insist language refers to language, not reality. Language is an attempt to comprehend and communicate the various contexts, levels, and limits of meaning that humans find in their experience. As de Gramont puts it, "Language is essentially about itself, not in the literal

---

36. Rosenau, *Post-modernism and the Social Sciences,* 96, 95, 97.

sense of being what it represents, but in being about its possibilities for generating meaning." Postmodernists use language in self-mocking, self-referential ways to subvert and deconstruct any conscious or unconscious identifications between language and a singular reality. They use language in ways to call attention to its protean ability to trigger simultaneously – with the same sounds and signs – alternative imaginations, multiple possibilities and outcomes. Rosenau writes, "There are no precise meanings for words, no definitive versions of a text, in short, no simple truths." J. Hillis Miller adds, "If meaning in language rises not from the reference of signs to something outside words but from differential relations among the words themselves, if 'referent' and 'meaning' must always be distinguished, then the notion of a literary text which is validated by its one-to-one correspondence to some social, historical or psychological reality can no longer be taken for granted."[37]

Knowledge as Story

Since, as we just saw, knowledge and language are coextensive, we can say that language is what gives truth its particular shape and construction. Therefore, if one wishes to understand truth in a postmodern framework, one has to understand how language "makes," constructs, and defines knowledge while also establishing limits and conditions to its claims.

The language form favored by postmodernism as paradigmatic of its understanding of truth, knowledge, and reality is story. This is because story, by its very nature and definition, explicitly acknowledges its own truth as fictive, that is, "made up," constructed, fabricated, "something invented by the imagination."[38] Story does not claim to repre-

---

37. de Gramont, *Language and the Distortion of Meaning,* 93; Rosenau, *Post-modernism and the Social Sciences,* 79; J. Hillis Miller, "The Fiction of Realism," in *Dickens Centennial Essays,* ed. Ada Nisbet and Blake Nevius (Berkeley: University of California Press, 1971), quoted in Rosenau, *Post-modernism and the Social Sciences,* 79.

38. *Webster's Seventh New Collegiate Dictionary,* s.v. "fictive."

sent or reflect any external objective reality. Rather, the modality of story's language wholly "constitutes" and "mediates"[39] a narrative reality that is first, last, and always an imaginative one. Thus, story knows that if it has any claim to truth, it is to an analogical truthfulness only, not any empirical factuality. The truthfulness to which story invites is completely unverifiable according to any external norms or objective standards. That truthfulness is also clearly delimited by the specific partiality of its own context and perspective and by the subjectivity of its participants.

Story, therefore, is very careful to make no universal claim whatsoever about the absolute nature of objective truth or external reality. In fact, story intentionally defines itself in contradistinction to science by its own inherent epistemological limits, subjectivity, particularity, and bias. It is precisely this epistemological humility, circumspection, and intrinsic tentativeness towards the knowledge it conveys that recommends story as model and paradigm to postmodernism.

Bruner calls such story-based knowledge the "narrative mode of thought" and opposes it to the "logico-scientific mode of thought."[40] By helping to select, arrange, and organize so much stimuli into manageable clusters, story "provides a framework for understanding the past events of one's life and for planning future actions. It is the primary scheme by means of which human existence is rendered meaningful."[41]

A narrative epistemology, therefore, calls us to a way of knowing that is entirely different from a scientific one. This is because it includes (rather than excludes) personal relationship and interaction, an awareness of subjectivity, and the acceptance of the contextual limits and relativity of knowledge. Story does not dismiss truth that is individual, unique, and particular but prizes it. Nor does story have any interest whatsoever in normalizing what is idiosyncratic, odd, or statistically deviant. Nor is story interested in developing absolute rules and generic principles applicable for all cases and conditions of possibility.

---

39. Lowe, "Postmodern Themes," 43. Emphasis in original.
40. Bruner, *Actual Minds*, 88.
41. Donald Polkinghorne, *Narrative Knowing and the Human Sciences* (Albany: State University of New York Press, 1988), 11.

Unlike scientific hypothesis testing, story doesn't need to eliminate or disprove all alternate possibilities to justify its truth. If anything, narrative truth finds itself enhanced and made richer by the simultaneous presence of multiple meanings and disparate interpretations. Unlike science, story does not see a less than categorical truth as diminished or defective. Quite the contrary. By respecting the specific limits of narrative truth, story honors that which is distinctive, differentiating, and intensely personal in one's point of view within the context of a given space and time. Thus, story has been adopted by postmodernism as epistemological paradigm precisely because it is "an explanation that makes no truth claims but admits to being the teller's point of view based only on his or her experience."[42]

Story does seeks to refine truth, however, not through its constriction but rather its expansion. Story refuses to attenuate or abstract anything that is singular, divergent, or unrepeatable. Story does not traffic in abstractions. Its truthfulness is respectfully inclusive of all the multiple meaning, alternate possibilities, and unconfined diversity of human experience – that "pied Beauty" which the poet Hopkins described as "all things counter, original, spare, strange;/ whatever is fickle, freckled (who knows how?)."[43] Thus, where science seeks to simplify and reduce reality into clear, precise, definable categories that can be tested for their "objective truth" and normativeness, story questions whether such attempts at classifying human experience are helpful or even desirable. In this way, story aggressively challenges the assumptions of modernity with its simplistic and reductionist notion of an "objective reality" wholly independent of a personal subject.

Endings in Beginnings: Conclusions in Premises

Ironically, scientists sometimes forget that their experiments are similar to stories in a very important way. Both presume provisional worlds that operate according to pre-

---

42. Rosenau, *Post-modernism and the Social Sciences*, xiv.
43. "Pied Beauty," in *The Poems of Gerard Manley Hopkins*, 4th ed., revised and enlarged, ed. W. H. Gardner and N. H. Mackenzie (London: Oxford University Press, 1970), 70.

established systems of premises, preconceptions, conditional hypotheses, unproven presuppositions, implicit values, and expectations. In story and scientific experiments, conclusions and outcomes depend to a large extent on the assumptions, contexts, perspectives from which they start.

Every story knows that how it ends depends entirely on how and where it begins. Thus, the story of Oedipus can only take place in the dark world of Greek myth with its assumptions about the irrevocability of fate, intergenerational enmity, revenge, murder, and incest. The story of Oedipus ends as it does because of its starting point and the operating rules of its "universe of discourse." In another setting, let's say a fairy tale world, the oracle might have told Laius and Jocasta that their son Oedipus was going to grow up to be a fine, healthy, well-adjusted loving son and "normal" boy. All three might have returned home with nothing to worry about "and lived happily ever after."

The important thing here, of course, is not to rewrite the story of Oedipus but to remember that neither version above, neither the tragedy nor the fairy tale, is more objectively "true," historically "real," or factually "certain" than the other. One's imaginative universe or concept of reality is defined, limited, and bounded by one's premises. Modern science forgot this and claimed that its assumptions were objective, transcategorical, and self-evident. But *all* assumptions are theoretical constructs only, premises granted a conjectural validity for the sake of argument.

For example, up until the nineteenth century, the principles of Euclidean geometry were assumed to describe "real space" and to form the substructures of all external reality.[44] Euclidean geometry so delineated and defined "objective reality" as to be considered identical with it. Logically, therefore, all reality had to conform to the premises of Euclidean geometry. Any evidence that contradicted those premises was dismissed as either wrong, irrelevant, or misleading, and excluded from any serious consideration. Thus, because it admitted no anomalies or contrary evidence, the Euclidean definition of reality came to be considered reality itself. Its premises went unquestioned and unchallenged "until it was realized that Euclid's was only one of any number of possible

---

44. Tarnas, *Western Mind*, 459.

geometries that could not only be different from, but even incompatible with one another."[45] With the development of non-Euclidean geometry and its application to the fourth dimension,[46] it finally became clear that "space is an assumption, and it can be described and controlled only so far as we assume it. In other words, there is no such thing as space. Instead, there are as many spaces as there are mathematicians and non-mathematicians, and that is measured in the billions. Even that number is too small. . . ."[47]

Throughout the last three centuries, modern science has believed that, because it could offer proofs that seemed to work, its mechanical principles and assumptions were actually "true," that is, final, definitive, and essential, revealing the objective nature of reality for all times and places. But Watzlawick cautions us:

> It becomes obvious that anything is real only to the extent that it conforms to a *definition* of reality – and those definitions are legion. To employ a useful over-simplification: real *is* what a sufficiently large number of people have agreed to *call* real – except that this fact is usually forgotten; the agreed-upon definition is reified (that is, made into a "thing" in its own right) and is eventually experienced as that objective reality "out there" which apparently only a madman can fail to see.[48]

This is what Watzlawick means when he says that "man has an apparently very deep-seated propensity to hypostatize reality,"[49] that is, to objectify his premises about reality and to forget that those premises were constructed by him in the first place. As the premises of modern science became "reified"[50] and given an objective status as undeniable "facts" and "truths," the whole conjectural, speculative, and

---

45. Watzlawick, Bavelas, and Jackson, *Pragmatics*, 261.
46. In 1824, Carl Friedrich Gauss posited non-Euclidean geometry. Ferris, *Coming of Age*, 199; Van Doren, *History of Knowledge*, 271-72.
47. Van Doren, *History of Knowledge*, 272.
48. Paul Watzlawick, John Weakland, and Richard Fisch, *Change: Principles of Problem Formation and Problem Resolution* (New York: W. W. Norton & Company, 1974), 96-97.
49. Watzlawick, Bavelas, and Jackson, *Pragmatics*, 259-60.
50. Ibid., 259.

fictive nature of the assumptions were forgotten and suppressed. As a result, the contextual nature of the conditional, limited truth claims of the conclusions were also forgotten. The heirs of Newton identified their own "modern" views, ideas, presuppositions, and assumptions *about* reality *as* reality itself and conferred upon them an absolute, objective, unchangeable value and status. They forgot that what they had created or constructed in the first place could be constructed in entirely different way as well. Watzlawick writes, "While the number of potentially possible interpretations is very large, our world image usually permits us to see only one – and this *one* therefore appears to be the only possible, reasonable, and permitted view."[51] A single world image may be extremely helpful in functioning, but it can also prevent the imagining of alternative constructions of reality, other possible interpretations of an experience, or taking a fresh look at reality from a different set of premises – all of which are essential functions in inquiry and problem solving.

Unfortunately, however, we too often mistake our premises for empirical facts or *a priori* conditions of how things *must* be now and always. A particular interpretation or version of "truth" is often awarded an exclusive status, thus making it not only "the" truth but the *whole* truth, and *nothing but* the truth, so help us God.

But story knows that it offers only one possible and very limited perspective of reality and, therefore, it does not attempt to establish that one perspective as an independent, universal, objective truth for all places, times, or conditions. In fact, because a story is always open and reapproachable, a story can be reentered, explored, and whole new meanings discovered amid the very same syllables and silences as before. In the world of story, therefore, many alternative perspectives or versions of reality may coexist, but none is ever allowed finally to emerge as the only definitive one, prescriptive for all. In fact, story thrives and deepens its significance whenever gradients of ambiguity, doubt, contradiction, mystery, and enigma create a chiaroscuro landscape of the imagination. The famous Japanese story, *Rashomon*,[52] with its various tellers, starting points, different assumptions, new

---

51. Paul Watzlawick, *The Language of Change: Elements of Thera-*

contexts and perspectives is perhaps the best example of the "polyphony"[54] not only allowed but encouraged by the narrative epistemology of postmodernism.

Story seeks an "archaeology" of knowledge, an exploration of the layers of meaning embedded within experience, a continuing reconsideration and reconfiguring of all possible evidence, and especially an ongoing search for what is "buried," missing, lost, or withheld from consciousness. Narrative epistemology continues to ask how the recovery of what has been missing, diverted, or suppressed from consciousness might yield different assumptions, perspectives, interpretations, and, hence, different conclusions from those of the prevailing and dominant models and paradigms of thought. Story, therefore, is not afraid of the discovery of the unexpected and unthinkable or the simultaneous existence of variations, anomalies, disparities, contradictions, or multiple alternative views. Story, unlike science, knows that the expectation of a "singular solution" or "grand unified theory" is finally naive. Thus, story does not feel its truthfulness compromised but enhanced by the possibility of alternate worlds in tension, each leading to different destinations, endings, and conclusions.

Recovering What Was Lost

Postmodernism seeks to rediscover all those questions, concerns, and assumptions that were excluded from modern science's project; it seeks to refocus attention "on what has been taken for granted, what has been neglected,"[55] omitted, or suppressed from the record of history. Michel Foucault has called these the "subjugated knowledges"[56]: those alternative traditions of knowledge that began with different assumptions or proceeded according to different methods of

---

peutic Communication (New York: Basic Books, 1978), 119.

53. Donald Richie, ed., *Rashomon* (New Brunswick, NJ: Rutgers University Press, 1987).

54. Steven Fraade, *From Tradition to Commentary: Torah and Its Interpretation in the Midrash Sifre to Deuteronomy* (Albany, NY: State University of New York, 1991), 123-127.

55. Rosenau, *Post-modernism and the Social Sciences*, 8.

56. Michel Foucault, *Power/Knowledge: Selected Interviews and Other Writings* (New York: Pantheon Books, 1980), 82-84.

questioning and yielded different conclusions and versions of the truth. Rosenau lists some of those "knowledges" that postmodernism seeks to recover and reexamine today: "the forgotten, the irrational, the insignificant, the repressed, the borderline, the classical, the sacred, the traditional, the eccentric, the sublimated, the subjugated, the rejected, the nonessential, the marginal, the peripheral, the excluded, the tenuous, the silenced, the accidental, the dispersed, the disqualified, the deferred, the disjointed."[57]

Knowledge that comes to us through story-based epistemology asks us to suspend our belief in everything we hold certain and settled, to question not only our own most dearly held assumptions and expectations but those of our culture and society as well, to suspect the status quo versions of reality we individually and collectively objectify or "hypostatize,"[58] and to examine the *a priori* categories used to defend the prevailing dominant versions of social reality as if they were the *only* ones imaginable.

It is only by becoming aware of the premises by which we are currently operating that we can imagine alternate sets of premises or systems of mind yielding different conclusions and outcomes. By not equating any one set of premises with reality itself, we then are free to consider reality in multiple and various ways, which is what story delights in doing.

Narrative Epistemology

If story is not concerned about knowledge of facts and figures or laws of physics, then with what is it concerned? With the knowledge of meaning and significance expressed in and through language. Narrative knowledge prefers to construct its realities from the "texts" (in Greek, literally, "the weaving together") and personal subjectivities of its participants rather than from any impersonal, decontextualized "objective," expert perspective, or external set of rules or norms. Narrative epistemology requires personal relationship, interaction, an awareness of subjectivity, and the acceptance of the limits and relativity of knowledge. In other words,

---

57. Rosenau, *Post-modernism and the Social Sciences*, 8.
58. Watzlawick, Bavelas, and Jackson, *Pragmatics*, 259.

narrative knowledge does not aspire to any independent existence apart from its participants, namely, teller and listener.

By its very nature, story constructs "reality" from multiple perspectives the way the mind structures knowledge from its "multiple intelligences,"[59] the way the stereoscopic eye combines two images into one without destroying distinction in each point of view. In fact, it is those very gradations of difference in perspective that afford clarity, depth, and a greater ability to see. Thus, the inclusion of multiple perspectives both in story and vision transforms perception. The juxtaposition of multiple two-dimensional images structured as field and foreground in one frame permit a three-dimensional view of reality that cannot be explained by the analysis and dissection of the eye.

Story can bear the asking of such questions; story can bear ambiguity, doubt, contradiction, mystery, and enigma. Story can tolerate the obscure, the imprecise, the suspect, the indeterminate. Story knows more is said than can ever be articulated – through indirection, suggestion, tone, and dynamics. Story can neither prove nor define the way science claims its representational discourse can, but story at least can permit the paradoxical simultaneities of reality. In the world of story, it can make room for light's resemblance to *both* particle *and* wave, the coexistence of matter and antimatter, the continuity and discontinuity of love and hate mixed together in the same single heart.

Narrative in Psychotherapy

How would a narrative epistemology modeled after the paradigm of story affect theory and technique in psychotherapy? To answer this, I turn now to the work of Michael White and David Epston. Michael White and David Epston are family therapists who are developing a unique approach to psychotherapy using story and narrative for the epistemological models of their theory. "The meanings or stories that people carry about themselves and their views of the world, and the

---

59. Howard Gardner, *Frames of Mind: The Theory of Multiple Intelligences* (New York: Basic Books, 1983), 8-11.

use of language to construct those stories, are central to White's thinking and therapy."[60] White is codirector of the Dulwich Centre in Adelaide, Australia, and Epston is the codirector of The Family Therapy Centre in Auckland, New Zealand. Together White and Epston authored the book *Narrative Means to Therapeutic Ends.* They have also published many articles describing their work in various professional journals throughout the world. Their work is also attracting growing attention in the field and in research literature, especially because of their epistemological approach and its affect on technique. The most recent edition of the textbook *Family Therapy: Concepts and Methods,* edited by Michael Nichols and Richard Schwartz, includes an extensive description and analysis of their narrative work in therapy.

Lives as Storied

White and Epston embrace a narrative epistemology that rejects empiricism's distinction between object and subject, the observer and observed. "Since we cannot know objective reality, all knowing requires an act of interpretation." Thus, White and Epston see clients in the context of lives-as-storied: "The stories or narratives that persons live through determine their interaction and organization and . . . the evolution of lives and relationships occurs through the performance of such stories or narratives."[61]

Following the work of political philosopher Michel Foucault, White and Epston believe that our personal "stories" (and those of our parents and families) are not just individual, exclusive, or private. Our lives are shaped and determined by the official "stories," "knowledges," or "narratives of power" that dominate and contextualize society and maintain its institutions, rituals, and customs. These scenarios establish firm but invisible parameters of an official version of reality. That official reality functions to reinforce the status quo and severely curtail actual change and the possibility of imaginative alternatives.

---

60. Nichols and Schwartz, *Family Therapy,* 495.
61. White and Epston, *Narrative Means,* 2, 12.

Deconstructing the Normative. In psychotherapy, client and therapist must be aware together of how these "normative" sociocultural narratives become internalized within families and selves, thus defining and limiting the trajectory of personal lives and "objectivizing the subject," to use Foucault's term. Sheila McNamee and Kenneth Gergen explain: "We come to the field of observation bearing a lifetime of cultural experience. Most important, we not only bear languages that furnish the rationale for our looking, but also vocabularies of description and explanation for what is observed. Thus we confront life situations with codes in hand, forestructures of understanding which themselves suggest how we are to sort the problematic from the precious."[62]

White and Epston believe that we are born into our family's story of itself and its members. As we grow and develop within that family story, we also begin to interpret for ourselves the meaning of life's events and relationships as they happen to us. From the accumulation and interaction of meanings, we are constantly constructing stories for ourselves that we use to understand and define our self-identity and our significance in the stories of others.

"Problem-saturated" or "Totalizing" Stories. Sometimes, however, we get trapped inside what White calls "problem-saturated stories," that is, stories organized around a problem that continues to define the family in terms of pathology and return it to paralysis, dysfunction, and hopelessness. The despair and frustration generated by such a story keeps the family locked inside the same story without any hope of change or alternative versions. These stories "totalize" family life and completely define self-identity within the confines of this fixed, permanent, ongoing narrative. In time, a totalizing story is mistaken for objective reality and excludes all other possible versions, meanings, interpretations, or alternatives. As individuals organize and structure their relationships, behavior, and self-identities according to these totalizing stories, they get "stuck" inside them and feel

---

62. Michel Foucault, "Technologies of the Self," in *Technologies of the Self,* ed. L. Martin, H. Gutman, and P. Hutton (Amherst: University of Massachusetts Press, 1988), 18; Sheila McNamee and Kenneth Gergen, eds., *Therapy as Social Construction* (London: Sage Publications, 1992), 1.

compelled to live out their lives according to the character roles assigned to them by this narrative.

White and Epston work to destabilize these totalizing stories, to deobjectify them, and to suggest to families and individuals that these stories may not be as "total" as they thought. White and Epston look for exceptions to these stories, what they, following Erving Goffman, call "unique outcomes,"[63] that is, events that in some way contradict the totalizing narrative. White and Epston do this by asking clients if they can remember *any* event or behavior, no matter how small or insignificant, that did *not* comply with the plot demands of the totalizing story. If the clients cannot, they are invited to consult with friends, family, acquaintances and ask them if they can remember any such exceptions in the clients' lives. Usually, some exception to the totalizing story is found, even if it is just some vague dissonant feeling from the past or simply the desire for a different outcome in the future.

Reconstructing "Reality" by Restorying

White and Epston's process here is very important and follows narrative epistemology in a very original way. By choosing story as paradigm, White and Epston are "deconstructing" the "objective" nature of these "totalizing" stories. As long as these stories are confused with reality itself, they can only command passive compliance on the part of the client. But by recasting "reality" in the constructivist terms of Vico (that is, as *verum factum*, "truth that is made"), White and Epston motivate and empower clients to take responsibility for the creation of their own stories through their active participation in the therapy process of "restorying" their lives.

White and Epston also move the client into the active role of storyteller by almost exclusively doing nothing else in therapy but asking questions of the client. These questions are carefully phrased and sequenced to have the client become as active as possible in deconstructing the totalizing

---

63. Erving Goffman, *Asylums: Essays in the Social Situation of Mental Patients and Other Inmates* (New York: Doubleday, 1961).

stories she has been trapped in. This deconstruction or deobjectification of such defining narratives allows the client to "reauthor" her own life's story by generating alternative versions of the past in service of a new future.

Externalizing the Problem as Antagonist. By focusing attention on "unique outcomes" or exceptions to the totalizing story and by moving the client into an active role as author and teller of her own story, White and Epston also begin to separate the client from being identified with the problem. So often in totalizing stories, the client is identified with the problem to such a degree that the client is eventually seen as the problem. "To separate people from their problem-saturated stories, White *externalizes* their problem . . . . as if it were a separate entity, existing outside of any family member – an entity with a will of its own, which is to dominate the person or family."[64]

In other words, by externalizing the problem as if it were a character in the client's story, White and Epston break the internal identification between the client and the problem. This is not just a New Age psychobabble gimmick but a subtle linguistic move, which then forces the client and members of the family to speak about the *problem* as antagonist, not the client. "Neither the person nor the relationship between persons is the problem. Rather, the problem becomes the problem. . . ."[65] In this way, the client maintains a separate identity from the problem. People are not the problem; the problem is the problem.

The Case of Sneaky Poo

In one of White's more famous cases, a child by the name of Nick suffered from encopresis. After working with White, Nick and his family began calling the problem "Sneaky Poo" and were encouraged by White to talk about it always in the third person as if it were a separate character or entity.[66]

---

64. Nichols and Schwartz, *Family Therapy*, 495. Emphasis in original.

65. White and Epston, *Narrative Means*, 40.

66. Michael White, "Pseudo-encopresis: From Avalanche to Victory, From Vicious to Virtuous Cycles," in *Selected Papers*

Thus, Nick and the problem were always kept separate and distinct from each other. If the encopresis recurred, the parents would not say "Nick had another accident" but "Sneaky Poo snuck up on Nick last night." This way the problem was not defined as internal to or identical with the client. The problem was the problem, not Nick.

It is very easy for any family to become overwhelmed by feelings of anger, frustration, defeat, hopelessness, or impatience when they perceive themselves as failures in getting the client to change. The client perceives these negative feelings too and is further discouraged by his "failure" to do what is wanted by his family. This discouragement often produces more problematic behavior, and this only confirms and reinforces the identification between problem and client.

Using White's narrative approach, however, the focus of the family's energy did not go into attempting to get Nick to stop being the problem. Instead of fighting each other, the family joined with Nick *against* "Sneaky Poo." "In this sense, White is like an exorcist who casts the devilish problem out of the bodies or minds of family members and then helps them organize to tame it."[67]

Asking about the Story

As mentioned above, White and Epston use extensive sets of questions in therapy to involve the client and family members in an active "reauthoring" of their stories. These questions are not simply open-ended or circular as in some forms of Milan-style therapy or strategic family therapy. Instead they are designed to serve specific functions. "White's questions help people realize that: (1) they are separate from their problems, (2) they have power over the problem, or (3) they are not who they thought they were."[68]

White and Epston organize their questions according to categories borrowed from Jerome Bruner[69]: (1) *landscape of action* questions, (2) *landscape of consciousness* questions, and (3) *experience of experience* questions. Below I will give

---

(Adelaide: Dulwich Centre Publications, 1989), 118.
67. Nichols and Schwartz, *Family Therapy*, 496.
68. Ibid., 497.
69. Bruner, *Actual Minds*, 14.

White's description of what these different sets of questions are intended to do along with some examples.

Landscape of Action Questions. "Landscape of action questions encourage a person to situate a unique outcome in sequences of events that unfold across time according to particular plots."[70] This set of questions asks the client to explore how an alternative telling of his/her own personal story, one that is focused on unique outcomes and exceptions to the problem, would change perceptions of self in the past, present, or future. Friends and family members can also be involved in this reinterpreting of the client's "official" autobiography.

Thus, in exploring a past time in the client's history when he/she did *not* react to the problem in typical fashion, White and Epston might ask: "I would like to get a better grasp of this development. What did you notice yourself doing, or thinking, as a younger person, that could have provided some vital clue that this development was on the horizon of your life?"[71]

Landscape of Consciousness Questions. "Landscape of consciousness questions encourage persons to reflect on and to determine the meaning of those developments that occur in the landscape of action." This set of questions is aimed at evoking the preferences, desires, beliefs, and intentional states of the client and family members that now arise from the alternative version of his/her life story. White and Epston's purpose here is to help client and family transfer their commitment from the old "problem-saturated" story to the new one. An example of this kind of question is provided by White: "What do these discoveries tell you about what you want for your life? . . . How does this effect the picture that you have of [your son/daughter, etc.] as a person? . . . What does this reveal to you about your motives, or about the purposes you have for your life?"[72]

Experience of Experience Questions. Experience of experience questions "encourage persons to provide an account of what they believe or imagine to be another person's experience of them." White and Epston ask these questions to

70. Michael White, "Deconstruction and Therapy," *Dulwich Centre Newsletter*, 3 (1991): 30.

71. Ibid., 31.

72. Ibid., 30, 31.

encourage client and family members to recover what aspects of themselves have been forgotten or neglected over time and to explore how being perceived by self and others in this new way would affect them. Some examples given by White are: "How do you think that knowing this has affected my view of you as a person? What do you think this might reveal to me about what you value most?"[73]

White and Epston are familiar with family systems therapy based on cybernetics and computer processing and appreciate its emphasis on interaction and circular causality. But by embracing a narrative epistemology, they manage to avoid the pitfalls of systems thinking mentioned above.

Therapy: The Art of Storytelling and Listening

The power and potential of therapy based on a narrative epistemology, that is, therapy as the *art* of storytelling and listening, became especially apparent to me after I viewed a series of master videotapes of family therapists, including Salvador Minuchin, Carl Whitaker, Paul Watzlawick, Virginia Satir, James Framo as well as White and Epston, working with clients. White and Epston's approach was the most conversational, dialogic, and the least intrusive. In fact, White and Epston both maintained a reserve and reticence that was very deceiving. By almost exclusively confining their interventions to questions or requests for further elaborations, White and Epston drew out clients and their families more and more until they spoke most of the time. In this way, the clients and their families became the active agents and initiators of the therapy. A role reversal occurred. White and Epston made *them* "the experts." For who could possibly know their story better than the people who had lived and created it in the first place? White and Epston sustained this by maintaining and communicating a genuine curiosity and inquisitiveness that kept clients and families exploring the many possible interpretations of their alternative stories.

In this way, White and Epston cast themselves, not as "professional experts" who know all the "right answers" about the way things should be, but as storylisteners. Thus,

---

73. Ibid., 32.

White and Epston made their clients and their families the storytellers and gave them the power, authority, and pride of place in the therapy process. White and Epston functioned as collaborators. Their asking questions led clients to tell more of the story and the clients' elaborations led White and Epston to ask further questions.

By crafting a therapy that models itself after narrative, White and Epston avoid the mechanistic bias of modernism. Models deriving from empirical or systemic epistemology have optimal functioning and operating as their norms. But those norms obviously do not apply in story. In fact, the categories, "norm," "normal," and "normative," have no meaning in narrative discourse. Story does not evaluate or test averages but instead thrives on the unique, the exceptional, the individual, the peculiar and particular. Instead of norm, there is perspective in story, that is, an awareness that no objective outlook of reality exists. Every view is from some specific coordinates of space and time and limited to that particular point. In that sense, story willingly acknowledges its own bias and subjectivity and the limitations of its truth claims.

Thus, White and Epston's model restates postmodernism's major charge against the scientific tradition, namely, that it fails to take into consideration the biases or partiality of its initial assumptions and premises or the limitations of its own methods, procedures, and investigators. The scientific method then ascribes an absolute objective status to its findings as the "correct" or "normative" view of how "reality" *really* "is" or should be. Story obviates this problem by reframing the whole discussion and moving to an entirely different epistemological model where no such universal or absolute claims can be made.

And unlike those therapists who claim their approach is "nonnormative" or "bias-free" and thus render even the discussion of biases impossible, White and Epston announce their perspective in every one of their articles, books, seminars, and lectures. They thereby openly promote the direct discussion of models, norms, biases, and perspectives as one of prime importance for therapists and the field in general.

What is finally refreshing about White and Epston's narrative nonscientific approach to psychotherapy is that it encourages practitioners to engage in a much larger world of discourse than the one they have been used to. By replacing the need of psychotherapy to "prove" itself again and again in ever-narrowing self-referential research, White and Epston broaden the scope of discussion and allow the field to contemplate questions of meaning and significance together with other disciplines across a wide range of interests. White and Epston are raising substantial questions about the nature of knowledge and power, uniformity and diversity, the objectification and control of human beings, and the labeling of dissonance as "deviance." All of these issues have profound political implications for change and the nature of social institutions. Together with Jack Zipes, Ariel Dorfman, and John Hoffman,[74] White and Epston call our attention to how radical, subversive, and powerful stories can be in affecting change.

---

74. Jack Zipes, *Fairy Tales and the Art of Subversion: The Classical Genre for Children and the Process of Civilization* (New York: Methuen, 1988), 97-133; Dorfman, *The Empire's Old Clothes*; John Hoffman, *Law, Freedom, and Story: The Role of Narrative in Therapy, Society, and Faith* (Waterloo, Ontario: Wilfred Laurier University Press, 1986).

Part Three

Ways of Knowing and the Scriptures

Chapter Five

Walter Brueggemann and Israel's Storying

FOR THE LAST TWENTY YEARS, WALTER BRUEGGEMANN HAS sounded a prophet's warning against the forced exile of awe, wonder, and imagination from human knowing in the modern age. An author and lecturer of estimable reputation, trained in the finest traditions of biblical scholarship, Brueggemann, nevertheless, has spent much of his academic life questioning the categories of "modern" thought that have been rigorously used to define the nature of truth and reality to the exclusion of all others.

Brueggemann argues that the Enlightenment's passionate embrace of science, technology, and historical criticism as dominant modes of knowledge was accompanied by a "tyranny of positivism that takes political-economic form and that easily co-opts historical criticism. . . ." This incautious "naivete and ideological reductionism" has left us today in "a genuine crisis of humanness."

> All of us are children of the Enlightenment. That cultural reality of the last 250 years has brought us enormous gifts of human reason, human freedom, and human possibility. None of us would want to undo those gifts, but they are gifts not without cost. The reality of the Enlightenment has also resulted in the concentration of power in monopolistic ways which have been uncriticized. Moreover, it has generated dominating models of knowledge which have been thought to be objective rather than dominating.[1]

---

1. Walter Brueggemann, *Texts Under Negotiation: The Bible and Postmodern Imagination* (Minneapolis: Fortress Press, 1993), viii; Brueggemann, *Finally Comes the Poet: Daring Speech for*

Brueggemann has long been intent on examining "the inextricably intertwined and mutually reinforcing" relationship between modern modes of power and knowledge. A Christian of the Reformed tradition, he is concerned that the Church has also "tended to trim and domesticate the text [of scripture] not only to accommodate regnant modes of knowledge, but also to enhance regnant modes of power."[2]

By recruiting modern modes of knowledge to the exclusion and suppression of others, certain arrangements of power have been able to establish "hegemony, intellectual and political."[3] The status quo thus established then seems simply natural, given, neutral, objective, disinterested, just, legitimate, obvious, absolute, permanent, and, therefore, beyond all question.[4] It simply is how things are, what is called "normal." But, Brueggemann asserts, "modernity is not simply a situation coming after intellectual 'primitivism,' but . . . reflects a socio-economic-epistemological situation of those who engage in autonomous reason in defense of autonomous power."[5]

Brueggemann and the Postmodern Critique

Brueggemann reminds us that the "close alliance between *modern* context and *'objective'* method" was a project of the Enlightenment in which certain variant modes of knowing had to be discredited as "primitive," "superstitious," "premodern." These alternative modes included story, "probing

---

Proclamation (Minneapolis: Fortress Press, 1989), 4; Brueggemann, *Texts,* viii; Brueggemann, *Hopeful Imagination: Prophetic Voices in Exile* (Minneapolis: Fortress Press, 1986), 5-6.

2. Brueggemann, *Texts,* vii.
3. Ibid., 12.
4. Brueggemann, *The Prophetic Imagination* (Philadelphia: Fortress Press, 1978), 17; Brueggemann, *Texts,* vii, 5; Brueggemann, *Hopeful Imagination,* 6; Brueggemann, *Israel's Praise: Doxology against Idolatry and Ideology* (Philadelphia: Fortress Press, 1988), 13; Brueggemann, *Hope within History* (Atlanta: John Knox Press, 1987), 12; Brueggemann, *Hopeful Imagination,* 129; Brueggemann, *Texts,* vii.
5. Brueggemann, *The Prophetic Imagination;* Brueggemann, *Abiding Astonishment,* 51.

speech, daring rhetoric, and subversive text," all forms of knowing that encouraged interpersonal immediacy and interaction, subjective identification and participation, imagination and the questioning of the status quo. By discrediting the intersubjectivity involved in such transformative modes of knowing, the canonization of "objective" method in science and modern epistemology only reinforced the idea that "reality is a settled matter." Of course, that was good news for those who already possessed the means to control and direct that reality.[6]

But Brueggemann alerts us to the fact that this exhaustive overidentification between truth and objectivity was not always the case. "Interpretation informed by historical awareness was such a close and appropriate match for our context of modernity for the past two hundred years that we have scarcely been able to notice that the connection is culture-bound and did not always exist. That is, scientific positivism did not always determine the shape of knowledge. . . ."[7]

Brueggemann acknowledges that, as an increasing number of scholars begin to examine these "inevitable" arrangements of power and knowledge, "we are in a wholly new interpretive situation," one in which "we face a decisive turn in our ways of knowing." But this "quite new interpretive situation that constitutes something of an emergency" is also a "positive opportunity," one that "requires a new practice of knowledge and a new, derivative option in political power."[8] This is the moment of postmodernism: the chance to review the effect of the categories, assumptions, and modes of thought that have shaped modern arrangements of power and maintained them as normative, normal, real, and irreplaceable.

While Brueggemann has become more comfortable in recent years with explicitly using the language and categories of postmodernism to examine this new interpretive situation, he confesses he has no "zeal" for the word itself but uses it "as a convenient reference for the widespread erosion of what has been most recently seen as 'given.'" He writes, "It may be that 'postmodern' is too particular or too

---

6. Brueggemann, *Texts,* 1 (emphasis in original), 12, 1.

7. Ibid., 1.

8. Brueggemann, *Israel's Praise,* 13; Brueggemann, *Texts,* vii, 8, vii, 2.

ambitious a word for what is being noticed. That word, however, is useful to point to the changed epistemological context in which we must now do our work."[9]

Thanks to scholars like Kuhn, Brueggemann, and others, we are beginning to see how, right up to our own day, the model of truth and knowledge that was forged during the formative years of the Enlightenment has continued operating as if it were the one standard norm of all things and hence identical with objective reality itself. The postmodern critique, for all its own problems and convolutions, at least helps us remember that "modern" modes of knowledge were not so much inherently objective as they were simply preferred to other modes of knowledge that had existed up to that time. Applying a hermeneutical method learned from a lifetime studying the stories and texts of the Hebrew and Christian scriptures, Brueggemann has recently suggested that an understanding of the historical context of the Enlightenment might help us appreciate how this situation came about.

The Collapse of the Medieval: Origins of the Modern

Brueggemann asserts that the extreme reliance on scientific positivism and Enlightenment modes of certitude was a "desperate maneuver" to cope with the "enormous and profound anxiety" that resulted from "the collapse of the medieval synthesis in which a coherent, unified system of meaning and power was everywhere pervasive. The loss of that 'home' created deep dislocation and displacement."[10] Brueggemann also refers to the "terrible European wars of the seventeenth century," the resulting social upheaval, and the assassination of Henry IV of Navarre as just some of the factors that plunged Descartes and his generation "into disarray as the threat of chaos became a social reality. That is, Descartes's philosophical reflection was an urgent effort to fend off the coming chaos so evident in the world around him."[11]

When we consider the sense of loss, anxiety, despair, and fear of chaos that pervaded the intellectual culture of that period, Brueggemann suggests, we might have a better

---

9. Ibid., vii, 17.
10. Ibid., 2.
11. Ibid., 5, 3, 2, 3.

understanding of why the Enlightenment sought to establish norms of certitude that were so absolute and objective as to be impervious to similar political chaos, intellectual assault, and social upheaval. The skepticism of the period led to such forms of radical individualism, self-interest, and self-reliance as would locate certitude within the internal workings of the mind itself. "Descartes fashioned a new separated individual consciousness that in fact had no reference point outside itself. This new 'interiority' permitted the self to generate its own certitude, and the self became an absolute point of reference."[12]

Reliance on religion, trust, faith, communal tradition, oral witness, story, anecdotal evidence, or interpersonal experience was repudiated. Instead the "modern" mind strove for objective knowledge and epistemological certainty based on "rational, logical coherence, discerned by a detached, disinterested, disembodied mind."[13] "Modern" knowledge relied on pure reason; the separation of mind and body; extreme forms of individualism; reliance on empirical, mathematical, and experimental criteria for proof of truth, fact, and validity; the complete elimination of subjectivity; and the control of nature through science and technology.

Brueggemann reminds us of what Kuhn learned while rereading Aristotle: that other perspectives, methods, and modes of knowing, once considered invaluable and true within their own contextual worlds, actually remain open and accessible to us and can offer us alternative ways of viewing present reality. Therefore, in keeping with the postmodern critique, if we are to reach a more balanced and realistic appraisal of the modern mind and its limits, we must consider what these alternative modes of knowing were and how they shaped and affected what was known.

Scientific Method and Epistemological "Correctness"

It is interesting for our purposes that Brueggemann describes the shift from medieval (or premodern) modes of knowledge to modern ones as "a move from oral to *written,* so that what is reliable is what is written; a move from the

---

12. Ibid., 4.
13. Ibid., 5.

particular to the *universal,* so that real truth is what is true everywhere; a move from local to *general,* so that real truth had to be the same from locale to locale; and a move from the timely to the *timeless,* so that the real is the unchanging."[14]

As we saw with Ong's analysis of orality and literacy, knowledge that was written down and printed in books and texts and that employed language using universal, general, and timeless categories was considered to be more accurate, authoritative, objective, and scientific than knowledge transmitted by oral-aural narrative accounts and particular, local, contextual categories of knowledge.

To the heirs of the Enlightenment, truth could not be contextual. Mutually determining interrelationships between the processes and contents of inquiry had not yet been examined. Reality was singular, the same everywhere and forever. And this is precisely why such contemporary ideas today as coexisting paradigms or models of the world, multiple modalities of thought, and "cross-cultural" perspectives of society are termed "postmodern": because the scholars and intellectuals of the "modern" period could not even imagine them, let alone think them.

For such "modernists," the scientific method "worked" well enough when it yielded consistent, reliable, quantifiable results duplicable across space and time. That was enough for them. They had obviously found *the* "right" method. In an age when truth was necessarily single and error had no rights, that meant that the scientific method was the "correct" one. It did not just enjoy preferment; it actually usurped, demoted, and replaced all other methods; it preempted them entirely and made them obsolete. That meant that those methods of inquiry and expression that emphasized the oral, the particular, the local, and the contextual aspects of knowing were held suspect, discredited, and sent into exile.

The effects of this epistemological shift were also felt in matters of faith and religion. Interest in developing a theological method that could deduce an absolute, universal system of certitude from the development of rational, logical

---

14. Ibid., 5. Emphasis in original. Brueggemann is referring to the work of Stephen Toulmin, especially his *Cosmopolis: The Hidden Agenda of Modernity* (New York: Free Press, 1990).

arguments led to the mass printing of catechisms and manuals of theology. Debates raged about the historical facticity behind the biblical texts while the study of Israel's rhetorical practices, her long traditions of alternative speech, orality, and storying went into eclipse. Now all the wonderful, messy, contradictory narrative particularities of the biblical stories were seen only as intellectual embarrassments. "The outcome of such a procedure is that the texts themselves are largely dismissed, and words themselves do not count for much. So there is in modernity a resulting dismissal of rhetoric as 'mere rhetoric' and the discounting of speech."[15]

But for Brueggemann and postmodern scholarship, language is not accidental or ornamental. Language actually identifies what is to be considered true, real, and imaginable with what is expressed. Therefore, rhetoric and speech practices are important determinants of not only what is known but what can be thought and expressed. Furthermore, language determines how that knowledge is to be regarded and valued. Here then is the important point of intersection between Brueggemann's lifework and the postmodern critique. "We find ourselves in the interface between 'what happened' (history) on the one hand, and 'what is remembered' and 'how it is said' (rhetoric) on the other. Indeed, *what* happened' turns out to be dependent upon and determined by *how* the happenedness is shaped in the speech practices of the remembering community."[16] As we saw above, "inextricably intertwined and mutually reinforcing"[17] relationships between arrangements of power and knowledge derive from what can be thought, said, and imagined; and what can be thought and said depends on the kinds of language and speech available, that is, permitted.

Questioning What Predominates

As children of the Enlightenment, we still live so thoroughly immersed within its constructions of "modern" truth, reality, and power that we can easily forget that its models of speech,

---

15. Ibid., 6.
16. Brueggemann, *Abiding Astonishment,* 13. Emphasis in original.
17. Brueggemann, *Texts,* vii.

thought, and inquiry are not finally absolute, permanent, or definitive. As Brueggemann reminds us, the Enlightenment was "an episode or 'project,' . . . not an ultimate transformation."[18]

But, as we have seen, those modes of thought and order that come to enjoy dominance within a culture are often granted an irrefutable status, even though they are, in fact, not objective at all, only preferred. Since those who are already rich, powerful, and enfranchised are often the only people with the leisure, opportunity, and resources to transform their preferences into policy, they also have undue influence over what models and categories of thought will predominate as "normative," "neutral and apolitical," "invisible," and, therefore, "universally applicable." As Ellyn Kaschak writes, "The epistemology of a dominant group can be made to appear neutral, and its value base invisible, since it coincides perfectly with what appears to be society in some generic, universal form."[19]

Throughout history, by recruiting preferred modes of knowledge, epistemological categories of thought, and supportive technologies, and then identifying them as objective reality itself, ruling elites and dominant groups already in power have been able to establish a hegemony of mind and imagination. That a particular arrangement favors certain interest groups and not others is often left unspoken. Viewpoints that call attention to the interlocking substructures of thought, speech, knowledge, and power or that threaten to make visible what has been invisible are often considered too dangerous and subversive to be tolerated. Dissident opinions proposing alternative arrangements for the redistribution of power, wealth, and other social resources are ignored or criminalized and prevented from public hearing. Sometimes, depending on how threatening these alternative voices may be to the continuance of the *ancien regime,* they may be completely banned, outlawed, and then permanently silenced.

---

18. Ibid., 6.
19. Ellyn Kaschak, *Engendered Lives: A New Psychology of Women's Experience* (New York: Basic Books, 1992), 10, 211, 10.

Israel's Storying: Empowering an Alternative Reality

It was in Israel's "naming not just the unnamed but the unnameable, speaking not just the unspoken but the unspeakable"[20] that Brueggemann discovered how a narrative epistemology could sustain a community's sense of hope and history in the face of systemic repression and violence. Through Israel's tradition of storying, a defiant, shared imagination powerful enough to activate an alternative future reality had been born.

Brueggemann: Questioning the Modern

Ironically, in one of his first books, *In Man We Trust,* Brueggemann was passionately earnest in attempting to move the church and her views of God and biblical faith out of what he saw as an extrinsic, "culture-fearing, culture-negating tradition" into a real committed involvement with the pressing social issues and concerns of modern history. By re-addressing the wisdom traditions of the scriptures and applying them to such post-sixties issues as secularization, situation ethics, death of God theology, and black versus white theology, Brueggemann was challenging Christian theology to move out of the guarded palisades of ahistorical thought into a real engagement with the existential hope, despair, and struggles of contemporary "man" in the modern world. Brueggemann stressed "man's" responsibility to act and to choose, to shape and decide his future, to celebrate his "aliveness" in the world "here and now," and not just in the hereafter. He criticized theology for a "devaluing of the historical process, a disengagement from it, a cynicism about it, a rejection of it."[21]

But four years later in *The Land,* Brueggemann was beginning to question aspects of that historical methodology and to grow weary of the simplistic dichotomies of "the dominant intellectual tradition of the West" with its "silly and exhausting antitheses which hold no promise for us." Like Kuhn reading Aristotle anew, Brueggemann was rereading the biblical narratives and discovering new possible

---

20. Ibid., 225.
21. Brueggemann, *In Man We Trust: The Neglected Side of Biblical Faith* (Atlanta: John Knox Press, 1973), 14, 16, 15, 17.

alternative "categories of perception which will permit us to see the text differently and also permit us to discern ourselves and our history differently."[22] Thus, Brueggemann's writing of *The Land* was "intended to contribute to the current hermeneutical discussion, that is, to reflect upon our categories and presuppositions in interpretation, to probe the shape of the expectations we have of the text and therefore our discernment of what we find in the text."[23]

As he pursued his hermeneutical interests in the stories of scripture, Brueggemann found that the Bible is "about another agenda which calls into question our conventional presuppositions and our settled conclusions." Breaking with customary categories used in describing the Hebrew scripture, Brueggemann found neither the timeless space nor spaceless time of myth. "There is rather a *storied place,* that is a place which has meaning because of the history lodged there. There are stories which have authority because they are located in a place. This means that biblical faith cannot be presented simply as an historical movement indifferent to place which could have happened in one setting as well as another, because it is undeniably fixed in this place with this meaning."[24]

The odd specificity of Israel's stories moved Brueggemann toward a deepening appreciation of narrative epistemology and an increasingly hermeneutical method in his own work. Brueggemann found the hermeneutic method had the advantage of allowing him "to be alert to fresh possibilities and to critique our usual ones" and "to identify new interfaces or to discern old interfaces in new ways."[25]

---

22. Foreword by Walter Brueggemann and John Donahue to *The Land: Place as Gift, Promise, and Challenge in Biblical Faith* by Walter Brueggemann (Philadelphia: Fortress Press, 1977), xi, xvii.

23. Brueggemann, *The Land: Place as Gift, Promise, and Challenge in Biblical Faith* (Philadelphia: Fortress Press, 1977), 184.

24. Ibid., 184, 185.

25. Ibid., 184, 189.

Israel's Storying as Knowing

As he grew increasingly sensitive to the alternate values and modes of power and knowledge implied in a narrative epistemology, Brueggemann found the antithetical categories traditionally employed by modern criticism to be wanting, even misleading and false because of what they excluded or eliminated from human experience: "it seems clear that in the zeal to be freed from nineteenth century evolutionary approaches the posture of 'againstness' has caused an imbalance of categories."[26]

To correct this imbalance, Brueggemann submersed himself into the stories of Israel and, even more importantly, the mind of her storytellers. Leaving behind what he called the "phony polarizations,"[27] convenient dichotomies, and reductionist modes of modern critical thought, Brueggemann gained deeper and deeper appreciation for the narrative epistemology he found in the stories of the Bible, an epistemology of "abiding astonishment."[28] Thus, at the end of his study of Israel's relationship to the land, Brueggemann concluded that "it will not do . . . to say that God's history is simply a story of coming to the land promised. Nor will it do . . . to say that God's history is a story of homelessness. Either statement misses the main affirmation of the unexpected way in which land and landlessness are linked to each other."[29] The story of Israel and the land could not be reduced to thesis. Only the narrative tension of the stories could hold together the complexity of the revelation of God's relationship with Israel.

Israel's stories reveal disturbing, unfamiliar ways of knowing and relating that must finally defy easy capture by the antithetical categories, dichotomies, or "phony polarizations" of modern reason. For Brueggemann, the stories of the Bible reveal a relationship between Israel and her God that is so complex, inexhaustible, and fraught with all kinds of wild confusion, dark mystery, and shocking tensions that to

---

26. Ibid., 188. Brueggemann is referring here to the excessive individualism of existentialism and the historicism of "salvation history" approaches to the Bible.
27. Ibid., 193.
28. Brueggemann, *Abiding Astonishment,* 30.
29. Brueggemann, *Land,* 189-90.

try to reconcile what must ultimately remain irreconcilable can only be an exercise in futility and madness. That is why Brueggemann decides that it is only narrative modes of knowing and relationship that can embrace and tolerate such ambiguity, wonder, paradox, pain, grief, and surprise; it is only an alternative imagination called into existence through storying that can help us understand Israel's situation as a model of our own in this postmodern age.

Brueggemann's Paradigm: The Exodus Story

Brueggemann finds in the experience of Israel an example of a community that struggled to maintain its native narrative epistemology against the dreadnought assault of inevitable imperial and technocratic models. I wish to concentrate on Brueggemann's study of the Exodus story, since it is in my opinion his most seminal work and the key to most of his other writings on the biblical texts.

What we learn from Brueggemann is that the struggles of our world today are not at all unlike those of Israel thousands of years ago. The names may have changed but the realities are very much the same. The poor and powerless, the silenced and invisible, the oppressed and voiceless still struggle for their lives, their stories, their futures. In the end, the questions remain: how shall we live together as liberated (and mutually liberating) brothers and sisters, how shall we be free, and how shall we free our minds and imaginations from all forms of domination, trance, distraction, and disconfirmation?

To understand what it means to have our own story, it is necessary to consider what life is like before the moment of self-authorship and self-ownership. It is rare for any of us to be entirely without a story that shapes our lives. Usually we find ourselves recruited into someone else's story. That may be the story of a parent, family, tribe, community, or nation: some dominant power that has the resources, force, and will to articulate, publish, and promote its story as coherent, worthy of respect, and authoritative for others. This is Israel's situation in Egypt before she finds her own story.

Israel and the Imperatives of Technique

The Exodus narrative begins with Israel and her people already wholly subsumed by the constituted reality that is imperial Egypt. That public world, that unquestioned and unquestionable reality finds its perfect expression in the reign and power of Pharaoh. His empire is maintained by a "network of *technological instruments* which are legitimated if not absolutized by religious and *mythopoetic ideology.*" The empire and its managers are not interested in asking questions about this world or engaging in any "serious conversation." As far as they are concerned, this world is "closed and beyond transformation." It is perfect and complete as it is, because it is "stable and productive." The imperial bureaucracy is interested in only one thing: making this world work, sustaining it, controling it, guaranteeing that it will not change. Brueggemann describes this as "the reason of technique," that "'managerial' consciousness in which all reality is reduced to problem-solving. Speech and act become only modes of instrumentalism, for the satisfaction of needs and the productivity of payoffs. Absent from such speech is any practice of commitment that may raise any critical question."[30]

The social arrangements of this empire simply reflect "reality" as it has always been and always will be, as it is described and recorded in all official histories of the empire and in all the ancient texts revealing the sacred cosmology. These arrangements are structured into the everyday life and imagination of every person through the religious customs and institutional practices of the state until they have become the official traditions of government and culture. These arrangements are, therefore, perceived as nothing more than neutral, inevitable, and benign. They are simply what reality looks like, the normal state of things.

Egypt: An Imperial Sociology of Knowledge

Around this status quo an official sociology of knowledge has taken shape. Over time, certain categories and modes of

---

30. Brueggemann, *Hope within History,* 11 (emphasis in original); Brueggemann, *Poet,* 73, 106; Brueggemann, *Hope within History,* 11; Brueggemann, *Poet,* 3, 45-46.

thought have been preferred to others, so that now they are simply customary, presumed, without any need for further questioning. Thus, a paradigm of reality and knowledge has emerged. Its unquestioned assumptions have been legitimated and now form the presuppositions for all study and thought. By disallowing the possibility of any alternative, Pharaoh and his armies have established this version of "reality" as "normative." The court psychologists affirm conformity with this model to be "sane, healthy" behavior, demonstrating optimal brain functioning, as nature surely intended. The court philosophers find such thinking logical, consistent, irrefutable. All the professions and sciences agree: no other alternative is possible. "The empire . . . wants to establish itself as absolute, wants the present arrangement to appear eternal in the past as in the future, so that after a while, one cannot remember when it was different from this, which means having available to our imagination no real alternative."[31]

Thus does this "objective reality" emerge, divinely revealed, blessed forever by priest and king, church and state, science and technology. It is the dominant story for all who live within the borders of the empire. "Every individual person, along with the tribe and clan, is at the very outset placed in this world. One is not in a social vacuum, not even for a day. Life is not neutral or empty space. One has no innocence before one is in the world of the empire. One is from there and has one's being there."[32]

Domesticating the Mind. There is one problem. The economic maintenance of this world demands massive cheap labor. This, in turn, has required the gradual enslavement of large numbers of Israelites whose rights, claims, identities, and stories have been forfeited to the interests of the state. But these social arrangements cannot appear arbitrary, temporary, or negotiable. They must seem to be absolute and eternal. So a way must be found to break any possible resistance to these arrangements. Thus, the minds of the Hebrew slaves must be domesticated, their wills broken, and their imaginations disconnected from hope "in a way unlikely ever to be undone."[33] Their poets, storytellers, and

---

31. Brueggemann, *Hopeful Imagination,* 112.
32. Brueggemann, *Hope within History,* 11.
33. J. Anthony Lukas, *Common Ground* (New York: Alfred A.

singers must be silenced; their rituals criminalized and forbidden; their children reeducated, given up for adoption, or murdered. They are to be indoctrinated, catechized, and converted, and the "mythopoetic ideology" of the empire invoked until they are amenable to revealed truth.[34] "The gods of Egypt are the immovable lords of order. They call for, sanction, and legitimate a society of order, which is precisely what Egypt had. In Egypt, . . . there were no revolutions, no breaks for freedom. There were only the necessary political and economic arrangements to provide order, 'naturally,' the order of Pharaoh."[35]

Certitude and Domination. Given the superior resources and technology of the empire, such a campaign of propaganda, evangelization, and reconditioning cannot help but succeed. The "magisterial symbolization and political hegemony" of the empire come to be allied in "the neat fit of *certitude* and *domination.*" In time, without any possible alternatives available to them, the Israelites accept and internalize the only "reality" provided. "There is for Israel no 'pre-empire' experience of social reality. There is no initial innocence or freedom. . . . The empire is all-encompassing in shaping and defining life and reality."[36]

In the world seen from the throne rooms and imperial courts of history, it is established "fact" that these slaves have no rights, are only property, not people.[37] These foreigners,

---

Knopf, 1985), 106. Lukas is quoting here from the 1954 Supreme Court ruling in *Brown v. Board of Education.*
34. Brueggemann, *Hopeful Imagination,* 11.
35. Brueggemann, *Prophetic Imagination,* 17.
36. Brueggemann, *Texts,* 2-3 (emphasis in original); Brueggemann, *Hope within History,* 11.
37. In *Hope within History,* 11-17, Brueggemann writes exclusively about the slave experience of Israel in the main body of his text. But his notes for this section make constant reference to multicultural experiences of oppression throughout the centuries: for example, Eugene Genovese, *Roll, Jordan, Roll* (New York: Pantheon, 1974) on the experience of the enslaved in the antebellum South; John Gaventa, *Power and Powerlessness: Quiescence andd Rebellion in an Appalachian Valley* (Urbana, IL: University of Illinois, 1980) on corporate and economic violence in a twentieth-century mining town; Kim Yong Bock, ed., *Minjung Theology* (Singapore: The Christian Conference of Asia, 1981) on religious resistance movements to totalitar-

outsiders, strangers, and aliens are subhuman, dangerous, suspicious, subversive, criminal. They are dirty, diseased, rapacious, immoral, ignorant, promiscuous, obscene.[38] They are stupid, simple, lazy,[39] incapable of learning or training, and content with their condition. They are savage,[40] superstitious, evil, unreligious, prone to violence and murder, deviant, thieving.[41] As Brueggemann says, "We are now able to see that what has passed for objective, universal, knowledge has in fact been the interested claim of the dominant voices who were able to pose their view and to gain either assent or docile acceptance from those whose interest the claim did not serve. Objectivity is in fact one more practice

ian regimes in post-war Korea. In this way, while Brueggemann's main remarks focus on a conventional academic analysis of a scripture passage, he is also developing a subtext emphasizing the parallels between the biblical narrative and other sociocultural, political, and economic constructions and arrangements throughout space and time. As we shall see, this is the heart and genius of midrash.

38. Robert Edwin Herzstein, *The War that Hitler Won: Goebbels and the Nazi Media Campaign* (New York: Paragon House, 1987), 351-54, 64, 311, 314. Herzstein describes the Nazi propaganda campaign to portray Jews as "subhuman" by images and metaphors that compared them to plague-infested rats crawling out of sewers and swamps. This is in remarkable contrast to the Nazi attitude toward the British who were portrayed as "evil" and "cruel" but human because they descended from the Nordic race. On page 64, Herzstein writes, "Quoting Mussolini (out of context), Goebbels declared that to fight the Jew was social hygiene, a struggle against a bacillus. This metaphor was one of Hitler's favorites. . . ."

39. Cecil Woodham-Smith, *The Great Hunger: Ireland 1845-1849* (New York: Old Town Books, 1962), 27, 32, 76. In explicating the cumulative effects of the Penal Laws (1695-1829) on Ireland, Woodham-Smith offers contemporary British opinion describing the Irish as a race and people of "insignificant slaves, fit for nothing but to hew wood and draw water" (27).

40. Richard Barnet, *The Rockets' Red Glare: When America Goes to War – The Presidents and the People* (New York: Simon and Schuster, 1990), 84, 88, 91. Barnet discusses contemporary historical and political views of the "Indian" problem from the era of Jefferson to Van Buren.

41. Herzstein, *The War that Hitler Won,* 64.

of ideology that presents interest in covert form as an established fact."[42]

The Normalization of Violence. To be a Jew in Pharaoh's Empire, therefore, is to be born into a world where the expectation of violence is considered "normal," the toleration of such brutalization "socially adaptable," the absence of human rights "perfectly legal," an attitude of submission reasonable, and a sense of guilt and self-blame deserved.[43] The natural result of living in a world of such "soul murder"[44] is personal and social "disconfirmation." Disconfirmation occurs, according to Watzlawick and his colleagues, whenever "the function of constantly rebuilding the self concept, of offering this self concept to others for ratification, and of accepting or rejecting the self-conceptual offerings of others" is disallowed. Yet such confirmation of another's self-concept "is probably the greatest single factor ensuring mental development and stability. . . ." Without this, Watzlawick claims, "we would live in a world devoid of anything except the most utilitarian endeavors, a world devoid of beauty, poetry, play, and humor." Without this, "man is unable to maintain his emotional stability for prolonged periods."[45] Or as Martin Buber puts it, "In human society, at all its levels, persons confirm one another in a practical way, to some extent or other, in their personal qualities and capacities, and a society may be termed human in the measure to which its members confirm one another. . . . The basis of man's life with man is twofold, and it is one – the wish of every man to be confirmed as what he is, even as what he can become, by men; and the innate capacity of man to confirm his fellowmen in this way."[46]

---

42. Brueggemann, *Texts,* 9.
43. This internalized self-rejection and self-blame is found among severely abused children who often think that they somehow deserve the abuse, that it is their fault and for their own good. Cynthia Crosson Tower, *Understanding Child Abuse and Neglect* (Boston: Allyn and Bacon, 1989), 40.
44. Leonard Shengold, *Soul Murder: The Effects of Childhood Abuse and Deprivation* (New York: Fawcett Columbine, 1989), 20-23.
45. Watzlawick, Bavelas, Jackson, *Pragmatics,* 84 (n. 7), 84, 85.
46. Martin Buber, "Distance and Relation," *Psychiatry* 20 (1957): 97-104.

Disconfirmation: "You Do Not Exist." Simple lack of confirmation or even rejection would be bad enough, but "disconfirmation" is something else. R. D. Laing quotes from William James: "No more fiendish punishment could be devised, even were such a thing physically possible, than that one should be turned loose in society and remain absolutely unnoticed by all the members thereof."[47] Watzlawick interprets what this might mean for a contemporary audience: "There can be little doubt that such a situation would lead to 'loss of self,' which is but a translation of 'alienation.' Disconfirmation, as we find it in pathological communication, is no longer concerned with the truth or falsity – if there be such criteria – of *P*'s definition of himself, but rather negates the reality of *P* as the source of such a definition. In other words, while rejection amounts to the message 'You are wrong,' disconfirmation says in effect 'You do not exist.'"[48]

Hopelessness: Self-Blame, Self-Rejection. Contemporary literature on child abuse, torture, and thought control[49] reveals some effects of living in such an environment: the development of a truncated personality, an identity of internalized inferiority, and permanent "self-rejection,"[50] the loss of a sense of self; the invalidation of one's own most basic feelings, wants, needs, desires, experiences, and moral val-

---

47. William James quoted in R. D. Laing, *Self and Others* (London, Penguin Books, 1990), 98-99. No reference given by Laing.
48. Watzlawick et al., *Pragmatics,* 86. Watzlawick is referring to clinical research done by Laing and others in the 1950s that suggests that many children suffer profound emotional and psychological disturbance from "subtle, but persistent" forms of disconfirmation that "mutilate," often unconsciously, the child's sense of self and authenticity.
49. Tower, *Understanding Child Abuse;* Elaine Scarry, *The Body in Pain: The Making and Unmaking of the World* (New York: Oxford University Press, 1985), 18-20; Robert J. Lifton, *Thought Reform and the Psychology of Totalism: A Study of "Brainwashing" in China* (New York: W. W. Norton, 1961), 3-7.
50. Lukas, *Common Ground,* 106. Lukas refers to the doll studies of social psychologist Kenneth Clark and his wife Mamie among African-American children in the mid-1950s and their "evidence of 'self-rejection,' the 'truncating effect' it had on the children's personalities, and the cruelty of internalized 'racism.'"

ues; confused thinking; a profound sense of guilt, shame, and self-blame; identification with the abuser and his views and values; a feeling that one deserves such treatment; and a childlike sense of respect and affection for the abuser. As Michael Lerner puts it in his book *Surplus Powerlessness,* "[The abused] were convinced that nothing could be done, that the experts would make the decisions as they always had, and that they either didn't know enough to suggest specific alternatives, or that they didn't believe anyone would pay attention to what they wanted anyway."[51]

Psychic Numbness as Norm. To survive in such a punitive and unstable world, the personality tries to protect itself through "psychic numbing,"[52] the attempt to excise from consciousness all awareness of one's own feelings in the face of such real danger. In the case of the Hebrews in Egypt, "Every Israelite person comes to know very early that one is claimed and identified in the empire and, for Hebrew slaves, one may guess, numbered and tattooed."[53] No other alternatives are even imaginable; if they were, they would be punishable by death.

Soul Murder: The Categories of Cruelty

With this arrangement internalized, it becomes the "normal" state of things. Both the arbitrariness and the intentionality of the arrangement is suppressed from awareness. As long as the arrangement works and provides a level of optimal functioning for all concerned (i.e., the rich get richer and the poor get poorer), then no more inquiry needs be made. Reassured by the gods and government, delivered from the need for any further examination of this arrangement, all public energy in the empire can now be more constructively invested in the economical functioning of this system. Operationality, technique, efficiency, competence, order, control, and the beneficial management of resources becomes the

---

51. Michael Lerner, *Surplus Powerlessness: The Psychodynamics of Everyday Life and the Psychology of Individual and Social Transformation* (Oakland, CA: The Institute for Labor and Mental Health, 1986), 11.

52. Robert Jay Lifton, *The Nazi Doctors: Medical Killing and the Psychology of Genocide* (New York: Basic Books, 1986), 420-27.

53. Brueggemann, *Hope within History,* 11.

task of the human enterprise in Pharaoh's Egypt. For what could be more universally desirable than an "imperial world [which] is a stable, productive world that generates food and bestows life for all its adherents (cf. Gen. 47:13-26)."[54] Who could argue with such a progressive agenda?

No Other Stories Allowed. Pharaoh, after all, is only trying to do his job, which is to promote harmony, prosperity, a strong defense, good trade agreements, and the people's faith and trust in the official state government. His task, as that of all kings and rulers throughout time, is to guarantee the status quo, to assure the claims of the kingdom (no matter how extravagant), and to preserve the unbroken continuity of the system *ad perpetuum.*

> The task of the king is, by official charge and most likely by inclination, to assure continuity of the known world. That is, kings preside over and rely upon the consensus that this world is the one we have had and do have and will have. There is no other world except this one. The king's business is to nurture and manage that consensus and to keep it intact. About this world, kings must always make the affirmation, "as it was in the beginning, is now and ever shall be, world without end." Kings embody and represent the endurance of the present, the eradication of a different past, and the prohibition of a different future. . . .
>
> Kings cannot imagine that the present can ever end. The present life-world is the frame of royal responsibility. To think without the present configuration of power and order and norms is to invite anarchy. . . . To kings, ancient and modern, reality cannot be conjured outside this world.[55]

Managing Dissent. In this carefully controlled and managed world, there is simply no room for dissent or dissatisfaction, no room for critique or the entertaining of other alternatives or imaginations. Such license would be irresponsible and disruptive, could weaken military morale, promote anarchy, threaten national security, and expose the country to its enemies. Because no complaints or divergence from this view is allowed or even imaginable, then everyone *must* be happy!

---

54. Ibid.
55. Brueggemann, *The Creative Word: Canon as a Model for Biblical Education* (Philadelphia: Fortress Press, 1982), 57-58.

After all, the outstanding civility and efficiency of the imperial system is proof that this is "the best of all possible worlds." But "'well-offness' leads us finally to absolutize, so that we may say 'the system is the solution.' The system wants us to believe that, for such belief silences criticism. It makes us consenting, docile, obedient adults. The system wants to contain all our hopes and fears, wants us to settle for the available system of rewards."[56]

What cannot be expressed must, therefore, be repressed. This kind of psychic domination is more insidious than the subjugation of a people or the deprivation of freedom. This kind of psychic conquest demands the total evacuation of one's own reality, experience, and world and the complete and thorough internalization of the absolute worldview of those enslaving you. Alice Miller writes:

> [The abused] have no choice but to repress the experience, because the pain caused by their fear, isolation, betrayed expectation. . ., helplessness, and feelings of shame and guilt is unbearable. . . . If [they] are talked out of what they perceive, then the experience they undergo will later be seen in a diffuse, hazy light; its reality will remain uncertain and indistinct, laden with feelings of guilt and shame, and . . . these . . . either will know nothing of what happened or will question their memory of it.[57]

Enslaving the Mind: Doubly Bound. Here we have the crazy-making paradoxical situation described by Watzlawick in his comments on the "double bind" and Lifton on thought control.[58] It is not enough for those being brainwashed to recite the propaganda required by their torturers. They must also thoroughly convince their interrogators that they freely and spontaneously believe what they are being forced to say. They must actually desire to say what will only bring further torture if they do not. They must demonstrate that they have internalized what has been violently forced down their throats over long hours of torture. In short, they must convince their captors that they have actually changed their

---

56. Brueggemann, *Hope within History,* 80-81.
57. Alice Miller, *Thou Shall Not Be Aware* (New York: New American Library, 1986), 311.
58. Watzlawick, Bavelas, and Jackson, *Pragmatics,* 212-13; Lifton, *Thought Reform,* 3-7.

most interior beliefs, opinions, and worldview. Watzlawick continues, "This situation is frequently compounded by the more or less overt prohibition to show any awareness of the contradiction or the real issue involved. A person in a double bind situation is therefore likely to find himself punished (or at least made to feel guilty) for correct perceptions, and defined as 'bad' or 'mad' for even insinuating that there be a discrepancy between what he does see and what he 'should' see. This is the essence of the double bind."[59]

And who are these people who are labeled "bad" or "mad"? They are those outsiders "excommunicated and nullified and declared nonexistent" by the empire, those "people who do not fit," who do not simply go along with everyone else as all "good" Egyptians should. Brueggemann writes, "Are they bad? Are they nonpersons? We have a long history of denying their existence, the poor, women, Blacks, the handicapped, all kinds of disqualified people. The more rigorously the absolutizing [of the system] works, the tighter they are locked out and the more of them there are who are locked out."[60]

Israel is placed in a crazy-making situation. She is required to repress the awareness of her experience, suffering, and pain, so that Pharaoh can suppress knowledge of his injustice and tyranny. Israel is not permitted to groan or cry out, not allowed to complain. She must remain numb to her torment and instead bless her masters and give thanks to the gods for all her blessing and good fortunes under her benefactor, Pharaoh. Israel must identify completely with the story, self-perceptions, and experience of her oppressors. In other words, she must do without any self-concept, without any story of her own. This way there can be no imaginable disparity between Egypt and Israel, no disagreement to disturb the convenient serenity and peace that permits this interactive system to continue to function in all its rapacity and injustice. This way the imperial regime's ideology can never be challenged or opposed. Brueggemann comments, "Over a long period of containment, all parties begin to think that the way it is now is the only way it could be. The managers of the ideology carefully nurture such a view. After

---

59. Watzlawick, Bavelas, and Jackson, *Pragmatics,* 213.
60. Brueggemann, *Hope within History,* 81.

a while the oppressed feebly and helplessly but willingly begin to accept that view."[61] Egypt is thus able to consider herself "benign, neutral, absolute,"[62] generous, indulgent, beneficent. "The victims involved actually think they must blame themselves for what has happened."[63]

For Brueggemann, Israel-before-the-Exodus comes to symbolize all those people throughout history who have been denied their own stories – the poor; the oppressed; the neglected ones without voice, who have learned to be silent to survive; those who have been shamed into repressing their own experience as unacceptable to the imperial consciousness; the ones whose stories and memories have been omitted from the "official" histories; all those who have no existence or identity apart from that given to them by their overseers. If this "rabble" can be prevented from having their own stories, then their rights and claims can also be disallowed. And so the marginated are reduced to silence and their silence is taken as consent. After all, if they do not complain, they must be happy and content with their place.

Victims Blaming Victims. It is the cunning design of those in power to disconnect, isolate, and separate the powerless from their own experience, memories, awareness, and perceptions and to encourage self-blaming. This strategy is designed to convince the victimized that they are responsible for their own helplessness and inadequacy. According to Michael Lerner,

> Powerlessness corrupts. Powerlessness corrupts in a very direct way: It changes, transforms, and distorts us. It makes us different from how we would otherwise want to be. We look at our world and our own behavior, and we tell ourselves that although we really aren't living the lives we want to live, there is nothing we can do about it. We are powerless. . . . The greatest obstacle [to change] is our own internalized sense that everything has to remain the same, that the way people treat each other and live together and work together is part of some fundamental and unchangeable reality.[64]

---

61. Ibid., 20.
62. Ibid., 12.
63. Miller, *Thou Shalt Not Be Aware,* 308.
64. Lerner, *Surplus Powerlessness,* 2-3.

By preventing these people from having their own past, the authorities and custodians of bureaucracy can exclude them from the future and prevent them from demanding their fair share of society's goods, services, and commodities in the present as well. Without their own stories, such peoples are kept nameless, unknown, anonymous, and thus, powerless.

The Self as Prison. People in such worlds of oppression do not have lives; they work and serve the purposes of those in power. They do not have rights, only duties and obligations. They are incapable of sustaining family life, bonds of attachment, or personal relationships, because they are not people but property. They are only slaves who can be taken away, sold, or killed whenever the masters so wish. In fact, to survive in such a world, it is better not to think of oneself as a person but to remain numb and not feel anything.

Without the story of their own history and experience, the powerless are also prevented from becoming a community of solidarity. The official "disconfirmation" of their pain and the empire's disqualification of their suffering deprives them of all means of social support. Without stories, they are kept disorganized, fragmented, and impotent, a mass of isolated individuals without brother or sister, ally or supporter, comrade or companion. In this state of weakness and powerlessness, anything can be done to the nameless ones because they are alone, without verifiable claims on sanctioned reality. They are the undocumented of history, without passports or visas. They have no rights or privileges. They are the displaced other, the alien, the stranger. They are "not-us" but "them." They are not in the official story. And if they are not in the official story, they do not exist.

Storying and the Civic Order

Stories and memories that contradict the authorized version of reality are seen as dangerous, threatening, revolutionary, radical, subversive, destabilizing. If they are allowed to be told, allowed to be heard, they will plunge civil order into chaos and anarchy. Therefore, telling such stories must be considered illegal. Stories will disturb the legitimate peace and tranquility government requires to conduct business-as-usual, which is, after all, the state's supreme duty and sacred charge from the gods. Besides, how can such "lies" be entertained? Such "libelous" stories must be, at best, merely exaggerations and rumors of the disgruntled and dissatisfied, the shiftless, the lazy, the troublemakers and malcontents who cannot rightfully appreciate their blessings and fortunes and proper place or lot in life. "Egypt! Love it or leave it!" Such ungrateful people are dangerous and irresponsible because they disparage and disgrace the integrity, reliability, and good intentions of those governing for the "common" good.

Dissonant stories will only upset, threaten, and deabsolutize the prevailing versions of the established reality. If tolerated, these alternative stories will destabilize civic order with their controversial claims. Worse, they might force the reexamination of what always has simply been assumed to be the "truth." This is too threatening: "When our life-world is threatened, it is surely discerned as the end of the world. . . . The known world cannot tolerate speech about the end of our world."[65]

Such alternative versions will only cripple the public trust and foster insecurity, weakness, uncertainty, and doubt among the government and citizenry. It might even mean that the "official history" might have to be retold, rewritten, expanded, opened up. The "official story" might have to be reimagined. Can the old ways permit such newness? King, council, priests and generals all say No! So the usual silences must be enforced.

Silence and Powerlessness. Silence and the absence of story isolate, shame, and keep people disenfranchised and powerless. In silence, no response to experience is permitted; no relationship to the other is possible. In silence, one is cut off both from self and others, from one's own individual experiences, history, and memories, as well as those of others. As Lerner puts it, "The most fundamental assumptions of powerlessness are connected to people's beliefs that they are all alone and that others cannot be trusted to share their perceptions or common interests."[66]

---

65. Brueggemann, *Creative Word,* 57-58.
66. Lerner, *Surplus Powerlessness,* 39-40.

Suffering and pain seen in such isolated contexts is usually internalized as one's own fault, one's due or just desert. This internalization of blame for one's own suffering and pain produces sheeplike behavior and contributes to the systemization of powerlessness. By not hearing the stories of others, one remains ignorant of the fact that other people are also suffering in the exact same way. Isolated from this knowledge, people resort instead to self-blame, self-reprisal, and self-punishment, which is exactly what the dominant powers of the empire want because it preempts any serious attempts at systemic change. "The anger that might be reasonably directed against a social order which generates personal unhappiness is instead directed inwards. . . . As such, it may play into the self-blaming that is a central force in keeping people powerless."[67]

The Denial of Anger. Alone, divided, isolated, without support, without community, without even self-valuing, those denied access to their own stories internalize the oppressive stories of the dominant culture and believe they are deserving of pain and shame. They deepen their own inferiority and self-hatred by devaluing their experience and doubting its validity. This silence is equivalent to a participation in the demonic forces of death because it permits the reign of fear and shame to go unchallenged. Silence, coupled with self-blame, isolation, and helplessness separates us from ourselves, our dignity, our goodness, our worth, and the belief that we are human. Instead silence converts our fear into shame – with the result that we believe that we deserve persecution, oppression, and victimization. It is this experience of shame that convinces us we are fundamentally not-good, that is, bad, evil, unworthy of help or solace or comfort. The silenced image themselves as loathsome and despicable, deserving of their inadequacy and powerlessness. Silence keeps them trapped in their shame because they are afraid of what might happen if they did speak or call attention to themselves. "The psychodynamic dimensions of this process are striking: the justified anger that one might feel at a situation in which one's capacities are being thwarted gets repressed, and is directed inward at oneself. This process of internalization of anger is extremely destructive."[68]

---

67. Ibid., 9.

Communities Breaking Silence through Story. But then something happens, something astonishing and shocking, something that could never have been anticipated, planned for, or managed, despite all the technological instruments, mythopoetic ideology, and armies of imperial bureaucrats. The Israelites – with all the disconfirmed, the brutalized, the tortured, the voiceless, the criminal and outcasts of history – do the one last thing they can, the one thing that cannot be taken away from them. They cry out their pain. "The victims of the enmeshment must make the first move, but precisely because they are victims, they cannot make such a move. They are paralyzed, bought off, or intimidated through a carefully nurtured symbiotic relationship of dependency upon the system. This Exodus narrative, however, asserts a remarkable recognition. Subservience is what we would expect . . . but it is not so in Israel."[69] Perhaps there is no more shocking phrase in all the scriptures than "and we cried out" (Exod. 2:23). And with that cry of pain the Israelites in Egypt fracture the first commandment of imperial order: "What must not be, cannot be."[70]

One Voice, One Story: An Alternative Consciousness

For the first time in the empire's history, as the Israelites cry out their pain, an alternative voice breaks the consensus and silence. The perfect civil order is disturbed. The totalism of the state that has assured social control for centuries is shattered. And all it takes is one alternative voice, one alternative perception, what Brueggemann calls an "alternative consciousness."[71] That alternative perspective, even when just an inarticulate moan of pain or "mumbling word," offers a counterproposal to the "settled truth"; it "destabilizes all our settled 'facts,' and opens the way for transformation and the gift of newness."[72]

The moment of revolution, which dismantles the indestructible empire, comes with the outcry of pain, pain that can no longer be silenced by imperial decrees to the contrary.

68. Ibid., 30.
69. Brueggemann, *Hope within History*, 16.
70. Miller, *Thou Shall Not Be Aware*, 108.
71. Brueggemann, *Prophetic Imagination*, 13.
72. Brueggemann, *Poet*, 5.

"Think what a subversive, revolutionary move that is! It is not revolutionary to experience pain. The regime does not deny the reality of pain. Or, if one notices the pain, one must not credit it for much. Simply to notice the pain, though, is not the same as public processing. As long as persons experience their pain privately and in isolation, no social power is generated. That is why every regime has a law against assembly." It is Israel's embrace and expression of pain that becomes "an irreversible act of civil disobedience."[73]

With that primitive, guttural, choked growl of pain cracking her throat, Israel dares to articulate her own experience and that experience is unspeakable pain. There is no word for Israel's pain in Pharaoh's dictionary, no vocabulary or grammar to say what she must. Such pain is supposed to be unimaginable or at least unheard in the empire, but Israel can imagine it because Israel feels and experiences it second by second, day by day, year after year. If Israel can feel that pain, it must be real; it must exist. And if her pain exists, so does Israel. So, denied language, Israel cries out in pain, disturbs the universe with her presence, and tells her story for the first time. With that anonymous howl breaking her self-isolating silence, Israel takes her first steps out of Pharaoh's crumbling empire and into her own life, experience, identity, and history. Israel's moan is her birth pang, her life cry, and her first story. With this cry, Israel proclaims she exists, she lives in space and time, she dwells in a history that she knows will be spoken one day, a history that will include her name among the nations.

With her cry of pain as self-articulation, Israel moves into subjectivity, self-awareness, and narrative. Israel's self-expression is her move toward healing and salvation, as she begins to claim her own experience as meaningful and worthy, to regard herself as deserving of respect and her voice worthy of hearing. What Israel has repressed, she can now speak because she has found her self-identity. That identity may not be valued in the world in which Israel finds herself, but *she* has valued it and claimed that identity as her own. That is what is important, because now Israel has her own story.

---

73. Brueggemann, *Hope within History*, 16, 17.

Storying the Pain Together: Israel as Community

Freed from her own shame and self-loathing, Israel speaks her story and, by sharing it, finds she is not alone. Others share her experience, as they will throughout history, the history Israel is making possible with her cry. Israel's cry of pain connects Jew with Jew: the sob of a mourning mother, the wail of a hungry child, the moan of an old man in the mudpit, the rasp of a death rattle. What none of them could imagine happens: for each cry raised, someone hears them; for every speaker, a listener. A listener who hears herself for the first time in the cry of the other; a listener who identifies his life experience with the story of another. And in this process, the silenced find their own voices; listeners hear their very own stories coming from the opened throats and unstopped mouths of their neighbors. They hear the truthfulness of what these tellers speak and, in acknowledging that truthfulness, they give back the gift of validation, of confirmation. In this way, together, speakers and hearers find the stories that had been denied them.

For this is what story does: it creates relationships of shared experiences, of communality, of compassion and empathy. The "other" becomes my brother; "an-other" becomes my sister. Stories connect people in worlds where such human connections have been systematically severed over the centuries. And in the storying of human experience, an alternative world is evoked, an alternative world with alternative values, alternative ways of knowing and relating. Thus does the community of Israel find herself gathered together in the act of storying.

In this way, story creates community and communication and helps us to realize we are not alone nor are we blameworthy. "Interactions are supportive to the extent that they undermine self-blaming. This happens most effectively and most explicitly when individuals come to see that they are not alone, and that the situations they face are shared situations, based not on the individual's personal inadequacies but on problems that are external, problems that are faced by others, and problems that require connection and help from other people by whom one is also needed."[74]

---

74. Lerner, *Surplus Powerlessness*, 41.

The Power of Story in the Exodus Event. Telling their stories
and claiming their experience gives credence, power, reality,
and credibility to the marginal and oppressed. To have their
story heard empowers, gives authority and identity, and
liberates. The sharing of stories means the forging of alliance, the sharing of the world, the sharing of a common
reality, the sharing of power: "that is, transformative power
is found not only in the Exodus event but also in the Exodus
narrative."[75]

In a sense, the parting of the Red Sea must happen first
with an act of imagination, in the parting of the silence that
has prevented all previous action or engagement. The parting of the flood waters of death must happen first in Israel's
parting of her decreed future, a future decreed to be always
the same as her past. Without any hope of someone or
something new changing the royal story, Israel is enslaved
forever.

In the face of such impersonal, technocratic regimes as
that of Pharaoh and imperial Egypt, in the face of regiments
and armaments and ballistics, it is the speaking of another
alternative story that disarms and deabsolutizes the "official" reality.

> This moment of outcry in Israel is a moment of 'going
> public' in an irreversible act of civil disobedience . . . .
> The outcry is an announcement that Israel would no
> longer bow before the imperial ideology, because the
> slaves had noticed that the ideology did not square
> with the reality of pain in their own lives which no
> amount of ideology could lead them to deny. . . . They
> would no longer bow before the *ideology* offered by the
> ruling class. The "withdrawal" is surely liturgical,
> political, economic, and psychological – the end of the
> "known world" of Egypt.
>   Such an action is unheard of in the ancient world.
> It is a withdrawal from the "sacred canopy," a disen-
> gagement from the only known world, a rejection of
> the rules of the game, a denial of the theodicy spon-
> sored by the system. The cry of pain begins the for-
> mation of a countercommunity around an alternative
> perception of reality. The only source of such a coun-
> tercommunity is to trust one's pain and to trust the

---

75. Brueggemann, *Hope within History*, 8.

pain of one's neighbor which is very much like our own.[76]

Israel's God Hears and Responds. But it is not just the Israelites who hear one another in a new way, as if for the first time. For something else, just as astonishing and shocking as that first cry of pain, happens. There is a god in the pantheon of heaven who is moved by that cry, a god who apparently listens for such cries, who longs to hear the stories of men and women. If this god is anything, he is a good listener; in fact, as Brueggemann points out, he is something of an eavesdropper, listening even when he is not being spoken to. Perhaps this is because that god hears his own name as the people cry out their "I AM" with their stories of selfhood and identity. So YHWH, "I AM," responds. "This response on the part of Yahweh is a surprise. The first actor in the story does not know of Yahweh ahead of time. It does not say Israel cried out 'to him.' The cry was not addressed to Yahweh or to anyone, but nonetheless it evoked Yahweh's answer."[77]

It is Yahweh's listening, hearing, interpreting, and responding that turns howl and outcry into storying, into interactive dialogue, into meaning and enduring relationship. Thus does the conversation that is Torah begin, the conversation between God and the people of Israel. "As Israel tells its faith-forming narrative, the pain is received, resolved, and honored by Yahweh, the Lord of the Exodus: 'Yahweh heard our cry, knew our condition, saw our affliction, and came down to save.' That reception and response by Yahweh also belongs to the narrative, and without it the narrative would collapse."[78] No sooner has Israel dared to articulate her self-identity with her cry of pain than she is surprised to find that identity transformed forever by the response of One, the Holy One, who has heard her and who will now always be listening and looking out for her.

As it turns out, Israel's story is about storying itself. Israel learns that her identity is no longer single but dialogic. For now she can never be alone. She will always be heard; she will always be partnered in an ongoing coopera-

---

76. Ibid., 17-18. Emphasis in original.
77. Ibid., 18.
78. Ibid.

tive, mutual, collaborative relationship. Just as YHWH is called forth into history by the storying cry of Israel in Egypt, so Israel is birthed a second time, from pain to promise, from pit to womb by God's own love of listening and responding. Israel and YHWH are born together in an act of storying, in a mutual act of telling and listening, of disclosure and reception, an act of dialogue and interrelatedness. Story is the mother of this God and Israel.

A New Story for Israel. A new story is now heard on the earth, one that expresses long-buried human pain and proclaims the intervention of a new God, one whose name has never been heard before, who subverts the "business-as-usual" philosophy of the current dominant regime. This God is arrayed against the systemic injustice, oppression, and deceit that the status quo keeps in place. With this God, a new paradigm, a new world, a new set of stories enters into human consciousness. And these very first sojourns into story form Israel's own version of reality which includes Israel's God: "the coming of a new lord on behalf of a nameless rabble."[79]

This God does not depend on antecedents or precedents. This God is new, underived, abrupt, and discontinuous with the gods of old. This God responds to the groans of the oppressed and promises them freedom, dignity, equality. Israel is born of both the groaning of her people and the hearing of those groans by Israel's God. That God listens and wants to hear what the voiceless, the nameless, the storyless have to say, even if that can only be a wordless cry of pain. "The narrative of Israel is an announcement of a radically new resolve in heaven that from the world of the gods there emerges this one who is responsive to the groans of the uncredentialed. . . . This is simply a *disclosure*, a surprising announcement of something as true as unexpected, without accompanying commentary. Because of that unexplicated responsiveness from among the gods, there is a genuine newness on earth."[80]

---

79. Brueggemann, *Creative Word*, 28.
80. Ibid., 29. Emphasis in original.

Alternative Story, Alternative World

What does this mean for the empire and its reliance on technocracy, control, intimidation, and ideology? In the face of Israel's cry of pain and her storying evocation of a new alternative world with its new god, Egypt is completely defenseless. Her weapon systems and defense budgets are useless. For if there can be one story other than the "official" story, then the imperial story is no longer the only one. That one alternative story means that there are other ways of speaking of reality in new, refreshing, and shocking ways. That new story creates an alternative world that negates the regime's ideological claims as objective, universal, eternal, and categorical. Israel's story means that "reality" is no longer as simple, single, total, or so closed as Pharaoh's solemn court officials had claimed. With Israel's one alternative vision of the world, experience becomes diverse, multiple, nuanced, different.

Now with a story of her own, Israel is able to see how the benign, neutral, absolute world of Egypt and Pharaoh was only an imaginary construct, a convenient contrivance, arranged and maintained to guarantee dominance and preference for some at the cost of others in the empire. As it turns out, the empire was Egypt's story, a harsh, repressive "lifeworld" that could only survive with the exploitation of foreigners and slave labor. "The Egyptian-Canaanite technological-ideological lifeworld isn't benign, neutral, or absolute. It is a contrivance of the dominant powers which are viewed in Israel both negatively and critically, because that social contrivance of imperial legitimacy is organized against justice, freedom, and humaneness. . . ."[81]

Story as Home/Land in Time and Space. With this new awareness of herself as one always in dialogic relationship with YHWH, Israel will never be able to "go down to Egypt" again nor sojourn in the "land" of Pharaoh, because she no longer has to interiorize that imperial world as the only one available to her. Now there will always be an alternative land, an alternative imagination, an alternative story which will invalidate all claims that pretend to be absolute, "proper or normative." Israel may again find herself under the domi-

---

81. Brueggemann, *Hope within History*, 12.

nation of other imperial powers, but now she will not have
to sell her birthright or submit her imagination to the storied
worlds of her oppressors, for now Israel knows "that *we do
not belong to Pharaoh's world*. That is an alien world and
one must not be seduced there. . . . That imperial arrangement which enslaves Israel and which seems legitimated
according to imperial ideology is not for one minute to be
accepted as normative or deserving of either respect or obedience. Faith development consists in seeing the destructive
power of the empire clearly and in having the freedom to act
apart from and against it." Now all her rituals, in home, in
family, in public and private gathering, will tell and retell
Israel's first story so that it is never forgotten: she will
"practice a liturgy that intends to subvert that seemingly
absolute shaping of social reality."[82]

Story as Critique of Ideology. Brueggemann summarizes how
the Exodus story functions as an ongoing "critique of ideology":

> (1) The Israelite knows that he or she lives in a
> contrived world. Egyptian arrangements are not at
> all thought to be either absolute or worthy of trust
> and respect. (2) The contrivance is not a matter of
> accident or indifference. It is quite intentionally de-
> signed to serve the special interests of some at the
> expense of others. (3) Because this technological-ideo-
> logical world is a contrivance and not a given, it may
> be undone, and dismantled – *deconstructed*. The
> world may then be arranged in an alternative way if
> one has the courage and wits to do so. (4) The agent
> of such dismantling, deconstruction, delegitimation is
> *known by name – Yahweh*. The Israelite shaped by
> narrative recital is not a helpless, isolated victim but
> has an ally so powerful that the dismantling of the
> contrived empire is sure and can be counted on. That
> dismantling by Yahweh must be regularly and fre-
> quently replicated in liturgy, so that each new gen-
> eration does not for a moment submit to the
> contrivance. As the liturgy legitimates a posture of
> refusal, so the posture results in various concrete acts
> of refusal, acts of freedom, which are derivative from
> the alternative paradigm offered in the liturgy on
> which the text is based. What Israel enacts regularly

---

82. Ibid., 11, 11-12 (emphasis in original), 11.

in the liturgy may occasionally be embraced in arenas of real historical danger and possibility.[83]

What Israel learns from her experience in Egypt is that any lifeworld is constructed; it is a fictive world made from the stories by which we arrange and order our experience. No such world anywhere is identical with objective reality; none can ever be absolutized. Those lifeworlds that make unlimited claims upon our loyalty and command our unquestioning obedience should immediately arouse our suspicion. Those deserving our respect can tolerate our investigation, engagement, curiosity, and participation. Israel knows that absolute claims to objectivity and impartiality usually serve hidden special interests. Israel knows this now; and so, instead of invalidating her own experience in the face of the certitudes and assurances of others, Israel will ask questions, seek conversation, dialogue, and a good argument because she knows she will find truth where such participation is open and welcomed.

> The Israelite is given an identity of critical awareness and the boldness to begin to think through alternatives that lie outside the legitimated structure which is now dramatized as inadequate and tentative. . . . Israelites are certainly not to be like the Egyptians, exploitative of others, but they also are not intended to be victims of such a system. Thus identity has to do with faith and life lived *outside the imperial system* in a zone of freedom and justice. This is faith formation which nurtures persons to live outside the dominant system with the courage and imagination to construct countersystems of reality.[84]

Story as the Way into Hope. Israel knows that her storytelling will always be something of an embarrassment to some within the Hebrew community who would wish her more "modern," scientific, up-to-date, "techno-literate." But such intimacy, trust, openness, particularity, and honoring of the concrete experiential will always make Israel's storying fiercely antimodern; her modes of knowing "suspect and troublesome in the world"; her public memory "a counterexperience, a subversive alternative to an imperial consen-

---

83. Ibid., 12-13. Emphasis in original.
84. Ibid., 14. Emphasis in original.

sus."[85] So Israel must remember that "the proper telling of
the story" is her own special way into the promised land of
an alternative imagination where she can remain free from
dominance of all kinds.

> We might wish for a more scientific analysis, but this
> community does its serious critique in narrative form.
> Israel knows that the dominant ideology will be de-
> stroyed by the proper telling of the story. That is why
> ancient Israel "loved to tell the story" and why "those
> who knew it best seemed hungering and thirsting to
> hear it like the rest." The retelling of the text is to
> remember who we are. The mode of the story is the
> only way to get at the concreteness of the hurt that
> will lead to action. The story both discloses how Israel
> was enslaved and mediates the power to undertake
> transformative, liberating action.[86]

Story as Israel's Primal Mode of Knowing. Brueggemann
calls story "Israel's primal mode of knowing," for "it is the
foundation from which come all other knowledge claims we
have." And, he continues, the "story can be told as a base
line. It is given by adult to child with confidence, nerve,
passion, delight. . . . with *firmness*, because it is undoubted
– with *graciousness*, because there is eagerness to share –
with *authority*, because the speaker both owns and is possessed by the story."[87]

The story is Israel's chief defense because it is her chief
reality, her fundamental articulation of who she is, and the
truth that continues to liberate her.

> Israel's narrative is a partisan, polemical narrative.
> It is concerned to build a countercommunity – counter
> to the oppression of Egypt, counter to the seduction
> of Canaan, counter to every cultural alternative and
> every imperial pretense. There is nothing in this
> narrative that will appeal to outsiders who belong to
> another consensus, or who share a different ethos and
> participate in another epistemology. To such persons,
> Israel's narratives are silly, narrow, scandalous, and
> obscurantist. The narrative form of the Torah intends

---

85. Brueggemann, *Creative Word*, 27, 26.
86. Brueggemann, *Hope within History*, 15.
87. Brueggemann, *Creative Word*, 15, 22, 23, 18 (emphasis in
    original).

to nurture insiders who are willing to risk a specific
universe of discourse and cast their lot there.[88]

Story as Container of Awe and Astonishment. The form of
story is what is important to the process of change. Simple
discursive accounts of intellectual insight are not enough to
move people's minds and hearts in ways they will never
forget – especially across cultures, generations, and the
passage of millennia. But stories do have that power, the
power of conveying and transforming personal pain and
experience.

Israel knows that pain, like story, can never be abstract
or universal, so she trusts the details of both. Israel knows
that long after all the dissertations have been read, defended, and forgotten, her stories will remain: It is her
mission.

> Social criticism and exposure of the dominant ideol-
> ogy are important. They, however, only give insight,
> and insight never liberated anyone. They do not give
> power or authority to make a move of withdrawal or
> delegitimation. Such power and authority to move in
> the face of imperial definition of reality come from *the*
> *public processing of pain.* By "public processing" I
> refer to an intentional and communal act of express-
> ing grievance which is unheard of and risky under
> such an absolutist regime.[89]

For Israel, that public processing of pain and grievance
is always expressed in story. The storying of the Jews binds
the suffering of all together into the one story of Israel and
keeps the pain, the power, the hurt, and the hope fresh, alive,
and immediate as only story can. That is why the Exodus
story speaks over the centuries, because ". . . stories live
across the generations. Not all of Israel's storytellers lived
at the time of Moses or Samson or Elijah. So when we say
[stories are] experiential, we must not understand that notion in personalized or privatized or immediate terms.
Rather, we must talk about the *public experience* of Israel
which encompasses each new generation."[90]

---

88. Ibid., 27.
89. Brueggemann, *Hope within History*, 16. Emphasis in original.
90. Brueggemann, *Creative Word*, 25. Emphasis in original.

Torah: The Work of Storying

In the spirit of Brueggemann then, let me propose that Torah is not just a noun but a verb as well, an active verb. Torah does not just refer to a body of content but it also denotes a dynamic process, a way of knowing, of being, of relating. One could even say without blasphemy that storying is the work of Torah and the vocation of Israel. For what is Torah if not the continuing artful constructing or storying of that "nomos" or "lifeworld" which is "an articulation of world coherence, as a shaping of reliable order, as a barrier against the chaos that waits so close."[91]

Storying in Israel then is mitzvah, prayer, and worship all at once, both "offering that life-world and creating that life-world." The whole community of Israel "engages in the construction of a world, the formation of a system of values and symbols, of oughts and mays, of requirements and permissions, of power configurations."[92]

The telling of her stories across the generations of space and time binds all of Israel into a single community of shared imagination. That imagination is nothing less than the mind and heart of God, the God who delights in Israel's storying and in whose image she is created to play and to story.

> There is a crucial match between the mode of story and the substance to be told. Trouble surfaces in the community of faith whenever we move from the idiom of story. As soon as we make this move, we create an incongruity between our convictions and the ways we speak our convictions. When we are saddled with this incongruity, we spend our energies on alien questions: Do you believe the Bible is inerrant? Do you believe Jesus was raised physically from the dead? Do you believe we should ordain homosexuals?[93]

Israel and God: Called by Story

The storying of God, God's eagerness to speak and listen, is the mother of Israel and her relationship with YHWH. In fact, Israel and YHWH are born together in story: Israel from

---

91. Ibid., 19.
92. Ibid., 20.
93. Ibid., 22.

within God's own telling of himself; YHWH from Israel's listening and storying about what and who she has heard, experienced, and known. From Egypt on, every successive generation of Israel is then both nurtured with and socialized through an active engagement with a whole tradition of storying that is Israel's life. "What Israel knows is that if the story is not believed, nothing added to it will make any difference"[94] – not more commandments, rituals, or laws.

Thus, Israel's storying, more than anything else, becomes her home, her land, her common ground through space and time. The place of consensus provides Israel with enough of a "secure base" to allow her to wander and explore, to question unceasingly, to wonder and consider new possibilities. "Israel's imagination is liberated and liberating. That does not mean unlimited and undisciplined, as though anything goes. . . . It is the consensus on which stories are based that defines the arena for free imagination." Because of the safe, secure, consistent boundaries of her tradition and heritage of stories, Israel is spared a life "in chaos, in alienation, in narcissistic subjectivity." Without tradition, the world is always in danger of becoming "a jungle of competing, savage interests" where "desire is skewed, emptied, failed, boring."[95]

Reason as Exile, Mystery as Homeland. Israel's storying also prevents her from becoming entrapped in modern modes of knowledge such as "explanation," "proofs," or "rational understanding" where she knows she has no business being. Instead, Israel's storying honors an epistemology whereby "many things are not known in this community, and some ways of knowing are precluded. Many things are bracketed out, not known, not asked about. The Torah does not answer every question. . . . It concedes ignorance. More than that, it honors mystery. It assures the child that there is much we do not know and cannot know." In this way, Israel's storying can communicate her most sacred beliefs while respecting the limits of her knowledge, her "deep convictions" and the "precariousness" of her knowledge, "how provisional so much must be." In this way, Israel wisely "refuses to be sucked into other knowledge games, refuses to know too much" and is

---

94. Ibid., 23.
95. Ibid., 24-25, 20.

taught to be wary of those people and powers "who want to know too much for the wrong reasons."[96]

Israel and the Truths of Story. Such attitudes as Israel's circumspection and humility about reason and inquiry are enough to qualify her tradition as completely antithetical to "modern" knowing. Israel turns to story and the "limited" knowledge that comes from such pre-, non-, antimodern modes of consciousness. "Story as a distinctive way of epistemology is especially appropriate to Torah" because "story is *concrete*. It is about particular persons in particular times and places. It does not flinch from the scandal of specificity. There is no pretense of universal truths." And it is precisely by means of such specificity and particularity that story avoids "every universalizing temptation," the temptation that modernism could not avoid. For a mind that does not hesitate to universalize will not hesitate to dismiss the individual and the anomalous for the elegance of the absolute and categorical. But Israel knows where such a mind leads and so "Israel does not propose to offer a story which is true for everyone all the time. Israel makes no claims or assertions of 'eternal truths.' "[97]

Israel and the Inexhaustible Tellings of Her Story. Israel's preference for narrative is also because story is *"open-ended in its telling."* The stories of Israel have definite shapes, boundaries, and trajectories of integrity that are always honored and respected, but the community of Israel also knows that good storytelling must always be fresh, immediate, original, and on edge. Thus, Israel always encourages creativity and inventiveness in her storytellers and so gives them the full range of their imagination to play with. Thus, "there is no comparable insistence that [the stories] be told in a certain way." As Brueggemann says, "The storyteller, once he or she has been claimed by these stories, has enormous freedom for the telling – freedom not only to give different nuance and accent, but freedom to turn the wordage in one direction or another." Thus, Israel's insistence on the consensus of tradition in her stories is also what allows her such tolerance and flexibility in their performance. "The community was not concerned to communicate static mean-

---

96. Ibid., 22, 23, 22.
97. Ibid., 23 (emphasis in original), 27.

ings or flat memories to Israel's new generation. Rather, it was concerned about creating a context, evoking a perception, forming a frame of reference which went beyond and did not depend on any particular version or nuance of any particular narrative." Israel does not want a community of parrots but a *shul* of wild songbirds singing all her multivarious versions of her story.[98]

Freedom to Hear and Decide. Israel also prefers storytelling for her epistemology of choice because of its encouragement of the "practice of imagination" in both the teller and the listener.

> This means that the listener has nearly as much freedom as the speaker in deciding what is happening. The listener is expected to work as resiliently as the teller. The communication between the two parties is a bonding around images, metaphors, and symbols that are never flattened to coercive instruction. Israel has enormous confidence in its narrative speech, sure that the images and metaphors will work their own way, will reach the listener at the point of his or her experience, and will function with a claiming authority.[99]

This bonding of two parties in a relationship that is dialogic, interactive, and mutually respectful and cooperative is the heart and mystery of Israel's relationship with her God.

Just as YHWH has entrusted himself to being revealed and known in Israel's stories, so Israel trusts her children with a comparable freedom to hear and imagine the stories for themselves. There is no coercion, pressure, or threat of force used to restrain the freedom of the listener. In storying, "there is an open field of speech between the parties that admits to many alternative postures. . . . The listener has freedom to hear and decide, and is expected to decide."[100]

---

98. Ibid., 23.
99. Ibid., 24.
100. Ibid.

Trusting the Story

Israel's trust extends not only to listeners but also to the stories themselves. Israel trusts her stories, trusts them *as* stories, knowing them to be more telling and revealing of Israel's own posture and relationship with truth than any other mode of knowing available to her. "Story in Israel is the *bottom line*. It is told and left, and not hedged about by other evidences. . . . Israel has confidence in its stories, in and of themselves. Israel understands them not as instruments of something else, but as castings of reality."[101]

The intense intimacy and even erotic involvement of Israel's relationship with YHWH is heightened with each new instance of their encounter in the direct, immediate, and experiential communion and exchange of stories. "That is, the [stories] tell what happened, what we have seen and heard, what happened to us. They are told by participants, not by objective third parties who tell someone else's stories. The adults do not ask children to believe stories by which they themselves are not claimed." That intimacy is fresh and new with every generation of storytellers and storylisteners because "stories live across the generations."[102]

Stories, thus, remain intensely personal and immediate as if they were happening for the very first time here and now. And, in fact, they are – in the telling and the hearing, the giving and receiving and the giving back again. Each telling and each listening is unique, new, and individual, open to the freedom and creativity of participants.

The Nurturing of Public Experience. But this experience of intense intimacy and immediacy, while unique and individual, is also always public, common, shared; it is never privatized. It unites each new hearer of the story with all other listeners throughout space and time in the ongoing community which is Israel – that same Israel who has heard the one, same, single, consistent, authoritative story throughout the millennia but who has heard it in countless new and different ways. "The Torah is for the nurture of public experience. . . . Not only is private experience not adequate for

---

101. Ibid., 26. Emphasis in original.
102. Ibid., 25.

life, it is a deception to speak of private experience; for all human experience is deeply social."[103]

Such intimacy, trust, openness, particularity, and honoring of the concrete experiential makes Israel's storying fiercely antimodern, her modes of knowing "suspect and troublesome in the world," her public memory "a counterexperience, a subversive alternative to an imperial consensus."[104]

This is because the inherent tensions that make storying dangerous and exciting will not permit any reduction of the human person in either a culture of "narcissistic individualism" or a "mass society:" "Israel's storytelling, however, denies both of these temptations, so that one is not free to have a *private faith* and not free to embrace the *common myths of the dominant culture*."[105] Instead, because each Jew is thrust into a social world, a community of blood and stories, no Jew stands alone or apart. Every Jew is linked throughout space and time with every other Jew. Yet that heritage of story assures that each Jew remains uniquely individual, irreducible to any other. In this way, the human person is more his or her own self when also most identified with the community. And it is only by dwelling within the storying process that this can happen.

Story Thwarting Modernity. The narrative of Torah is of such shocking newness and unexpected disclosure that it is wholly unconventional and antimodern in another way. "Such an incredible narrative is a claim against all conventional religions, ancient or modern. Characteristically, all conventional religion wants to derive and extrapolate, to stress the continuity, to explain everything in terms of antecedents. That is because conventional religion, in its reasonableness, does not believe there is a newness that can come against the system." But Israel's stories are not reasonable. They do not follow any logic, system, or method of proof. Instead, they are completely underived and discontinuous, without precedent, explanation, or prior cause. "No speculation is offered which would preoccupy the philosophers or entice the scientists. This is simply a *disclosure*, a

---

103. Ibid., 25-26.
104. Ibid., 27, 26.
105. Ibid., 25. Emphasis in original.

surprising announcement of something as true as unexpected, without accompanying commentary."[106]

The stories proclaim a strange new God whose name has never been heard before, whose abrupt appearance and impetuous intervention into history could never be anticipated or prepared for. This fiercely incalculable God owes his existence to no power other than the hopeful imagination of childlike Israel who has called this God forth with her cry of pain. As a result, this God is dangerous because so free, so uncontrollable, so uncompromised. He is contemptuous of every protocol, custom, or procedure. "Israel's story is against every reasonable explanation, every congenial interface with administered human culture."[107]

What makes Torah such an embarrassment to the "modern" critical mind is its irresponsible indulgence of such epistemological naivete, illogic, and imaginative abandon. But, to Israel, the child's uninhibited first response to the stories is not only warranted but unqualified. It cannot be improved on in any way. Primitive, childlike awe, wonder, and what Buber calls "abiding astonishment"[108] is the perfectly appropriate reply to Israel's stories of her wild, untamed God. "The ethos to which the children are invited is one that assures we shall never cease to be astonished, or never be so satiated or numbed or co-opted that we forget the abruptness in heaven and on earth that has caused us to be. We shall never become so domesticated that our lives are not jolted and our cages rattled by the discontinuity. . . . The narrative consensus assures an abiding restlessness with every present arrangement."[109]

God, Children, and Stories: Wild and Uncontrollable

Perhaps we now begin to glimpse why the responsiveness of Israel's children and their storying are so threatening to the modern mind: because the stories are finally as uncontrollable and wild as the God they summon, coming as they do out of an unbridled imagination that is as intractable, capricious, and ungovernable as it is creatively illogical.

---

106. Ibid., 28, 29. Emphasis in original.
107. Ibid.
108. Brueggemann, *Abiding Astonishment*, 30.
109. Ibid., 30.

"Now we can see why this substance must have the mode of narrative. How else shall we speak of an urgent matter which defies all the reason and logic of the empire?"[110]

In other words, these stories in no way respect the power games of modernity nor will they submit to any of the acceptable rules of formal logic, grammar, or syntax. As stories, they are finally defiant of the "real" world. They refuse to have their wild wanderings tamed or confined by any of the necessary requirements of external space or time. Thus, angels can dance up and down cosmic ladders; seas can part; the sun can stop still in its track. The stories are only as limited as the imaginations that inspire them.

But, perhaps, in the eyes of the power brokers and managers of technology, the stories are guilty of an even greater heresy. As we saw in our discussion of oral preliterate modes of knowing and storying, stories stubbornly refuse to claim that they have anything "objective" to say about that real world. They, thus, avoid entering the playing fields of power and control, where the rigged rules of empiricism and evidential argument wait to destroy their credibility. With calculating ingenuity, the stories claim that they are just stories, child's play, nothing more, certainly nothing to be taken too seriously. The intrinsic self-constraint of narrative epistemology reasserts the modesty and self-limiting humility of its truth claims. The stories are about nothing, that is, no-thing, at least, not in the world of any external space-time reality.

But because the stories are about no-thing and make no claims about the conditions of that external world, the stories can also never be refuted or disproved. Ironically, by admitting that they are about nothing, the stories guarantee the eternality and radical independence of their power and influence. They do not have to rely on federal funding, NEA grants, or ecclesial imprimaturs to be told. They are, after all, just harmless stories about no-thing. All they need to be told is a teller and a listener. And that is why stories are so dangerous. Like the imagination, they cannot be controlled.

> The agenda of the Torah . . . is about the transformation and redistribution of power in human affairs. The narrative must be left in its raw unacceptable subver-

---

110. Ibid.

siveness. It will not be reduced to safe religion or
personal introspection. There is no child so young that
the miracle and gift of power, and the threat of power,
is not a primary agenda. The reality and ambiguity
of power is fundamental to humanness. . . . But Israel
addresses that issue as its beginning point. The disclosure (revelation) of this narrative is that power has
been reassigned.[111]

---

111. Ibid., 31.

Chapter Six

Midrash as a Way of Knowing

WE HAVE BEEN EXAMINING HOW OUR MODELS OF REALITY
influence and shape our ideas and practices of knowledge
and relationship. I have suggested that Kuhn's contribution
of paradigms has helped us appreciate the importance of
context in the understanding, interpretation, meaning, development, and transmission of truth. I have referred to the
contemporary shift in the models of human knowledge that
is occurring presently across many fields and disciplines,
that shift known as the change from "modern" to "postmodern" categories of knowledge. I have examined this shift in
the therapeutic work of Michael White and David Epston
and the writings of scripture scholar Walter Brueggemann.

In considering the postmodern critique of the modern
era, I have indicated how its advocates today propose storying as a model for an epistemology of meaning as an alternative to a scientific epistemology of causation. Some locate
the trajectory of postmodern understandings of truth within
the hermeneutic tradition that arcs from Vico in the eighteenth century through Heidegger in the 1920s to more
contemporary authors.[1]

However, there is a much older tradition of a narrative
epistemology of meaning and context that has often been
overlooked in contemporary accounts of postmodernism. A
consideration of the midrashic tradition in Judaism has
much to offer us in comprehending and appreciating how
narrative approaches to knowledge and relationship have
existed for thousands of years and are not just recent discov-

---

1. Rosenau, *Post-modernism and the Social Sciences,* 5; Martin
   J. Packer, "Hermeneutic Inquiry in the Study of Human Conduct," *American Psychologist, 40* (10): 1081-82.

eries or passing intellectual fads but true alternatives to dominant technological modes of thought.

The Gap between Jewish and Gentile Ways of Knowing

It is interesting, if not shocking, that two recently acclaimed histories of secular knowledge and Western thought, purporting to be highly inclusive of multiple perspectives and diverse cultural traditions, should continue to present Judaism primarily in caricature from a Christian viewpoint. In these texts, the Jewish God is presented once again as an angry God, while the Christian God is a God of mercy. Judaism's relationship with God is reduced to strict obedience (or an imperfect obedience rooted in fear) of the law.[2] Christianity is seen to have a more enlightened and benign attitude to the law, one which is fulfilled in the love of God, thus eliminating the need for repressive obedience.

I do not believe that the authors of these texts consciously intended to be so dismissive of Judaic tradition or to present such condescending parodies of Jewish attitudes to the Torah. But these examples show how commonplace misrepresentations of Judaic thought and tradition still are even among recognized contemporary scholars.

One could attribute these caricaturizations of Judaism to subtle, if unconscious forms, of anti-Semitism in the academic community. And that may very well be the case. But I would also like to suggest that a significant contributing factor to this continuing misunderstanding of Judaic tradition is the gap between the epistemologies of Jew and Gen-

---

2. A more accurate understanding of "law" is presented in *Back to the Sources,* ed. Barry Holtz (New York: Summit, 1984), 84. The use of the word "law" to describe the Torah comes from the Greek translation of *devarim,* literally "words," into *nomos.* "Learning" is closer to the Hebrew meaning of Torah. As with so much of Hebrew, Torah conjures up multiple meanings, associations, all with various colors and shadings. The reduction of Torah to a set of laws to be obeyed scrupulously is a misrepresentation by what it leaves out. If Torah is anything, it is an invitation to an infinite number of opportunities of love and communion with the God of Israel through the most ordinary moments of a most ordinary day.

tile. This has not been appreciated until the recent postmodern critique with its awareness of "the interface of midrashic methods of interpretation and contemporary practices of deconstruction."[3]

One could rehearse the familiar reasons why Jews have been persecuted, penalized, ostracized, expelled, tortured, and murdered throughout the ages: the charge of being "Christ-killers"; the anti-Semitic tone of the Gospels and Christian scriptures; the libeling of their rituals as "blood sacrifices" in which Gentile children were rumored to be killed; such forgeries as the "Protocols of the Elders of Zion," which alleged worldwide schemes and plots to "take over" the world; and "nativist" envy of their success and social status.

It is obvious that much of the fear, hatred, and suspicion of the Jews can be attributed to their "otherness." In the very midst of aggressively dominant Christian societies that had little toleration for non-conformity or difference of any kind, Jews were able to maintain their own distinct alternative culture, religion, customs, institutions, and language through clever forms of adaptation that, by and large, prevented total assimilation, or, until the Holocaust, widespread, systematic annihilation. Many of the differences between Jews and Gentiles were obvious and overt: dress, language, diet, their restriction to certain professions and areas of the cities. Of course, the most obvious difference was the area of religion, especially since religion was the most predominant factor in social control and social cohesion for centuries in these Christian societies.

Thinking Differently: Epistemological "Otherness"

But, I suggest, that the essence of Jewish "otherness" was not so much just the accumulation of these different factors, although they definitely had a role to play. I suggest the major difference was "the ways in which Jewish modes of thought and speech operate[d] outside of and over against 'Western logic.' "[4]

Earlier we looked at how our ideas of reality and the categories of our thought, knowing, and relating are "con-

---

3. Brueggemann, *Texts,* 100.
4. Ibid., 97.

structed," shaped, and influenced by language and forms of speech. By studying the Hebrew scriptures through the analysis of Brueggemann, we considered how the community of Israel lived and survived in biblical times through a narrative epistemology based on her ability to hope and imagine through storying with and about God and about their unique relationship together.

This narrative epistemology did not end, however, with the destruction of the Second Temple and its cult in 70 C.E. If anything, it became even more important during the late Talmudic period when Israel made the hard transition to nonpolitical status and became "a society held together not by political power but by religious belief."[5] "The only sacred possession that the Jews had left was their Torah."[6] According to Gershon Cohen, "With the dissolution of the high-priesthood and its cultic authority, the Jewish people could be governed only by the Torah. The Jew was obligated to fulfill whatever parts of the Torah could be fulfilled in the absence of monarchy, prophecy, Temple, and priesthood. The only problem that remained for the Rabbis to resolve was the specific ways in which the Torah was to be applied."[7]

Toward the end of the first century C.E., the canon of the Hebrew Bible was considered to be "closed": "nothing could be added or taken away."[8] Following in the footsteps of Ezra who, upon the return from Babylon in 538 B.C.E., had begun "the task of interpreting the Torah so that its law could actually be practiced,"[9] the rabbis of the first centuries C.E. undertook the project of interpreting and explicating the Torah in an organized and systematic way. In Holtz we read, "Convinced that Jewish life could recover from its defeats at the hands of Rome only through renewed dedication to 'Torah,' rabbis organized themselves to spread their teaching, gain disciples, and achieve the largest possible role

---

5. Gershon Cohen, "The Talmudic Age," in *Great Ages and Ideas of the Jewish People,* ed. Leo Schwartz (New York: Modern Library, 1956), 163.
6. Don Rossoff, "The Midrashic Process," (Master's Thesis, Hebrew Union College-Jewish Institute of Religion, 1979), 15.
7. Cohen, "Talmudic Age," 165.
8. Bernhard W. Anderson, *Understanding the Old Testament* (Englewood Cliffs, NJ: Prentice-Hall, 1975), 597.
9. Rossoff, "Midrashic Process," 15.

in Jewish life."[10] What drove the rabbis was "a sense that the laws of Scripture should be expanded to cover all life, not limited to their own originally intended contexts."[11]

Breathing Life into the Scriptures and Law: Midrash

As Rabbinic Judaism sought to provide some coherent method for maintaining Jewish identity and cohesion grounded in biblical tradition, the rabbis realized that the Hebrew scriptures needed to be adapted to life in gentile culture for Judaism to survive. "By the time of the rabbis much had changed. The social and political realities of the biblical world had given way to Greek culture, and the influence of Hellenism was crucial in the world of rabbinic Judaism."[12] The epistemological problem that the rabbis faced was exactly *how much* of a balance to strike between the Torah and host cultures.

To articulate a body of laws adapted from the Torah to their new circumstances, the rabbis engaged in long, complex, and complicated legal discussions. Much of this rabbinic discourse was codified towards the turn of the third century C.E. when the Mishnah was completed. "The discussions of the rabbis then became centered on what was in the *Mishnah.* These later discussions on the *Mishnah* were then added on to the *Mishnah.* The term used for these discussions was *Gemara.*" And from these works came the Talmud: "broadly speaking, Mishnah plus Gemara constitutes the *Talmud.*"[13]

But, as we have already seen in studying the writings of Brueggemann, Torah has never been thought of as just written texts, a body of content, or a collection of literature. "Torah for the Jewish tradition is a multifaceted term. On one level it refers to the first five books of the Bible, the content of the scroll found in any synagogue. In another more expanded sense, Torah is the Hebrew Bible as a whole. But

---

10. Holtz, *Back to the Sources,* 129.
11. Ibid., 130-31.
12. Ibid., 181.
13. Rossoff, "Midrashic Process," 15-16; Susan Handelman, *Slayers of Moses: The Emergence of Rabbinic Interpretation in Modern Literary Theory* (Albany: State University of New York Press, 1982), 301.

Torah stands for more than one text or one book. Torah is revelation, the entire revelation and the entire activity of Jewish study throughout the generations."[14]

Throughout the centuries, Torah has been more than anything else a persistent, enduring, ongoing way of thinking and acting by which Israel continues to define her identity and come to know herself within the variables of history and culture. Torah remains that conversation between God and Israel which cannot end. Like any conversation, it consists in the reciprocal dialogue, play, and relationship among participants and involves the communication, reception, interpretation, and interaction of personal presence through what is said and what is not said, what is stated and what is implied, what is articulated in speech and what is left to silence.

With the canon of scripture closed and no new narratives possible, Israel needed to find some way for her dynamic storying relationship with God to continue growing, developing, and deepening while also being absolutely faithful to the Torah. "Midrash arose as an attempt to keep a sense of continuity between the ancient traditions of the Bible and the new world of Hellenistic Judaism."[15]

By once again including a narrative epistemology in her repertoire of knowing and relating, Israel found a way to be faithful to Torah that was both utterly new and absolutely consistent with her tradition. Through midrash, she entered into a careful reminiscence and reappreciation of her shared life with YHWH by telling stories *about* her stories, weaving elaborate catenae of new stories around and through her old stories. In this way, her ancient stories were kept intact and inviolate, dynamically fresh and immediate. "We are speaking here of the texts known as Midrash, a type of literature so significant that in many ways it can be seen as the central enterprise of almost all Jewish religious writing until the modern period."[16]

---

14. Holtz, *Back to the Sources*, 12.
15. Ibid., 181.
16. Ibid., 177

Midrash: The Multiplicity of Meaning

No one knows exactly where midrash begins or ends.[17] Some rabbis would say it began in the beginning, when God created. Others would say it began when God gave the Torah to Moses at Sinai.[18] Some find midrash already interwoven throughout the texts of the Bible.[19] Some say midrash begins in the last century B.C.E.[20] Most agree, however, that the "flowering" of midrash did not occur until between 400 and 1200 C.E.[21] Some authors claim the great outpouring of Hasidic stories during the eighteenth and nineteenth centuries should be considered midrash while still others declare that midrash continues even to the present day.[22] Of course, it all depends on what one means by midrash. "What, then, is Midrash? It it helpful to think of Midrash in two different, but related, ways: first, Midrash (deriving from the Hebrew root 'to search out') is the process of *interpreting*. The object of interpretation is the Bible or, on occasion, other sacred texts; second, Midrash refers to the corpus of work that has collected interpretations, works such as Midrash Rabbah."[23] Most scholars would accept this as a good, basic definition of how the word "midrash" is used to describe both an activity and a literature.

Jacob Neusner, however, expands this into a larger discussion of culture and continuity, tradition and change.

> Midrash understood as a distinctive process of the reading of Scripture . . . presents us with a sustained and sizable sample of the process of interpretation, by one group in a distinctive context, of a received text created by another, earlier group in a different cir-

---

17. Judah Goldin, "Midrash and Aggadah," in *Judaism: A People and Its History,* ed. Robert Seltzer (New York: Macmillan, 1989), 107.

18. Burton Visotzky, *Reading the Book: Making the Bible a Timeless Text* (New York: Doubleday, 1991), 34.

19. David Stern, "Midrash," in *Contemporary Jewish Religious Thought,* ed. Arthur Cohen and Paul Mendes-Flohr (New York: Scribners, 1987), 614.

20. Goldin, "Midrash and Aggadah," 107.

21. Holtz, *Back to the Sources,* 178.

22. Visotzky, *Reading the Book,* 10; Jo Milgrom, *Handmade* Midrash (Philadelphia: The Jewish Publication Society, 1992), 3.

23. Holtz, *Back to the Sources,* 178.

cumstance. As such, Midrash provides us with insight into the continuity of culture over a changing era, a striking and interesting example of the general hermeneutical possibilities of accommodating change through exegesis of the received in light of the givens of a new age.[24]

Stern echoes this opinion and sees this engagement with cultural issues to be as "ancient as the biblical text" itself. "Later biblical authors can be seen to have re-used earlier sacred traditions in the new contexts of their times, elaborated upon fixed ideas and words, harmonized conflicting texts, and transformed old imagery in order to respond to changing needs."[25]

Midrash, then, is primarily a particular way of thinking, of knowing the world, of constructing reality according to the shapes of an Hebraic imagination: it is "the *process* by which we seek out the underlying truths and meanings of the Torah as well as the *product* of that seeking."[26] According to Handelman, "The midrash searches Scripture to clarify ambiguities, applies it to contemporary needs, probes for deeper meanings, supplements gaps in the text, speculates about history and philosophy."[27] Thus, midrash is not a single book or literature. It is a form of the narrative knowing that is at the heart of Israel's whole self-identity and her relationship with God as expressed in the writings of Brueggemann.

Midrash is, therefore, both the process and the results of the rabbis' study of Torah. As we saw above, however, while the Torah, of course, includes the first five books of the Bible, it is much more than that.

> The key point, the point around which everything revolves, is the rabbis' conception of Torah itself. Torah, to the rabbis, was an *eternally relevant book because it was written* (dictated, inspired – it doesn't

---

24. Jacob Neusner, *Invitation to Midrash: The Workings of Rabbinic Bible Interpretation* (San Francisco: Harper & Row, 1989), 6.

25. Stern, "Midrash," 614. Handelman characterizes the book of Deuteronomy as "a kind of midrash on the first four books." *Slayers,* 302.

26. Rossoff, "Midrashic Process," 14. Emphasis in original.

27. Handelman, *Slayers,* 302.

matter) *by a perfect Author,* an Author who intended
it to be eternal. When we keep this essential fact in
mind, much of the midrashic process falls into place.
The rabbis could not help but believe that this won-
drous and sacred text, the Torah, was intended for all
Jews and for all times. Surely, God could foresee the
need for new interpretations; all interpretations,
therefore, are already in the Torah text.[28]

In fact, the rabbis claimed that since God knows and foresees
everything, all later interpretations of Torah "had originated
at Sinai in the same divine revelation in which God had given
Israel the written text of the Torah."[29]

The Oral Torah: The Storying Relationship Preserved

Scholarship still tends to emphasize "a disproportionately
print-oriented hermeneutic in our study of the Bible,"[30] a
result of the "chirographic bias" of Western culture,[31] and
the technology of the "Gutenberg galaxy."[32] A fundamentalist view sees sacred texts as the simple oral dictation of God
to a human amanuensis. Another naive but once common
view saw scripture as the simple written record of "*the
original* form of oral materials."[33] But the result of these
attitudes is that "we treat words primarily as records in need
of interpretation, neglecting all too often a rather different
hermeneutic, deeply rooted in biblical language that proclaims words as an act inviting participation. We like to
think of textuality as the principal norm of tradition,
whereas I [Kelber] wish to show that speaking was a norm
as well, and writing often a critical reflection on speech, and
also a transformation of it."[34]

It is a commonplace that the so-called book religions
"trace their lineage in some fashion to the Hebrews, the

---

28. Ibid., 185. Emphasis in the original.
29. Stern, "Midrash," 614.
30. Kelber, *Oral and Written Gospel,* xv.
31. Ong, *Orality and Literacy,* 24.
32. McLuhan, *The Gutenberg Galaxy.*
33. Kelber, *Oral and Written Gospel,* xv.
34. Ibid., xvi.

prototypical 'people of the book.'" But any view that does not include the "Hebrew 'genius for hearing'"[35] with its ongoing appreciation and celebration of oral-aural psychodynamics would be only a crude caricature of Jewish tradition. For "word" [*dabar* in Hebrew] is an event of effective power, an experience of intense interaction and personal engagement. "Spoken words of their very nature entail real, not imagined, personal relations, since the audience is on hand and reacting. . . ." Moreover, these relationships entail "the present use of power, since sound must be in active production in order to exist at all. . . . Sound can induce repose, but it never reveals quiescence. It tells us something is going on. . . . Force is operating."[36]

The power and force of the word in Jewish tradition, however, is more than just solemn. It is playful and hence numinous. "In an oral culture, verbalized learning takes place quite normally in an atmosphere of celebration or play. As events, words are more celebrations and less tools than in literate cultures. Only with the invention of writing and the isolation of the individual from the tribe will verbal learning and understanding itself become 'work' as distinct from play, and the pleasure principle be downgraded as a principle of verbalized cultural continuity."[37]

It is in this context of orality's presence, power, play, and relatedness that I wish to discuss the Oral Torah. For the orality of the spoken tradition is never a negative value, the result of not being able to transcribe verbatim accounts of the rabbis' sermons because of the Sabbath prohibition against writing. Instead Jewish tradition has wisely seen the importance of an ongoing dialogue and interaction between fixed text and contemporary speech throughout history. This is the weave of the Torah scroll that unrolls the future. It is from this vantage point that we can prize the relationship between the Written and Oral Torah given together at Sinai.

The Written Torah is that collection of love letters, stories, songs, poems, memories, and recollections of the

---

35. Visotzky, *Reading the Book*, 51.
36. Walter Ong, *Presence of the Word: Some Prolegomena for Cultural and Religious History* (Minneapolis: University of Minnesota Press, 1981), 113, 112.
37. Ibid., 30.

relationship that have been judged the most valuable, treasured, and enduring through time. Comparable to a hope chest or family album, the Written Torah is an attempt to make tangible and present what in essence must always remain evanescent but undying. And so, using the developing technology of writing in the West and under constant threat of dispersion and cultural annihilation, Jews risked blasphemy to fix in space and time what must remain living, changing, indeterminate.

Torah: Text as Presence

This they did with whimsy and play. Hebrew letters were mystic: shifting forms, trading black foreground with white background, changing place and meaning on the page, chanting encrypted numbers in secret languages, cramming volumes in unsounded vowels. In this way, the sages found a way to write that best captured not only what they knew but the very way they knew. And what they knew to be truest was presence. That was how Yahweh had revealed himself to Israel and the name they called this presence: "I AM."

But this presence from its very revelation has always been an interactive one. Consequently, the language of presence had to be ever an interactive one as well. Thus, the paradoxical mercurial fixity of the Hebrew alphabet; the Torah in all its quantum possibility, beyond measuring, predicting, or determining, always becoming real but only in the actuating moment of the present, a present that emerges out of a past and future of infinite potential; the Torah scrolls as the bride of heaven being danced from beginning to end and back again on the night of Simchat Torah.

In a sense, the Torah does not exist until it comes into an interaction of presence. Not until a Torah scroll is unraveled, be that in public chanting, private study, or the telling of its stories, does Torah become activated. Its letters remain inert, lifeless, and meaningless until they are configured by sound into a relationship of presence – not abstract sound but the particular sound of a single human voice or the polyphony of a congregation.

Just as the Torah demands a human voice, so too the "Torah *demands* interpretation."[38] Torah demands discovery. There is no Torah that is not interpreted, not discovered. In other words, there is no aboriginal, absolute, definitive, infallible Torah of some prior, pristine existence independent of human speaking, hearing, or interpreting. And it is that Torah, discovered, interpreted, sounded, and passed on in oral-aural story and tradition that takes precedence over the literal text of Torah.[39] "The framers proposed, not to lay down, but to discover rules governing Israel's life. . . . For the Judaism of the dual Torah rejected as insufficient and incomplete the (merely) written record of the revealed Torah at Sinai and announced itself as more than the religion of the written Torah."[40] This approach to sacred scripture may stop the heart of a fundamentalist but not a Jew. All interpretations are already in the Torah, including those of the rabbis preaching in the synagogues.[41]

According to Visotzky, most of the rabbis' "early sermons were delivered on the Sabbath, when it was prohibited to write." Unlike the extemporaneous preaching of the Church Fathers which was "copied by shorthand experts and edited and revised for written circulation" among the early Christian communities, the teachings of the Jewish rabbis could only be preserved in memory and communicated by word of mouth. This is how both the midrashic method of the rabbis and the narrative content of their sermons on the Written Torah came to be known as the Oral Torah. "The Rabbis called their interpretation of scripture, legends, stories and laws the Oral Torah." In this way the "loose canon" of Oral Torah and midrash came to function not just as commentary but as Torah itself within the community. As we read in Holtz, "Midrash, in other words, was already in God's mind when the Torah was conceived."[42]

But as with all communications by word of mouth, the oral transmission of this Jewish homiletic material suffered from "inaccuracy."[43] But as we have already seen, such

---

38. Holtz, *Back to the Sources,* 17. Emphasis in original.
39. Neusner, *Invitation to Midrash*, 267.
40. Ibid.
41. Holtz, *Back to the Sources,* 177.
42. Visotzky, *Reading the Book,* 14-16; Holtz, *Back to the Sources,* 185.
43. Visotzky, *Reading the Book,* 15.

categories as "accuracy" and "exactness" are intellectual criteria derived from "modern" techniques of knowing after the invention of the printing press and mass literacy movements. The orality of Jewish tradition included tolerance for "inexactness" and "inaccuracy." What to a modern mind might seem an inferior epistemology is to the Jew only a different one, an epistemology that encourages an alternative, pluralistic imagination. It is this attitude of the Jewish mind that explains why midrash is being rediscovered by postmodernist critics. "This beginning of a shift in approach from the modern, scientific worldview to a postmodern one offers an opportunity not only to learn about a characteristically Jewish path of thought but also to join in it and enrich it. The midrashic process is a particularly apt one to renew in this way because within itself is the assumption of open-endedness, unveiling, and enrichment."[44]

This is a very important point. By giving priority to the treasury of her stories, by insisting that they be maintained and transmitted in their narrative form, and by trusting the stories themselves and making them the actual bearer of Jewish faith, Israel continued to reaffirm her Exodus choice of a narrative epistemology over all others. Thus, Israel chose the inexhaustibility of truthfulness over the exactitude of certainty, exploration over arrival, the encouragement of inquiry over its foreclosure, the particular over the general, the detail over the abstract.

Midrash as narrative participates in the notion of truth's inexhaustibility. When applied to the scriptures, the Hebrew word *midrash* describes the activity of searching, seeking out, inquiring about the sacred texts.[45] Without any specific object being designated as their final end or purpose, therefore, these activities are, in themselves, ongoing, ceaseless without any limit or term. It is implied that there is always *more* truth to be found, searched for, sought out, inquired about.

---

44. Arthur Waskow, "God's Body, the Midrashic Process, and the Embodiment of Torah," in *Body and Bible: Interpreting and Experiencing Biblical Narratives,* ed. Bjorn Krondorfer (Philadelphia: Trinity Press International, 1992), 134.

45. Handelman, *Slayers,* 302; Rossoff, "Midrashic Process," 14.

Halakhah and Aggadah: Both/And Not Either/Or

While the Oral Torah "encompasses all of rabbinic teaching,"[46] it is usually subdivided into two major groupings:
halakhah and aggadah. "Often, when a section of the Torah
is legalistic, it attracted legal commentary, or *halachic*
midrash. Where the material is moral-didactic or narrative,
the commentary is a looser social-ethical type of midrash
called *aggadic. Aggada* simply means storytelling, and one
medieval rabbi defined Aggada as everything that is not
Halacha (law)."[47] However, it is important not to make the
very typical gentile mistake of reducing these to categorical
opposites or completely separate and distinct literary enter-
prises. "Yet while we can make distinctions between the two
types of midrash, the lines which separate them are sometimes blurry. In Judaism, ethical principles and moral lessons do not exist apart from ordinary, everyday living.
Jewish ethics and beliefs (*haggada*) are *made real* through
living the Jewish way of life (*halacha*). *Halacha* and *haggada*
are intertwined and interdependent – just as our dreams are
shaped by what we do and what we do is shaped by what we
dream."[48]

These two forms of midrash, halakhah and aggadah,
"grew side by side"[49] and "in intimate coexistence."[50] As
Joseph Heinemann puts it, "Indeed, a talmudic discussion
often inadvertently slips from rigorously analytical argu-
mentation on some halakhic point into the lighter and more
emotionally appealing aggadic mode of discourse. By the
same token, Halakhah is not absent even from the most
strictly aggadic midrashim."[51]

The relationship between halakhah and aggadah is
"reciprocal," with each nourishing and nurturing the other.
Though as different as bread and wine, the two forms of
midrash complemented one another: "Halakhah is charac-

---

46. Stern, "Midrash," 614.
47. Visotzky, *Reading,* 16-17.
48. Rossoff, "Midrashic Process," 16. Emphasis in original.
49. Cohen, "Talmudic Age," 182.
50. Joseph Heinemann, "The Nature of the Aggadah," in *Midrash
    and Literature,* ed., Geoffrey Hartman and Sanford Budick
    (New Haven: Yale University Press, 1986), 50.
51. Ibid.

terized as man's chief nourishment without which existence is impossible; but, like wine, Aggadah wears a smile. . . . Man does not live by bread alone; wine has something that bread lacks – there is no joy without wine and one does not sing songs except over wine." Just as stories of individual cases and specific instances offer judges a tradition of precedents to help them discern how a law is to be understood and applied differently according to the different circumstances, needs, and contexts of different people, so the stories of aggadah served halakhah, tempering the law's tendency to see blindly at times, that is, abstractly, without focal distinction or discriminating vision. In the same way, halakhah gave "aggadah a kind of permanency by evolving from it legal norms, that is, permanent patterns and life forms."[52] Abraham Heschel writes, "Halacha gives us the norms for action; agada, the vision of the ends of living. Halacha prescribes, agada suggests; halacha decrees, agada inspires; halacha is definite; agada is allusive. . . . Halacha, by necessity, treats with the laws in the abstract, regardless of the totality of the person. It is agada that keeps on reminding that the purpose of performance is to transform the performer, that the purpose of observance is to train us in achieving spiritual ends."[53]

Wisdom as Interplay of Story and Law. It should come as no surprise that from time to time even among the rabbis that law was considered more important than story. "As a general rule, the Halakha came first and the Aggada came afterwards to validate or rationalize it."[54] Judah Goldin says that some rabbis felt the need to "apologize" for their use of aggadah, while others insisted that "haggadic statements are not to be employed as authoritative teaching." Some rabbis were so embarrassed by "aggadic literalism" that they tended to reject the use of aggadah in interpretation: "You base nothing on and bring no proof from any aggadic statements and you don't raise questions because of them." Some scholars "who apparently feel superior to haggadah or feel that haggadah is superfluous" chose to study the law exclusively. But such scholars were considered "intellectual

---

52. Ibid., 51-52.
53. Abraham Heschel, *God in Search of Man: A Philosophy of Religion* (New York: Noonday Press, 1992), 337.
54. Cohen, "Talmudic Age," 201.

snobs" and compared to "the angels who tried to prevent the giving of the Torah to Israel." They are warned: "If you wish to cleave to His ways, study aggadah." Both the problem and the solution to this tension between halakhah and aggadah seems best stated by Rabbi Isaac's retort when confronted by two students arguing over their respective merits: "You know what this is like? To a man who had two wives, one young and one old. The young one keeps pulling out his white hairs and the old one keeps pulling out his black hairs. As a result he ends up completely bald!"[55] Both the restraint of halakhah and the freedom of aggadah are needed for the full revelation of God's truth in Torah: "what leads one to a proper knowledge of God and to attachment to his ways is to be found not in pursuit of halakhic studies (alone?) but in reflection on the acts of God as described in many places of the *aggadah*."[56]

Only those unfamiliar with the dynamic, creative relationship of mutual tension between halakhah and aggadah or ignorant of the long tradition of midrashic thought and story could characterize Jewish observance of the law as motivated by anything so simplistic as repressive obedience and fear.

The Scandal of a Storying God. Let us examine one midrashic story. I have chosen this one in particular because it is the one most often cited in the literature and because it serves as "synecdoche for the question of the Oral Torah as a whole."[57] I would like to call the reader's attention to some of the details that comprise the context of this story.

Ochnai is an enterprising stovemaker in late first century C.E. who believes he has built a better oven. It is made of alternating layers of clay and sand to satisfy the rules of purity for stoves, since stoves made only of clay could easily become defiled and have to be destroyed: "Bad news for the householders of Palestine; good news for the clay lobby." Ochnai realizes his invention may help him "corner the

---

55. Judah Goldin, "The Freedom and Restraint of Haggadah," in *Midrash and Literature,* ed. Geoffrey Hartman and Sanford Budick (New Haven: Yale University Press, 1986), 60-68.
56. Goldin, "Midrash and Aggadah," 114.
57. Daniel Boyarin, *Intertextuality and the Reading of Midrash* (Bloomington, IN: Indiana University Press, 1990), 34.

market on ovens in the Jewish community of Palestine," so he has enlisted the help of Rabbi Eliezer ben Hyrcanus, "known to his colleagues as Rabbi Eliezer the Great." The clay workers' lobby has apparently prevailed on the other rabbis who seem to be winning the day.[58]

The story continues:

. . . On that day Rabbi Eliezer brought all the proofs in the world, and the masters would not accept them.
He said to them: If the law is according to me, let this locust tree prove it.
The locust tree moved a hundred cubits. (And some say: four hundred cubits.)
They said to him: The locust tree cannot prove anything.
Then he said to them: If the law is according to me, let this stream of water prove it.
The stream of water turned and flowed backward.
They said to him: The stream cannot prove anything.
Then he said to them: If the law is according to me, let the walls of the House of Study prove it.
The walls of the House of Study began to topple.
Rabbi Joshua reprimanded them:
If scholars are disputing with one another about the law, what business is it of yours?
They did not fall down out of respect for Rabbi Joshua, and did not straighten up out of respect for Rabbi Eliezer, and they are still inclined.
Then he said to them: If the law is according to me, let the heaven prove it.

A voice came forth from heaven and said:
Why do you dispute with Rabbi Eliezer?
The law is according to him in every case.
Rabbi Joshua rose to his feet and said:
    "It is not in heaven" (Deut. 30:12).
    What is the meaning of: "It is not in heaven"?
Rabbi Jeremiah said:

The Torah has already been given once and for all from Mount Sinai; we do not listen to voices from heaven.

---

58. Visotzky, *Reading,* 52.

For You have already written in the Torah on Mount
Sinai: "After the majority must one incline" (Exod.
23:2).[59]

Visotzky highlights both the shock and affectionate
humor of this story: "Rabbi Yermiah is far more chutzpahdik
than he seems, reading *Robert's Rules of Order* to God. He
rubs God's nose in it, as it were, by quoting from the Bible
that the rabbis follow majority rule and so Rabbi Eliezer is
outvoted, never mind what God's opinion on the matter may
be." David Wolpe puts it more bluntly: "God is unceremoni-
ously told to butt out of a legal discussion the Rabbis are
conducting!"[60]

The story is utterly serious and silly, dangerous and
shocking, hysterically funny and outrageous, bordering on
blasphemy, sedition, and sacrilege. The story begins with the
simplest and most mundane details of everyday life – prior
to self-cleaning ovens – and ends in the courts of heaven. But
perhaps what is even more startling, especially to non-Jewish ears, is the ending of the story:

Rabbi Nathan came upon Elijah.
He said to him: What was the Holy One, blessed be
he, doing at that moment?
Elijah said to him:
He was smiling and saying: My children have de-
feated me, my children have defeated me![61]

YHWH and Israel Wrestling in Story. What has happened to
YHWH, the mountain God of Sinai, the God of power and
might, the God of cloud, fire, lightning, and thunder, the God
of Exodus who struck down Egypt with plagues and pesti-
lence and drowned Pharaoh and his armies in the sea and
threatened terrible punishment to all who did not observe
his commandments and worship him in fear and trembling?
How could this same God permit these rabbis to defy him so
openly, to disobey him, to contradict what He himself pro-
nounces to be the true, right, correct interpretation of the

---

59. Nahum N. Glatzer, ed., *Hammer on the Rock: A Short Midrash
    Reader* (New York: Schocken Books, 1962), 96-97.
60. Visotzky, *Reading,* 54; David Wolpe, *The Healer of Shattered
    Hearts: A Jewish View of God* (New York: Henry Holt and Co.,
    1990), 63.
61. Glatzer, *Hammer on the Rock,* 96-97.

Torah? Why does God not strike these rabbis dead on the spot for their scandalous contempt and impertinence? Should not their immediate annihilation serve as warning to anyone else who may be contemplating treating God so disrespectfully? But, most of all, how is it possible for this God to smile at such abusive behavior by his children? Is this God a wimp? A masochist? An overindulgent parent who by tolerating such defiance among his children has contributed to their damnation? Isn't this God just encouraging further acts of rebellion against his authority and power by his lack of swift reprisal?

As we have seen throughout this study, story communicates multiple meanings simultaneously: some in what the story says, some in what it does not say, and some in what it could say but hasn't, at least, not yet. Sometimes the different meanings seem to complement each other, sometimes to contradict. This midrash story is a wonderful example of the narrative epistemology we have been talking about as all its various meanings strain and contend with one another for preference, closure, and resolution. But it is precisely such simplistic epistemologies that story resists. By encouraging this *agon,* this contest of meaning, story strains against all notions of truth as singular or simple and compels storylisteners to become actively engaged in the ongoing process of narrative knowing. It forces them to imagine what else this story could mean or imply within the given circumstances and lives of all its audiences – from the very first listeners of the story to themselves, the present hearers. By doing this, the story leads its participants into a domain of open knowledge and alternate possibilities, where the canons of science, reason, logic, and deduction ultimately fail.

YHWH's Respect for Israel. Let us look at just some of the possible meanings of this midrash story, especially what is *not* said, mindful of the adage that what is not said is often the loudest thing heard.[62]

I would like first to suggest that there is an implicit association with the story of Exodus here, although it is never mentioned. That is because the midrash story deals not only with the relationship between God and Israel but

---

62. Watzlawick, *Language of Change,* 86.

also with the very nature and identity of this God. How can the God of the midrash be the same as the God of Exodus?

Story does not refute; by juxtaposing alternatives, story enlarges and complicates what was previously simple. The story of the rabbis above does not refute any of the stories of the Lord in Exodus. It does not diminish in any way God's power, might, or awesomeness. In fact, by assuming all that, it cleverly plays off the discrepancy between that God and the other face of God it is daring to reveal. In fact, by juxtaposing a portrait of this other, very different kind of (smiling!) God with the terrifying God of Exodus, the rabbinic story sets in motion a process in which the dichotomy and contradistinctions between these different images must now be entertained simultaneously. The dynamic relationship that results from this unresolvable tension yields not only new intellectual knowledge about this God but a different kind of relational knowledge that only story and narrative can generate.

In a sense, this story is a comic version of Exodus, a counter-Exodus, or, if you will, an "exodusspiel." The God of power and might does not lead any eager band of obedient and awed rabbis through the vast unexplored tracks of the Torah into the promised land of sure truth, certitude, and knowledge. Instead, this motley, bickering band of sages bluntly tells the Holy One, blessed be He, that his contributions are not appreciated, and would he mind falling in line behind them as *they* lead the way into the Law, thank you very much.

To our amazement, this God seems to enjoy the forwardness and freedom of his rabbis, not to mention their clever, if somewhat tortured, exegesis of scripture. Visotzky comments, "How ironic that at the very moment when the Rabbis assert their right to interpret Scripture, Authorial intent be damned, they justify it by simply breaking a verse of the Bible into pieces."[63]

How un-Pharaohlike this God! As we saw in Chapter Five, the job of kings and gods and all those with power is to enforce present arrangements that favor them, preserve

---

63. Visotzky, *Reading,* 54.

their interests intact, and make even the consideration of any other possibilities wholly unimaginable.[64]

To insure this, only certain forms of discourse can be permitted and others must be outlawed entirely and banned. No familiarity can be tolerated. No jokes, play, humor, ambiguity, or imagination of any kind can be permitted. Brueggemann, in commenting on the darker aspects of David's kingship, notes how court rhetoric, if it is to serve state power and policy rather than truth, must be stripped of all playful language and flattened into monotone and monosyllable.

> It is then no wonder that free, impressionistic narrative has been superseded by a tight line of imperial reasoning that does not find it amusing when people criticize or think in alternative modes. . . . then there is no room for ambiguity or playfulness or exploration. And indeed the rhetoric wishes precisely to eliminate all such room, for the banishment of playful room makes things secure. State truth tends not to be marked by a sense of humor. . . . The language must be as one-dimensional as the purpose.

Such flattened language may secure deference and compliance for a time, but, in the long run, it fails to win trust, loyalty, or devotion among the people. As Thomas Gordon puts it, "It is a paradox: Use power, lose influence. Several factors operate in concert to cause this. First, power creates the very responses that eventually will weaken it, among which are resistance, rebellion, retaliation, avoidance, withdrawal, deception, organizing alliances to balance the controller's power, law breaking, and so on."[65]

---

64. Brueggemann, *Creative Word,* 57-58.
65. Walter Brueggemann, *David's Truth in Israel's Imagination and Memory* (Philadelphia: Fortress Press, 1985), 79; Thomas Gordon, *Teaching Children Self-Discipline* (New York: Times Books, 1989), 94.

Paradoxes of Power:
God as Storying Friend of the World

In Exodus, YHWH had manifested himself as the One more powerful than Pharaoh, and, therefore, deserving of Israel's obedience. His superior strength and overwhelming force in destroying Pharaoh and his armies were perhaps the most compelling reasons for the Israelites to put themselves under his protection and commit themselves to him as their God. Thus, the whole issue of comparative power was an important one in Exodus. YHWH had to compete with the power of Pharaoh and prove more powerful or else he would have been dismissed as ineffectual, a false God who misled the people, who could not stand up to the might of Pharaoh or save them from the powers of the world that oppressed them.

But the God of the midrash story above appears to be an embarrassment. Where is his power? His displays of divine anger and wrath against those who would defy him? This God is the butt of their jokes, a buffoonish fool who is not only outwitted and outsmarted by these insolent and arrogant rabbis but who even seems to enjoy their chutz-pah.[66]

One of the subtexts of this midrash story is, I believe, precisely how God is *not* like Pharaoh, how this God seeks a different relationship with Israel, one that is *not* based on repressive obedience, fear, or language too terrified to tease. Michael Goldberg writes, "Indeed, were she now [at Sinai] to find herself in the position of being forced or pressed into [the Lord's] service, what would the exodus have in the end accomplished? The Israelites would have merely gone from serving one Pharaoh back in Egypt to serving another Pharaoh in the wilderness . . . . For the narrative to make sense, the Lord must be a significantly different kind of king, a

---

66. Mordechai Rotenberg, *Re-Biographing and Deviance: Psychotherapeutic Narrativism and the Midrash* (New York: Praeger, 1987), 137. "The Talmudic term *Chutzpah* refers originally to man's dialogical corrective obligation and optimistic ability to argue with and influence Heaven's decrees."

significantly different kind of *character,* than the king of Egypt."[67]

Wolpe comes closest to capturing the scandalous intimacy that the God of the midrash seeks with Israel: "God is, in Rabbinic parlance, 'the friend of the world.'" He continues, "No more audacious example could be adduced to show how confident the Rabbis were in their sense of integrity before God, and in their almost collegial relation with Him."[68] This familiarity is not bred of contempt but of a comfortable presumption of friendship which, to someone outside this relationship, might seem shockingly disrespectful. But not to God himself who seems to enjoy this mystical foreplay and teasing impudence most of all. The irony, of course, is that this God communicates even more power by his serene self-assurance, easy forbearance, and calm composure than any irritable, overanxious, oversensitive king or god ever could. This God takes utter delight in being the willing playmate, jesting partner, and roughhouse companion of his people. Such knowledge is shocking and wonderful. And only story could be the angel-messenger of such scandalously unsettling good news.

Story as Divine Love: God's Self-Limitation

There is an important, if subtle, relationship in the story among power, relationship, and knowledge. God's power is very different from that of Pharaoh. For God, it is not a zero sum game in which one participant must lose all power for another to have any power. As a result, God does not have to cling to his power the way Pharaoh did. By giving away power to others, this odd God of Israel creates more power for all, including himself. Power with this God is not like bread, a scarce commodity that must be fought over before it is entirely consumed and disappears forever. Power with this God is a renewable resource, like love, which only increases the more it is given away.

---

67. Michael Goldberg, *Jews and Christians, Getting Our Stories Straight: The Exodus and the Passion-Resurrection* (Philadelphia: Trinity Press International, 1991), 122. Emphasis in original.
68. Wolpe, *Healer,* 62, 63.

Thus, by this God's willing limitation of his own absolute power and his sharing of it with Israel, he creates a relationship of intimacy, mutual interdependency, and affection that leads to new kinds of knowledge and truth. Rotenberg refers to this in his comments on the midrash story above. He sees this as an example of "God's volitionary, space-evacuating contraction that urges man to use his '*chutzpah* power,' which is effective even in relation to Heaven." He sees God's laughter over the rabbis' "defeating" him as "not only His permission for man to use *Chutzpah* in interpreting His divine law but also as a sign that this was the wish inherent in God's self-contracting space evacuation for human volitionary actions, in the first place."[69]

Rotenberg is referring to the paradoxical but root idea in Jewish mysticism of *tzimtzum*. The word itself, meaning "concentration" or "contraction," applies crude but characteristically vivid spatial concepts to the act of God's creating. For God to be able to create "out of nothing," there had to be some part of the universe which was not already suffused with God's glorious presence, that had to be a space of literally no-thing, but that would be impossible since God has been "all in all" always and everywhere. So, with that wonderful blend of folk wit, naive literalism, and unbounded invention that characterizes the rabbinic imagination, the idea came about that God "concentrated" or "contracted" his glory to create an empty space in which the universe could come into being: "the first act of all is not an act of revelation but one of limitation," – "not a step outside but a step inside, a movement of recoil, of falling back on oneself, of withdrawing into oneself." In every minute of creation, therefore, there is "a double strain," a "perpetual tension" occurring within God, an "ever repeated effort with which God holds Himself back" at the same time that he is actively filling and sustaining all that exists with his glory and presence.[70]

I suggest that the idea, later articulated as the mystical notion of *tzimtzum*, is already implicit in the scriptures as early as the flood accounts. God's promise never to destroy humankind again is an important revelation in the nature,

---

69. Rotenberg, *Re-biographing*, 7.
70. Gershom Scholem, *Major Trends in Jewish Mysticism* (New York: Schocken Books, 1961), 260-65.

character, and identity of this God. A God who is willing to limit his absolute whim, impulse, and power; to curb his anger and wrath; to consider the effects of his actions *before* acting, these are all examples of the very different kind of God that Israel comes to know.

Knowledge of God is, therefore, always contextualized by relationship with this self-limiting God, a God who wants his relationship with his people to be characterized by dialogue, partnership, reciprocity, mutual interdependence. Thus, in discussing the nature of God in his two famous essays, "The Divine Pathos" and "God in Need of Man," Heschel constantly keeps calling our attention back to the fact that for Israel knowledge of God is never abstract, a matter of theoretical content or ideas, but always an invitation into relationship. "The prophets never ask: '*What* is God?'"[71] Instead the scriptures ask over and over again and in different ways: "Who is God?", "What do we know about this God from how he relates to us?", "Who am I?", "Who is Israel?", and "How are we to interact and respond to this God in what we do?"

This God refuses to play at absolutes, whether that is power or knowledge. This God seems more interested in the conversation than the outcome, the engagement than the truth. Instead of compliance and mind-numbing agreement, this God most wants his creatures to speak their minds, assert themselves, contribute the wisdom of their interpretations and opinions, even disagree with him, just as long as they keep talking with him in real honest dialogue. "The Torah is theirs," God seems to say, "not mine. Let them play with it, have fun with it, find out why it's there for them. Let them enjoy all the secrets and stories I've hidden in it for them." As Rotenberg puts it, "The Torah has been given to humans and . . . it is thus for them to interpret the law as they understand it in the relativistic terms prevailing during their life times, even if they are at times wrong."[72]

To state the obvious, therefore, the modern idea of truth as something absolute and objective in and of itself is "nonsense" to the God of the Torah. For this God, "the law must

---

71. Abraham Heschel, *Between God and Man* (New York: Free Press, 1965), 116-24, 140-45, 116.
72. Rotenberg, *Re-biographing*, 7.

be human, subjective, and relative." Decisions must be made
on the basis of human understanding and interpretation
even if they are wrong. "These Midrashic stories demonstrate . . . that the rules governing legal interpretations were
not fundamentalistically set according to the a prioristic
voice of the written word of Heaven, but left open to the will
of humans . . . ."[73]

Midrash can be seen then as the use of stories to
humanize interpretation of the law. Decisions did not precede from abstract "fundamentalistic authoritative heav-
enly" principles or theories of truth and law. Rather the
context for the rabbis' debate and discussions about the
Torah was always to be the needs of the people and the
circumstances of this particular community. "Whenever the
Halacha is uncertain so far as the court is concerned and you
do not know what is to be done, go out and see how the
community conducts itself and do likewise."[74] It is this that
is God's desire, his wish, and his will. God desires that his
creatures make abundant and prodigal use of the very powers he chose to limit within himself and to share with them
instead, so that they, his people, rude, rancorous, dissenting
children though they may be, could dwell with him in partnership.

Midrash and Story as a Sabbath Art

As stated above, the midrashic activity of searching, seeking,
and inquiring of the text is ceaseless and ongoing. Since
midrash never has any one specific object designated as its
final end or purpose, arrival is not the point; the journeying
is. Thus, whatever is found in the process of midrash is never
a final end point or terminus. In other words, there is never
any one correct answer, which, when found, provides *the*
solution to the question posed by the text; no exact content
which, when discerned, retires the problem from all further
inquiry definitively and finally. There are always more possible constellations of meaning by which to chart new
courses into the truth.

---

73. Ibid., 8.
74. Ibid., 8, 7.

Without an objective end point as its goal, midrash lacks any immediate pragmatic purpose or utilitarian function. Midrash is not technically a necessary activity for Israel nor is it explicitly commanded in any prescribed way *per se* by the Torah or Jewish law. Instead God seems to have created midrash because he thought his people might enjoy it. "The word's power does not consist in its explicit content – if, generally speaking, there is such a thing – but in the diversion that is involved in it."[75] So, on one hand, midrash is superfluous, unnecessary, unproductive. On the other hand, the activity of midrash is as necessary to the survival of Israel as food, sex, love, joy, or prayer.[76]

For Israel, midrash is that sacramental expression of her most fundamental and essential being: a people who bless and praise their God in every possible imaginable way in every possible moment. Midrash effects what it symbolizes. The act of Israel's storying, like the act of praising found in the psalms, is both constitutive and responsive.[77] Her storying, like her praising, constitutes Israel, her identity, mission, and purpose because it is yet another way to respond to the wooing of her God. Midrash is Israel's response to a relationship of such "abiding astonishment" with her God that her playful storying cannot help but enhance, deepen, extend, and expand the dynamics of her relationship with YHWH and further intensify them.

Midrash continues to evoke and actualize the power of Israel's storying imagination, first realized in the Exodus event and celebrated and exercised each Shabbat "where," as Heschel puts it, "the goal is not to have but to be, not to own but to give, not to control but to share, not to subdue but to be in accord."[78] Midrash is like play: "a form of letting

---

75. Chaim N. Bialik, "Revealment and Concealment in Language," quoted in Samuel C. Heilman, *The People of the Book: Drama, Fellowship, and Religion* (Chicago: University of Chicago Press, 1983), 160. No reference to source of Bialik quotation given in notes or bibliography.

76. Some might even say midrash is *more* necessary. Corey Fischer, founding member of A Traveling Jewish Theater based in San Francisco, has created a one-man show entitled "Sometimes We Need a Story More Than Food."

77. Brueggemann, *Israel's Praise*, 4.

78. Abraham Heschel, *The Sabbath: Its Meaning for Modern Man*

go, merging freely into experience, immersing oneself totally in the moment so that there is no distinction between self and object or self and other. Energy, life, spirit, surprise, fusion, awakening, renewal are all qualities of play . . . it is free flowing form, opening, and expanding in unexpected and unpredictable ways."[79] By saying that midrash is like play, I mean to imply that midrash is one of those activities that is diametrically opposed to the technological-imperial mindset of Pharaonic Egypt. Midrash is an act of dangerous defiance and open rebellion against all forms of human objectification, diminishment, dominance, degradation, or control.

That is because midrash is finally one of the Sabbath arts, practiced whenever Israel reclines with her resting, satisfied, rejoicing God. It is in that unguarded moment that Israel engages in her most significant "work": the appreciation of creation, the cherishing of beauty, the joy of union, and the utterance of ineffable cries of blessing for such gifts of grace. This is the "work" that God requires, the knowing to which God invites, the labor that God demands of Israel because it is paradoxically the only way that God can both seduce and shock Israel into remembering their first storying together in Egypt. And through that remembering, Israel realizes once again who she is at heart in the eyes of her Beloved: utterly free, conceived in laughter and love, with an untransferable dignity and beauty. Israel is to engage in this serious "work," the midrashic storying about her stories, with all the ecstatic eroticism of the mystic at contemplation, with all the absorbing seriousness of a child at play. This is definitely not an Israel to succor the modern mind.

Midrash and Postmodern Thought

Recently non-Jewish scholars have begun to study the epistemological implications of Israel's storying in midrash. Brueggemann, in his recent writings, has indicated a grow-

---

(New York: Farrar, Strauss, and Giroux, 1987), 3.

79. C. Moustakas, *Rhythms, Rituals and Relationships* (Detroit, MI: Center for Humanistic Studies, 1981), 20, quoted in Charles Schaefer, *The Therapeutic Powers of Play* (Northvale, NJ: Jason Aronson Inc., 1993), 42.

ing interest and curiosity in the "interface" between midrash and postmodern thought: "Jewish midrash . . . dares to imagine a wild textuality that carries and voices more than we can entertain." Brueggemann's growing interest in midrashic modes of thought and speech is, I believe, related to his reevaluation of his own "modern" schooling, education, and training as a scripture scholar. In some of his most recent work, Brueggemann acknowledges how he has been influenced by such predetermining categories of the modern mind as "Hellenistic modes of rationality," historical criticism, and other "hidden criteria" which "decide[d] beforehand what would be included in a text" and what would be disposed of as "unacceptable to modern consciousness."[80]

What a refreshing alternative Brueggemann offers to the two intellectual historians discussed at the beginning of this chapter. Unlike them, Brueggemann, at least, is one scholar who, instead of repeating the settled caricatures and certitudes from his own tradition, training, and education, seeks rather to expand his understanding by learning from what is "most characteristically Jewish in the text. For Jewish reading honors texts that are disjointed, 'irrational,' contradictory, paradoxical, ironic, and scandalous." Midrash's emphasis on the story in all its undomesticated oddity, specificity, wild poignancy, and "scandalous particularity," "the little story . . . free of systematic perspective, and especially of systematic theology," is what is most shared in common by both midrashic and postmodern approaches to narrative knowing and relating.[81]

Let me close this chapter with an invitation by Brueggemann to his Christian colleagues trained in the academies of modern thought.

> Thus I propose a fresh honoring of the ambiguity, complexity, and affront of the text without too much worry about making it palatable either to religious orthodoxy or to critical rationality. I propose that the church become, in fidelity to its legitimating text, a place of rhetorical disjunction in which the text and its proposed "as" fail to conform to or reinforce the dominant hegemony. . . . This approach, however, requires interpreters of the text to unlearn much that

---

80. Brueggemann, *Texts,* 22, 58.
81. Brueggemann, *Texts,* 58-59.

we have valued, much that has made us respectable in the church and the academy. Moreover, such a practice destines the church, insofar as it takes the text seriously, to give up much of this preoccupation with great metaphysical reality and great moral certitude. After all, if God has been mediated to us through Jewish consciousness and Jewish rhetoric, and if this word is the word of this irrepressibly Jewish God, we might expect enormous epistemological displacement in our characteristically gentile hearing of the text.[82]

82. Ibid., 59.

Chapter Seven

Storying and Midrash in Preaching Today

ART IS OFTEN BORN OF FRUSTRATION AND DESIRE. SO WERE
the stories contained in this chapter. Before looking at these
story-homilies directly, I'd like to share how they emerged
from my own experience as priest and preacher.

Ordained as a deacon in the Roman Catholic Church in
1978, I was trained in seminary to make generous use of
stories in my preaching. But it was always understood that
stories were there only to serve theology, either as quick
"attention grabbers" or as colorful illustrations. Stories existed in sermons, not in or of themselves, but only to entertain and dispose the mind of the listener to a favorable
hearing of the serious (and, therefore, important) theological
discourse. The theological material or main body of the
sermon was to be organized around the progressive development of three points as in a logical argument and presented
in a discursive manner appealing to the intellect and reason
of the listener. Story was only admitted to set the table and
clear the dishes; its place was not at the table of the Word
but in the scullery.

After years of preaching according to my training, I
found my homilies becoming dull and predictable. There just
wasn't that much new to be said theologically. I became
bored and discouraged as did my congregants. The only
difference was that, as good loyal Catholics, they had become
resigned to tedious preaching as a measure of their faith and
devotion. Faced with the painful evidence of my inadequacy
in the glazed eyes of my congregants, I came to dread preaching and so spent even less time preparing. How might I tell
the same theological truth over and over again? How might

I make the same homiletic point year in, year out? I tried to reassure myself that the constancy of form and expression was the whole point of theological truth: it doesn't have to change over time. In fact, it isn't supposed to.

After several years of this, I had occasion to return to the parish where I had first served as a newly ordained priest, when preaching was still a passion and adventure for me every time. During my visit, many parishioners – old and young, conservative and liberal, garrulous and grim – told me how much they had enjoyed my "preaching." This, as it turned out, was not entirely true. What they really meant was how much they had enjoyed the *stories* I had told. It was the stories that had remained with them all this time and affected their lives, *not* the theological content or homiletic points.

I was amazed at how well they remembered the stories. Sometimes they reprised the stories verbatim. Other times the stories were slightly changed in a detail here, an emphasis there. And sometimes they were completely transformed, new creations in their own right. In any case, those parishioners had remembered the stories and the stories had touched and changed their lives in some way. They did me a great service, for they confirmed something I had suspected all along. The story *was* the homily, *was* the preaching. It was the stories that people remembered, the stories that stayed in their hearts. I needed to trust the people and the stories.

So I made a decision to act on that trust in my preaching, to let story convey wholly whatever needed to be said theologically. After all, it had worked for the authors of the scriptures – Hebrew and Christian – all these years. I would tell stories, nothing else. I have never regretted that decision. Nor, do I think, have my congregations. They might be furious or fractious about something they *heard* in the story, whether I *said* it or not. They might object to an ending or an image other than what they expected, to a halo slightly tarnished or atilt on some favorite saint's head, or to a miracle slightly modified. They might be shocked, surprised, even horrified, by something they "saw" in their own mind's eye.

But, at least, now they can let me know. Stories don't intimidate them the way theology did. Where before they slipped out of church, smiling, nodding, but silent, now they stop and converse about the stories – proof, I submit, of story's ability to change both thought and relationships. Now they stop to tell me the story *they* heard or wanted to hear, the story as they would like to tell it to someone else, or the story they thought I *should* have told! They are surprised when I don't bother to refute, correct, or argue my story against theirs, for story doesn't engage in such debates. Instead I find myself listening to their stories and replying, "Wow! Now that's a great story. Did you know you were a storyteller?" This is a response of awe at the storytelling abilities people still possess despite a technology and culture that determinedly represses such narrative creativity. As we depart from church, as storylisteners to one another's storytelling, our stories continue their dialogue in mind and memory, expanding not only the truth of the scriptures we have heard together but also the capacity of our hearts to receive them.

Method in Storying

I continue to conduct my narrative preaching in a spirit of learning, study, and experiment. Much of what has preceded this chapter has been the fruit of scholarly research into stories. What follows is the pastoral harvest of my narrative preaching in cathedrals, large churches, small congregations, cloistered abbeys. What is impossible for these texts to convey, however, is the interplay of oral-aural dynamics that occurred in each telling and listening. The printed word cannot convey the ineffable languages of breath, body, face, eye, or silence nor tell how the language of listening affected and changed the language of telling.

The homilies contained in this chapter were *not* written out, memorized, and then delivered orally. Though this is how most preachers I know are trained, I thought it an important part of this experiment to compose the stories orally and not to write them down as texts prior to their delivery. In effect, I had to learn how to do this as I went along.[1] The stories were audiotaped instead as they were

---

1. The oral-aural language of storying has its own grammar of

delivered during the liturgies and the spoken words then transcribed to their textual forms below.

Christian Midrash?

Following the midrashic methods of the rabbis, I composed the homilies here to be theological in their narrative form and process more than in their explicit content. Scriptural allusions and intertextual relationships – theological, linguistic, and rhetorical – are implied, never stated, thus, inviting the associative participation of the congregation. The storylisteners are engaged as creative hearers and thinkers to speculate and wonder precisely because of what is *not* said. In this way, the homilist is no longer the sole vessel of truth and they merely the receptacles. Instead both speaker and listeners must "theologize" together. Together they become the instigators of knowledge, knowledge that must be shared, that can only be revealed in dialogue, knowledge that is, by its essence, conversational, interactive, dynamic, and communal. This knowledge is neither objective nor an object. As Ivan Illich and Barry Sanders put it, "In the oral beyond, there is no 'content' distinct from the winged word that always rushes by before it has been fully grasped, no 'subject matter' that can be conceived of, entrusted to teachers, and acquired by pupils (hence, no 'education,' 'learning,' and 'school')."[2] Because the story-homilies partake in the openness of a narrative epistemology, they remain "winged," unfixed, generating many possible meanings, interpretations, and alternate stories among both listeners and tellers. They are not mere narrative illustrations of a theological "point."

In the Catholic homiletic tradition, however, many scripture readings have been long identified with certain

---

colloquial sound and rules of "illiteracy" that must be respected. The difficulty comes when this oral-aural language is then committed to print as text. Then a wholly different set of "literate" rules applies. Since the grammar of literacy is the one we have been trained in all our lives, the grammar of sound and speech may *look* shockingly incorrect on the page. I ask the reader to bear this in mind.

2. Ivan Illich and Barry Sanders, *The Alphabetization of the Popular Mind* (San Francisco: North Point Press, 1988), 7.

theological topics: for example, the story of Martha and Mary (Luke 10:38-42) with the tension between contemplation and action; the coin of tribute (Luke 20:19-26) with the relationship of church and state; the raising of Lazarus (John 11:1-45) with the resurrection of the body. Most Catholics who have grown up in this oral-aural tradition, thus, "hear" simultaneously the scripture passage *and* the particular theological "lesson" or homiletic "point" that has customarily been presented as *the* meaning and purpose of that scripture.

After awhile it is no longer possible to hear a scripture story anymore, except as a narrative frame to hang a "moral" message on. The story is eviscerated and stuffed instead with theology; it becomes a skin to cover a carcass. Seeking to return to the mode of theology practiced by the original faith communities in Judaism and Christianity, I sought to reassert in my story-homilies the primacy of narrative. It was necessary, therefore, in composing them to subvert the traditional theological associations and homiletic expectations among most Catholics, so that the freshness of the story could be reopened and attention directed to the flexibility of the narrative form itself.

The Stories

Like the midrashim, the stories here enter "the spaces between the lines" of the texts and create alternate narratives that explore just some of the inexhaustible multiple meanings buried like treasure in the same field of story. "We read the same Book, differently. We seek to hear the same Voice, differently."[3] And we respond to the same story, differently.

In the sections below entitled "Scripture of the Day," I have briefly paraphrased the scripture readings from which these stories grew. The first two story-homilies demonstrate how the exact same set of readings for the same feast day in the Roman Catholic liturgical calendar can create two entirely different "possible worlds," each with their own truth.

---

3. Visotzky, *Reading,* 69, 13.

FAMILIES ARE THE HARDEST THING

Liturgical Occasion: Second Sunday of Advent
A Cycle
First Reading: Isaiah 11:1-10
Second Reading: Romans 15:4-9
Gospel: Matthew 3:1-12

Background

April may be the cruelest month if we are to believe the poet T. S. Eliot. But, from my experience as priest, confessor, and counselor, I would say that the liturgical seasons of Advent and Christmas are, for Christians, the most conflicted. The very real biological, psychological, and elemental effects of diminishing sunlight, lengthening darkness, and increasing ice, cold, snow, and rain on all animal organisms at this time of year are not so much celebrated as denied. The resulting cognitive dissonance is suppressed and intensified in the subconscious where it lurks menacingly. As family therapists Evan Imber-Black and Janine Roberts observe, the intense social pressure among many families to be unquestionably happy and joyous and to celebrate the holidays in certain prescribed ways can lead to all kinds of tension and anxiety, fights and arguments, as well as feelings of dread and depression, "either because of the predominance of certain religious traditions, or media bombardment about what to buy, eat, how to decorate, or when to get together. Both parents and children are subject to idealized images of what the family should look like and be doing. We have talked to many people who feel like they fall short of these 'perfect' families."[4] The story below, "Families Are the Hardest Thing," of course, makes no explicit reference to contemporary families or holiday celebrations. It doesn't have to. Instead it evokes them in unconscious ways that are particular to each listener and his or her personal circumstances. Though all hear the spoken words of the story, each hears it differently.

---

4. Evan Imber-Black and Janine Roberts, *Rituals for Our Times: Celebrating, Healing, and Changing Our Lives and Our Relationships* (New York: HarperCollins Publishers, 1992), 19.

Scripture of the Day

First Reading: Isaiah 11:1-10. A vision of God's holy mountain in the messianic age when wolf, lamb, and lion will dwell together. The Lord's anointed will judge with such wisdom and understanding that even the Gentiles will seek out this kingdom.

Second Reading: Romans 15:4-9. God is the source of all patience and encouragement, so we should live in perfect harmony with one another and accept each other as Christ accepts us.

Gospel: Matthew 3:1-12. Great crowds from Jerusalem and Judea are going out into the desert to hear John the Baptizer. He is preaching that the reign of God is at hand, a time of upheaval and wrath, of cutting down and burning in unquenchable fire. In fact, someone so powerful is coming to judge the nations that even John isn't worthy enough to touch his sandals. People should repent and change now and be baptized in water rather than wait and be baptized in fire and spirit.

Families Are the Hardest Thing

Families are the hardest thing. That's what Jesus thought as he watched his cousin John there at the Jordan River. Families are the hardest thing. He looked at John with love and pride and yes, also with some sadness. You see they hadn't talked with one another in several years.

Now, they had always been different. But growing up together as kids, it never seemed to matter much. They used to talk about being disciples together, disciples of the Messiah when he came. Together they would call all the people and announce the good news that the Messiah had come.

But as they grew up, they began to have different ideas, believe in different Gods, hope for different heavens, and wait for different Messiahs.

It was at their last meal together, during the Hanukkah festival, when all the family had gathered together, sometime around dessert – when most arguments and family fights tend to break out – when the different ideas of John and Jesus had come to a head.

"No, Jesus, you're wrong, dead wrong. The Messiah will come but only when people are different, when they're changed, when they're finally sinless, and spotless and holy."

"You're so thick and stubborn, John, and just because you're a few months older than I am, you think you know it all. Look, the Messiah will come and love us just as we are – weak and silly, petty and selfish, cruel, kind, corrupt, shameful, yearning to be brave and decent and good, wanting to be more than today and always failing by tomorrow."

"Don't blaspheme, Jesus. You've been studying all that wishy-washy theology stuff again, haven't you? But, you're wrong, Jesus, you're dead wrong. People must change and repent or else the Messiah will come in wrath with axe and fire of eternal flame to purge and punish and purify."

"No, John, it's you who's wrong. The Messiah may come with fire but it will be the fire of love and forgiveness, to warm cold hearts and brighten the darkness inside of people, and to melt the frozen pain of families and nations with his mercy and compassion.

"And I wouldn't be at all surprised if the first thing he'll do when he comes is call sinners to his side, break bread with them, drink wine, sing songs and dance with them and throw a party of celebration and rejoicing that hasn't been seen since Solomon's day!"

John's anger was glowing white hot. He couldn't stand it any longer. He turned and walked into the desert and stayed there for the next five years while Jesus shut himself up in his carpenter's shop, pounding nail after nail into wood. They hadn't talked since.

Families are the hardest thing. But all during that time, they thought of one another and missed each other and wondered how the other was. But they were so different, too different, as different as a lion and a lamb. They would never be disciples together now. Their dream of childhood would have to die unfulfilled. They would go their own way and be alone.

But then Jesus heard that John was at the Jordan. He thought to himself that he would go and hide among the crowd just so he might catch a glimpse of his cousin and hear what his cousin was saying these days.

And as he watched the people go down into the river, as he watched them tell John their sins and open their hearts to him and unburden themselves of their guilt and shame, something opened up inside of Jesus too, something broke open.

And he thought to himself: "How stupid I've been! All these years I've been waiting for John to change, to be different! John will never change!"

And then before he knew it, Jesus was plunging into the water until he was face to face with his cousin. And then he broke the silence that had been a desert between them: "John, I'm sorry. Please forgive me. We're family."

John looked at Jesus. And that stern stoneface cracked and softened just a little. "Jesus, if the Messiah can come to two stubborn cousins like us, then I guess he can come any way God wants him to." And with that, John dunked Jesus under the water of the river and held him there a little longer than usual, the way he had when they were kids together.

When Jesus surfaced, spitting and sputtering "Amen to that," a smile, frown, and hiccup were all playing at once on his face.

And there they stood looking into one another's eyes, the lion and the lamb of God, as different as fire and water, but family nevertheless. And up above a dove was hovering on the air.

Additional Reflections

This story-homily makes explicit the theological differences between the earliest followers of John and Jesus but in narrative form. It frames this disagreement within the story of familial relationship between John and Jesus as borrowed from the Lucan tradition. But this time John and Jesus are two adult family members estranged from one another as the result of their opposing theological views. The shock of the story is the recontextualization of human misunderstanding, anger, hurt, and disagreement within the relationship of two "good," holy and sacred figures personally and intimately associated in the minds of Christians with God the Holy One. But instead of preaching only the "sinfulness" of such conflict, the story offers an imaginative account of going through the conflict to reconciliation, a process that demands awareness of one's own contribution to the conflict, the admission of responsibility, and the request to be forgiven, all personalized in the actions and character of Jesus. Making Jesus such an active participant in this story casts his divinity in terms of his humanity, a humanity that learns and is changed by relationships with men and women, a humanity that is close and approachable and not one beyond all space and time.

JOHN AND JESUS

Liturgical Occasion: Second Sunday Advent – A Cycle
First Reading: Isaiah 11:1-10
Second Reading: Romans 15:4-9
Gospel: Matthew 3:1-12

Background

The following story was presented two years earlier as the homily on the exact same readings as presented above. (Certain nonverbal cues and suggestions about gestural language and tone of voice are included in brackets in the text. They are written as suggestions for the one storyteller who, through body and voice, assumes the different roles of John and Jesus.)

John and Jesus

Now John was continuously being interviewed by people like this day and night. Last week the Eyewitness News Team had come out to interview him there in the Jordan River. Tonight he's supposed to be on *Nightline*. And next week, both Rosie and Oprah want him on their shows. I mean John is "big time" now, a real celebrity. Did you see that headline in *USA TODAY*? "New Wildman Heard Preaching in the Desert; Says Baptism by Water Now But Fire Next Time!" Yep, that was John!

Hundreds of people from Jerusalem have been coming out here to see John and hear him preach: soldiers, rabbis,

Romans, Pharisees, Levites, lawyers, politicians, even some
of those running for election.

Now on this one particular day, hundreds of people had
come out from Jerusalem to hear John preach and among
them, he recognized his country cousin, you know, from
Nazareth, the carpenter's son, called Jesus.

Well, Jesus was so impressed with his cousin John
being so popular, that he came up and asked John: "John,
could you give me some lessons on how to preach like you."

So John told his cousin Jesus: "Look, kid, I think you
ought to know that organized religion is not a pretty thing –
I mean, it can get real ugly and rough at times – what with
all the competition for cable these days.

"But look, I'll give you my secret. Now listen very
carefully, Jesus. What you want to remember every time you
preach is this: sin, guilt, fear, shame, and punishment. Yes,
sir, works every time. You hit those things and the people
will come crawling on their knees begging for God's mercy.

"Now, let's give it a try, okay? Let's see. . . I know. Let's
play a game. I'll start a story and then you finish it. Simple,
right? That ought to be a good way for you to start out
preaching.

"Now, let's see . . . how's this? There's a man who has
two sons and they live out in the farm country. Now the
younger son is a real, rotten s.o.b. and he doesn't want to
stick around any more. He wants to skip town and go off and
see life and have a good ole time for himself. So he goes up
to his father and asks for money and well, sure enough, the
father gives it to him. And the very next day, he gets on the
bus and where do you think he goes? He goes to Tahoe and
Reno and Las Vegas – even flies clear across the country so
he can try his luck at Atlantic City too. Blows all the money.
Thousands and thousands of dollars. Now there's a bad
recession in the country and this kid can't get a job for
himself. Well, he might be a rotten kid, but he's a shrewd
kid, so he says to himself: 'Hmmmm, if I go back to my father
and plead for mercy, I bet he'll give me my ole job back again.
Couldn't hurt.' Well, here's the rotten young son coming up
the road now to see his father and ask for his old job back.
Now the father has been waiting all these years for this very
moment and sees him coming up the road. So he goes to the
tool shed and gets out this long wooden stick that he uses to

beat the mules with and . . . Okay, Jesus, your turn. Just
finish the story."

So Jesus is standing there, thinking for a while, when
finally, he says: "Okay, I've got it. He's got the stick, right,
and he's steaming angry. I mean, the kid blew the family
fortune for God sake's and here he is back again! So the old
man starts to walk to his son and he's furious and he feels
that stick burning in his hand. . . . But then he sees his son
and . . . his mind goes blank and he's, well, just so happy to
see his son alive after all these years that he breaks the stick
in two and throws it away. And then, you're never going to
guess – he starts to run. Can you believe it? He starts to run.
He runs as fast as he can and he doesn't care how silly or
ridiculous he looks – him, a grown man running towards the
very son who cheated and bilked him and the whole family!
And when he gets to his son, he throws his arms around him
and hugs and kisses him and says: 'Thank God, you're alive.
We're going to have the biggest celebration and party this
valley has ever seen.'

"Yeah, that's it. Okay, John, how did I do?"

Now, as you can imagine, John realized that Jesus
hadn't heard a word of advice on preaching that he had given
him.

"Where did you get that drivel? That's the silliest thing
I ever heard. Now what parent would treat a child like that
after the kid had spent all that money and made a fool out
of 'em. That's crazy. You don't think God would be like that,
do you?

"Okay, so you blew that one, but, hey, I'll give you
another chance. Only this time try and remember what I told
you: sin, guilt, fear, shame, and punishment. That's what
you go for! Okay, I'll make this one easier for you.

"Here's a woman who is of real loose virtue and she is
found with a married man in the very act of adultery, I mean,
right in the middle of committing sin, right? You got that?
So the good townspeople drag her to the village square, after
letting the man go because it's obviously not his fault. And
they throw her down in the dirt. Well, you and I both know
that a woman caught in the act of committing that kind of a
sin is deserving of death, so all the people reach down and
pick up stones. Now I'll make this very easy for you, Jesus:
they're starting to wind up, right? with their stones in their

hands. [Mimes winding up for a baseball throw]. You got that? . . . Okay, take it from there. What happens next?"

[Jesus: picks up John's miming gesture and continues it, as if all set to throw a stone.]

"Okay, let me make sure I got this. They're winding up with the stones and she's a sinner, right? And then they look at her and they say: Yep, she's a sinner all right. . . . [Jesus stops his wind-up and his arm comes down to his side very slowly and quietly.] But then I guess we're sinners too. And she's no worse than we are and we're certainly no better than she is. And then they drop the stones [Jesus mimes the dropping of his stone, so that closed fist goes to open hand] and they reach out to her and they pick her up and they brush her off and they say they're sorry.

[Jesus very quietly:] "How was that one, John? Any better?"

[John's face registers disgust at this nonsense.]

"Look, that's two you blew, Jesus! I'm trying to make this real simple for you. I mean, it's your first lesson and everything, but, you have to concentrate. Okay, here let me give you just one more. And if you blow this, maybe God doesn't want you to be a preacher, Jesus. So here it is. And please try to remember what I told you."

[As Jesus:] "Yup, I will: sin, guilt, fear, shame, and punishment."

[John:] "That's right. Okay, here it is. There's a bunch of lepers coming down the road. Now you and I both know that a leper is unclean and has probably sinned to have deserved the leprosy. Now these lepers are covered with awful sores and they reach out their hands to touch you, Jesus. Now let me give you a real simple hint – there are a lot of sticks and stones and rocks lying right by you which you could easily pick up and use, you know? So what do you think you do?"

[Jesus:] "Well, I think I'd be scared. I think I'd turn and start to run away. Yeah, that's what I would do. . . . But then, maybe I'd stop and ask myself what am I afraid of? Why am I running? And then I'd think I'd turn around. And then I'd look at them reaching out to me. . . [Looks long and silently at the faces of the congregations.] Boy, I think I'd see how much pain they're in. And I'd start to feel their pain inside of me. And then I'd realize they probably haven't been held in so long, not touched by anyone. Can you imagine what that would be like? [Jesus enacts the following embrace very slowly, using the liturgical garments to "speak" their language of vesture.] So I think I'd walk up to them and I think I'd reach out and I think I'd want to hold them. Yeah, that's what I would do, I'd hold them, each and everyone. And then I'd thank them."

[Jesus is very quiet, and, though he knows his response is not what John wanted to hear, Jesus has become more confident in himself and fascinated by the stories himself. He doesn't know where they have come from, but he'd like to find out.] "I don't think that's what you wanted to hear either, was it, John?"

[John:] "Well, kid, I'll put it to you this way. You go home to your mother in Nazareth and make sure you give Aunt Mary my love, okay? And tell her that she's very lucky to have a son who's such an excellent carpenter – who, I think, should stay a carpenter! Religion's not for you, kid."

[Jesus is obviously disappointed.] Jesus started to walk away. But a kid in the crowd came up to him and said: "Hey, mister, mister, your sandal strap is untied."

And Jesus looked down at him and [brightening] said: "Hey, you know, you're right. Would you mind helping me fix it?"

Additional Reflections

Unlike "Families Are the Hardest Thing," this story does not focus on family dynamics at holiday time or the problem of reconciling estranged family members. Instead, it proceeded from the (rather loud) public discourse occurring at the time in the popular media around such issues as politics, election campaigns, televangelists, prejudice, the economic recession, unemployment, farm policy, AIDS, and others. Again, these are never stated, only suggested, in the story. As we saw with the story of Ochnai and the politics of baking and the oven lobby in Chapter Six, midrashim addressed very immediate, contemporary, and mundane concerns of the community. They also made use of humor that came from deliberate anachronisms (here as references to famous gambling casinos) or local and regional references.

For example, AIDS is never mentioned in the story, but the parish where this story was preached was just beginning to confront it together as a community at the time of this homily. Parishioners knew friends and loved ones who had died or were dying from that disease; some were very active in various AIDS ministry programs just starting in the area; others worked nearby in an AIDS hospice. Some listeners, hearing about the leper's sores, "saw" Karposi-Sarcoma lesions. Others in the parish had very different opinions about people with AIDS and had voiced fears about close contact or touch with such people, especially during the eucharistic celebration itself, for example, at the kiss of peace and the sharing of the cup. The above story "spoke," apparently loudly, to both groups of people and their differing opinions, precisely by *not* mentioning – directly or explicitly – the whole topic of AIDS at all. Story not only permits such "hearings;" it encourages them.

Another midrashic device employed in the above story is the reference to other scriptures known to the congregation and held in oral-aural memory. These would include the parable of the prodigal son (Luke 15:11-32), the woman taken in adultery (John 8:1-11) and the cure of the leper (Mark 1:40-45). Here they are evoked in very different ways by the storying of both John and Jesus. John sets up the story according to one system of beliefs and presuppositions, the conclusion being implied by the unfolding logic of that system. But, from the imagined personal encounter between the characters in the story and Jesus as storyteller, alternate "possible worlds" are evoked that lead to entirely different conclusions and endings that shock, anger, and antagonize John.

But also embedded within these stories as Jesus now tells them are additional implied reframings of the congregation's own belief system, so that the congregation finds itself identifying at some level with the reactions of John as well as those of Jesus. The storylisteners themselves experience the tensions between both characters and their worldviews. When Jesus says, "But then I guess we're sinners too. And she [the woman caught in adultery] is no worse than we are and we're certainly no better than she is," he himself is offering a shocking alternative possibility to the strong insistence in Christian doctrine that Jesus was always and forever without sin of any kind.

The sinlessness of Jesus is a nonnegotiable in Christian theology. The above story does not at all contradict that dogma but asks the hearers of this word about the Word to consider, however briefly, the imaginative possibility of Jesus identifying himself with sinners. This is something that cannot even be suggested without furious outcries and charges of heresy in any language of discourse except story. Because of its fictive language and frame, the impossible is made possible in story.

JOSEPH'S DREAM: THE NIGHT ICHABOD SPOKE

Liturgical Occasion: Feast of the Holy Family
A Cycle
First Reading: Sirach 3:2-6, 12-14.
Second Reading: Colossians 3:12-21
Gospel: Matthew 2:13-15, 19-23.

Background

The following story grew out of a particular experiment in the interaction between verbal and visual theology, what Jo Milgrom might describe as "handmade midrash." It is included here to demonstrate how, in a narrative epistemology, the creative imagination can be enriched by the dialogue between two different modal languages: word and figure, story and image. The story is an example of how both verbal and visual/nonverbal language "can work together and enrich each other in biblical and religious studies."[5]

For several years, I spent Christmas with a community of contemplative nuns. The arts and imagination played an important part in the spirituality, prayer, and ritual life of the community there. One of the customs that was scrupulously observed every Christmas season was the making of the Christmas crèche. Since it was the core event around which the entire Christmas festival at the monastery was developed and the context of the following story, I will describe it briefly.

First, the scriptures describing the birth of Jesus were read and a period for reflection and prayer provided. (Some years the scriptures were read in juxtaposition to the writings of contemporary authors, poets, playwrights, storytellers, or

---

5. Milgrom, *Handmade Midrash*, ix-xi, 3-12, 17, 3.

mystics. Other years discussions of the meaning and mystery of the incarnation of the Divine Child took place.) Next, a drawing was held in which those present chose at random the figure they would make for the crèche. A time was set, a fire prepared, and music played as each participant fashioned clay into form and figure. A bell was rung, and then, in silence, a solemn placing of the figures took place. Finally, when all the figures, including Herod, had found their places and the year's crèche was completed and assembled, a silent procession of adoration and prayer took place.

It is hard to describe the anticipation and excitement among those who regularly participated in this event. This was because the figure chosen (or, as most in the monastic community would say, the figure that chose you) became one's personal guide and mentor into the Christmas story, rituals, and prayer throughout the festival. In other words, the ancient mystery and story of the birth of Christ was perceived from the perspective of one of the characters in the story. The story remained the same but it was experienced fresh and anew.

One year I made the donkey for the Christmas crèche. I was then asked to preach on the following set of scripture readings on the day after Christmas. This is the story-homily that resulted.

Scripture of the Day

First Reading: Sirach 3:2-6, 12-14. Sirach teaches the importance of honoring one's parents. Sons are especially urged to care for their fathers when they are old, weak, or when their minds fail. Such kindness will not be forgotten and, in fact, will serve as a sin offering.

Second Reading: Colossians 3:12-21. Put on mercy, kindness, humility, meekness, and patience. Bear one another's burdens, for you are members of one body. Wives, be submissive to your husbands; fathers, don't crush your children with your nagging and correcting.

Gospel: Matthew 2:13-15, 19-23. After the wise men leave, an angel appears to Joseph in a dream and urges him to flee with Mary and the child into Egypt, since Herod has sent soldiers to kill the child. After Herod dies, Joseph has an-

other dream in which an angel tells him to return to Israel.
In yet another dream, an angel tells Joseph to settle in
Galilee, not Judea.

Joseph's Dream: The Night Ichabod Spoke

[As Joseph, the husband of Mary:] Just between you and me,
I wish I had never met Mary. Not that she wasn't a wonderful
wife, very loving and caring. No, don't get me wrong. It's just
that after I met her, I never had another full night's sleep.

Every night angels would keep coming and waking me
up with one dream or another. Gabriel was the worst. Sometimes he'd come three or four times in one night.

"Joseph," he'd say, "get up and burp the baby."

"Joseph, get up and close the window; there's a draft on
Jesus."

"Joseph, get up and tuck Jesus in; the covers have come off."

The next morning, I'd wake up – exhausted. And I'd
saddle up my mule, Ichabod, and I'd go off to the forest to
chop wood for the day's work. Now I'd never tell my troubles
to Mary because she had enough to worry about, what with
the baby and all, so instead I'd tell them to Ichabod.

[The congregation hears one half of an imagined conversation:] "Yeah, Ichabod. Last night. Yeah, again. Three
times I had to get up! That's right, our ole friend Gabriel.
You know, Ichabod, I don't mind doing it for the baby, oh no!
I love the baby and would do anything for him. It's only that
every time Gabriel comes he always reminds me: 'Now
Joseph, remember you're just the foster father. God is the
real father.' Well, you know what, Ichabod, that hurts. Sometimes I come so close to saying, 'Oh yeah? Well, if he's such
a great father, why doesn't he come down and do some of the
dirty work himself!' But I never do."

Now on that last night when we were in Bethlehem, when
Gabriel came and told us to flee into Egypt, I had had it.

"Look, Gabe, you've got it all wrong. You see, the three
wise men were just here and they said Herod is delighted
that we're here in his territory. In fact, he plans to come out
tomorrow and worship the baby himself! Yeah, I wouldn't be
surprised if he wants me to quit my carpentry business and
move into the palace with Jesus and Mary. Or maybe he

wants to build us our own palace! I could help with the design and the blueprints and the building. What's that?"

Suddenly, in the dream, I saw soldiers beginning to arm, saddling their horses and sharpening their swords. And Gabriel was yelling: "Joseph, it's a trap! Flee, run for your life, for the baby!"

And I just stared, dumbfounded . . . and angry . . . at God. How can this be? What kind of a father would let this happen to his own son! He's just a baby!

I woke up Mary very gently. I didn't want to upset her too much. She took Jesus in her arms and I put her and the baby on top of Ichabod. Ichabod was extraordinary. It was as if he knew what was going on. I didn't have to kick him or push him or drag him at all. He flew! I had to run to keep up with him. And as we fled, so many feelings came up inside of me. Of course, I could only tell them to Ichabod.

"Ichabod, I don't understand God. Here he created the world in seven days, parted the Red Sea for us, makes kings travel from the east just to see Jesus, and sets the stars to singing and angels to dancing. Well, he's certainly good on the luxuries and the pyrotechnics, but I'll tell you this: I could do with a lot fewer angels and kings and some more practical necessities, thank you very much. Like a week ago, when I was knocking on all those doors in Bethlehem and they kept slamming in my face and no one would take us in. You'd think he'd be able to come up with some clean, dry, warm space for Mary to deliver their baby, but no! All we get is a drafty, cold stable with a lot of stinking animals. Oh! No offense, Ichabod.

"Or what about tonight? You'd think he could create a sandstorm to hide us or give us a head start or one of the magi's camels or a fine Arabian pony, but no, here I am, in the middle of the pitch-black night, I can't see where I'm going, with, of all things, a mule who, if you don't mind my saying so, is slightly over the hill. Now don't get huffy. I didn't mean any offense. Yes, you're doing quite well for yourself tonight. In fact, I'm very proud of you tonight, but let's face it, you're not the fastest creature in this night, are you?

"And where does he have me fleeing to? Egypt. Egypt! Where they're still pretty sore about Moses and the ten plagues! I doubt if we're going to be all that popular down there. I tell you, some father God is!"

We went as far as we could that night before all three of us needed to sleep. You'd think that, given these special circumstances, I'd at least be allowed to get a good forty winks – undisturbed. But no. I had another dream. Only this time it wasn't Gabriel who appeared. It was Ichabod and he was talking to me. And he was shaking his head and saying:

"Humans! Go figure. Who can understand them? They can be saints and poets, artists and architects. They can build beautiful cities and bridges, palaces and pyramids. But who does all the dirty work? We mules, that's who! We cart the bricks and the stones and the lumber back and forth and we never complain. Carry all their commerce and produce from one end of the empire to the other. We carry their young men as soldiers into war and cart their weapons behind them. And then we bring back their broken bodies to their waiting mothers. And all they ever do is kick us and beat us and call us stupid and stubborn and silly.

"Joseph, I just want you to know that I'm proud to be known as Ichabod, Joseph's ass. I'm proud to bear your burdens and to carry what you cannot, to do whatever you are unable to do. And you know what, Joseph? God asks you to be his ass, to bear the very burdens he cannot, to carry in your arms what God cannot, to do what he is unable to do, to be the father to Jesus that God can never be. And you know what, when you're up at three a. m. walking Jesus in your arms, God is so jealous of you. Oh, what he'd give just to be able to do that, but he can't. Don't kid yourself, Joseph; you're more father to Jesus than God ever could be and he knows it. He needs you. . . to be all the father he wants to be.

"And you know what, if you'll be God's ass, then he makes this promise to you. He'll be the ass of all humankind and carry on his broad back every man, every woman, and every child and all the burdens they carry with them, all the burdens they can't put down or let go, the very things they can't share with anyone else, especially the burdens they are most ashamed of. He'll carry all of that on his own shoulders until everyone is brought safely home out of the desert and out of the night. Not a bad family of asses, we three, you, me, and God. Asses all."

And then in my dream, the next thing I saw was Gabriel putting a wreath of flowers around Ichabod's great big ear and forehead. And then Gabriel came forward, but very shyly, almost shamefaced, and he said: "Joseph, I'm sorry. I want to apologize. I promise to never call you a foster father ever again. You're the best father Jesus could ever have."

And then he turned as if to go. But over his shoulder, he turned and said: "Oh. And Joseph? I hate to bother you but you better get up. Jesus needs his diaper changed."

Additional Reflections

Stories of talking animals abound in ancient and medieval legends, folktales, and fables; many have long been associated with Christmas.[6] Ichabod admittedly comes out of those rich narrative traditions, but his closest relative in story would be Balaam's ass (Numbers 22:22-35). Both number angels among their social acquaintances; both are gifted with speech and drafted into evangelical service by none other than God the Holy One. Both serve with quiet devotion, fierce loyalty, and long-suffering humility. The intimate alliance of ass and Holy One in the story in Numbers is shocking and moving. I sought to evoke something similar here in the implied association of Ichabod, Joseph, and God, "asses all," bearing one another's burdens – and those of humankind – in love and relationship.

WHEN JESUS BOWED DOWN BEFORE SATAN

Liturgical Occasion: First Sunday of Lent – A Cycle
First Reading: Genesis 2:7-9; 3:1-7
Second Reading: Romans 5:12-19
Gospel: Matthew 4:1-11

Background

Lent is a season of penance, renewal, and purification in which Christians prepare themselves to celebrate the festival of Easter. It is associated with the forty days and nights that Jesus spent in the desert immediately following his baptism by John. As the gospel relates, it was believed that

---

6. Richard Horsley, *The Liberation of Christmas: The Infancy Narratives in Social Context* (New York: Continuum, 1989), 12.

Jesus was severely tempted by Satan during this period but never fell from grace. By juxtaposing the Genesis story, the excerpt from Romans, and the gospel passage on the very first Sunday in Lent, the church emphasizes how weak and sinful men and women are. When they are tempted, they cannot resist but fail and fall into sin. But when Christ was tempted, he did not yield to temptation, fall, or bow down to Satan. This is one of the things that makes Jesus divine in the Christian faith, his utter sinlessness. The Catholic homiletic tradition often associates this set of readings with that theological message: the sinlessness of Christ, the sinfulness of humanity.

In reading these scriptures, I found myself asking one of those questions that cannot be asked in any language but story. Could I still love Jesus even if he did "sin" or "bow down" before Satan? The immediacy of the answer in my imagination surprised me: "Of course! Maybe even more so." The following story came from that response.

Scripture of the Day

First Reading: Genesis 2:7-9; 3:1-7. Genesis 2:7-9 emphasizes God's creation of the man (that is, the male) in the garden of Eden. (This selection of verses anticipates the "one man" theme in the Romans 5 reading described below.) Genesis 3 describes how the serpent succeeds in tempting the woman and the man to eat the fruit that God has forbidden them.

Second Reading: Romans 5:12-19. Through one man (namely, the man in Genesis 2 above), sin and death entered the world. All of us descended from that man suffer death because all have sinned too. But through one man, Jesus Christ, grace has entered the world and brought life and the acquittal of our sins. Through one man's disobedience all became sinners; through one man's obedience all shall become just.

Gospel: Matthew 4:1-11. After forty days and nights of fasting in the desert, Jesus, weak and hungry, is tempted three times by the devil: first, to turn stones into bread; then, to jump from a great height; and, finally, to bow down in homage to Satan. Jesus defies him: "Away with you, Satan! Only God is to be worshipped."

When Jesus Bowed Down Before Satan

And as the angels comforted Jesus, he kept feeling that he had just missed an important opportunity. But he couldn't quite put his finger on what it was. He asked himself if he had done the right thing. It seemed so. Was there something else that he should have done? Something that he had forgotten to do?

Should he have turned stones into bread? No! He had come – not to turn stones into bread – but to turn people into bread that they might feed one another with their lives and hopes and strength.

Should he have jumped off the roof of the temple? For what? So that the people could look up and see the Messiah doing loop-de-loops in the sky? While a squadron of Blue Angels came swooping down from the heavens in fighter formation to save Jesus at the last moment?[7] Naaah. He had come to reveal that the Messiah was not in the sky. But upon the earth. The good and holy earth. Among the people. Especially those who had fallen and stumbled and among those who comforted the fallen and cared for them and helped to lift them up.

Should he have bowed down before Satan so he could have all the power of the world? For what? He had come to reveal that the people filled with the Spirit were the power of the world. With such power that could cause stone walls dividing nations and people to crumble into dust. Power that could take iron curtains of tyranny and oppression and tear them asunder.[8] Power that could fling wide open prison doors

---

7. This is an example of how local and contemporary allusions can be woven into story to create humor, immediacy, and intentional anachronisms. The angels in the scriptures have been transformed by rhetorical strategy into "a squadron of Blue Angels," an obvious reference to the air show performed the day before by U.S. Navy fighter jets over San Francisco Bay.

8. The references to "stone walls" and "iron curtains" allude to the fall of the Berlin Wall and collapse of Communism in Eastern Europe which had occurred just five months before

220 Ways of Knowing and the Scriptures

and let old men walk into the light of day and take a long walk to freedom to become the princes and leaders of the people.[9]

No. He couldn't think of what he would have done differently. And yet there was something, something that kept haunting him. Something, some missed important opportunity.

Well, days turned into weeks and weeks into months and months into years. And then one day, it came to him, came to him what he had failed to do. What he must yet do.

He awoke in the morning, a Sunday morning, eager to do what he had forgotten to do. But what were these strange, bloody swaddling clothes he was wrapped in. And what was this narrow stone manger he lay in? And this dark cave? Surely this was not Bethlehem and yet some new strange mysterious birth was happening to him. He untied himself from the bloody, binding clothes and went free. But at the mouth of the cave, he found a stone as large and heavy as death keeping him from the world he loved so much. He laid his bloody palm upon it and it seemed to fill with the light and air and yeast of hope until it was as light as a loaf of bread and rolled away.

No more time to waste. Now he must do what he had set out to do. He ran through the world he loved so much – from Golgotha tomb through Jerusalem to Galilee to Nazareth to Bethlehem through the desert and back to Egypt. Back to the garden, to the apple tree at the edge of the world. And he looked back at the world he loved so much and he loved it as he never had before. But he could not stop now from what he had to do. And so he let go and threw himself off the edge of the world, down, down, down into the deep, dark abysm of space and time. Down and down he fell through the chaos and void that had existed before creation until he landed in the Kingdom of Hell.

He hit the ground running and wherever he went, he kindled a little hope in hopeless hell and cast doubts of despair

---

this homily was delivered.

9. The parish where this homily was preached was ethnically diverse and had been involved in many actions and campaigns on behalf of social justice, both local and global. The release of Nelson Mandela from prison and the ending of apartheid in South Africa, which had just occurred, had been something the whole parish had prayed and worked for.

among the damned. But he kept on running until he saw him. Satan – cowering in fear and fright, wondering what dread revenge this carpenter would take upon him now. Hadn't he just broken that same body upon the gibbet of the cross forty-eight hours before? And yet now here he was – risen from the dead – to wreak some horrible vengeance against him.

But Jesus approached Satan ever so quietly and gently. And he looked deep into those hollow eyes, deep into those cavernous sockets, crammed with lies and deceits and dishonesty, stuffed with greed and lust and the hunger for power, and there in the deepest recesses of Satan, he saw a still small dim flickering tiny spark of light, sputtering in the howling winds of hopelessness and self-hate that raged inside Satan. And in that spark, he could still see what Satan had once been – Lucifer, the mighty archangel, the Beloved of God,[10] the Standard Bearer of Light, who had lit the sun and the moon and the stars with song that first day of creation.

And Jesus knew that as long as there was still even the tiniest spark, all was not lost. There was still hope.

And then he did what had come to do. Jesus made himself like one who had fallen, like one who had stumbled. Jesus the Holy One, Jesus the Mighty One bent down and bowed before Satan. Not in adoration, not in subjugation, but in the total abandonment of love.[11] He kissed Satan's feet and with tears of joy streaming down his face, he washed Satan's feet.[12]

Satan let out a howling scream, for what pain could be deeper than to still be loved by the very one you had tried to hurt and harm and hunt down, still be loved by one who will not give up on you even after you have given up on yourself. Satan could not bear such love and so in his agony, he

---

10. Many narrative traditions – from the Sufis to Milton – hold that Satan had once been God's closest friend, confidant, and favorite archangel, Lucifer, the bearer of light.

11. Here the act of Jesus's bowing down before Satan has been transformed from a sin into a shocking display of the love and forgiveness of God.

12. The language of this image evokes two other stories from the Gospels: that of the repentant woman who, in an extravagant display of sorrow and gratitude, anoints and washes the feet of Jesus with her tears and has her sins forgiven (Luke 7:36-50) and that of Jesus at the Last Supper, washing the feet of the disciples as a slave or wife might (John 13:1-17).

screamed out his pain, turned, and flew off into the darkness and chaos of space.

And as he fled, Jesus called after him: "You can run but you cannot hide."[13]

For Jesus knew that all space, indeed the universe itself, is curved, curved like a stone, curved like a loaf of bread, that doubles back upon itself. And so the further Satan tried to run away, the closer he was coming back to this very same place where Jesus awaited him – with open arms to embrace him, eyes filled with love. Try as hard as he might, Satan could never escape such fierce, forgiving, and faithful love as this.

Neither can you. And neither can I.

Additional Reflections

Instead of beginning the season of Lent with a homily focussing on the traditional topics of human sinfulness, contrition, and self-purification through acts of penance, mortification, and denial, I chose rather a different theological approach, one that did not emphasize human effort as much as the scandal and gratuity of God's mercy, love, and forgiveness. By alluding to the story of Easter on the first Sunday of Lent, I evoked the single festal unity of both seasons celebrating God's hastening to greet us with grace.

The event referred to in the story is traditionally known as the Harrowing of Hell: when Christ entered into the underworld on that first Easter morning and freed all the souls waiting there for deliverance. An icon favored in Byzantine Christianity depicts this event with the Risen Christ tenderly leading our parents Adam and Eve by the hand out of the kingdom of death and hell.[14] The mention of "garden"

---

13. This line of movie dialogue, used to convey toughness, here is placed in the mouth of Jesus. Only this time, it is a declaration of the tough relentlessness of God's love, mercy, and forgiveness.

14. In a private communication to the author, Professor Jo Milgrom has pointed out how the traditional Christian interpretation of Genesis 3 continues, however subtly, the history of supersessionism. It does this by reducing the richness of this passage to such exclusive, narrowly specific Christian theological terms as fall, sin, atonement, and redemption. In her discussion of the cosmic clock in Marc Chagall's painting *Homage*

and "apple tree" in the story refer to this iconographic tradition as well as to the Genesis story in the first reading.

By using the same language as the gospel passage ("stones"/"bread," "jump"/"fall"/"throw self off," and "bow down"), the story-homily acts as midrashic companion to the story of the temptation of Christ in the desert. In the allusive rhetoric of the story-homily, Jesus "yields" to temptation and performs the very actions that would have been sinful in the gospel: Jesus turns a stone into "bread," jumps from a great height, and even bows down to Satan. A paradox: the same actions but now with entirely different meanings, no longer sins but acts of grace, not a capitulation but a glorious victory, one in which no one loses and nothing is lost.

THE RAISING OF LAZARUS

Liturgical Occasion: Fifth Sunday of Lent – A Cycle
First Reading: Ezekiel 37:12-14
Second Reading: Romans 8:1-11
Gospel: John 11:1-45

Background

The story of the raising of Lazarus contains many dark and troubling features that are usually suppressed in preaching on the episode. Why did Jesus wait so long to return to the

---

à *Apollinaire* in *Handmade Midrash,* 76-77, Milgrom offers a very different view of this same passage from a Jewish perspective. By way of a midrash story "probably known to Chagall from his childhood shtetl learning," Milgrom demonstrates the playful ambiguity of the Hebrew mind. The story weaves together the "mistake" of God's tardiness and "frantic haste" in creating Adam and Eve with their "mistake" in transgressing. Creation, commandment, transgression, judgment, and pardon are all of "a single liturgical day, Rosh Hashanah, the new year, and the anniversary of Creation." In the mouth of the storying rabbis, the Genesis account has become a story of human will and accountability matched by the Holy One's pardon and forgiveness. Milgrom concludes: "Thus 'original forgiveness' in an early rabbinic text offers a powerful alternative to the oppressive guilt of original sin. . . ."

side of his friend Lazarus who was so gravely ill? By delaying his return, did Jesus "allow" Lazarus to die? Was he using Lazarus to showcase his own powers? What were Lazarus and his sisters thinking when Jesus did not return as expected? Were they angry? Did they feel betrayed, let down, disappointed, abandoned?

Scripture of the Day

First Reading: Ezekiel 37:12-14. God promises his people that he will open their graves and have them rise from them. He will put his spirit into them that they may live. Then shall they know he is God. "I have promised, and I will do it," says the Lord.

Second Reading: Romans 8:1-11. If Christ dwells within you, the body may be dead due to sin, but the spirit is alive because of justice. And the Spirit which raised Jesus from the dead will raise your mortal bodies to life.

Gospel: John 11:1-45. Word is sent to Jesus that Lazarus, the one he loves, is gravely ill. Jesus remains where he is for two more days. He then announces that Lazarus has died and he is going back to Judea to raise him. The disciples do not think this is a good idea, since people there have recently tried to stone Jesus to death. When Jesus arrives in Bethany, Lazarus has been in the tomb four days. When he sees the sisters of Lazarus and the other mourners in tears, Jesus, troubled in spirit and moved by the deepest emotions, weeps. He then calls Lazarus to come forth from the tomb and Lazarus does, bound and covered in winding cloths. "Untie him and let him go free," Jesus cries out.

The Raising of Lazarus

[A visual cue has been pre-established with the congregation. When the preacher as Lazarus raises his hand to his ear, the congregation calls out: "Lazarus, Come Forth."]

[As Lazarus, moving some of the furniture in the sanctuary and talking to some invisible presence in the tomb with him:] "Now I think we should put the sofa there and the chair over here. What do you think? What color do you think we should . . . ? Black? But you say everything should be black. The sofa, the chair, and you're always dressed all in black. You know, I used to think it was a cultural stereotype that black was Death's favorite color. But it's true. You're all dressed up in black.

"You know, I think you get a bum rap. I know when I was alive outside in the world, I was afraid of you. Everyone is so afraid of you, Death, I don't understand it. You're the one person who keeps your promises. I had friends that said they'd be my friends, but when I needed them, they weren't there. They let you down; they break your heart. But you, I know, you will always stick by me. You'll be here forever and I'll have peace, eternal peace. . . I won't have to care about anyone or anything anymore. What a relief! So . . ."

[Cue: Lazarus raises hand to ear.]

People: "Lazarus, Come Forth."

"Did you hear something? [pause] Ah . . . It's probably just the wind. So what about the curtains? Where do you think we should . . . . Oh, you're right. I forgot . . . There are no windows in a tomb.

"So I don't see the sunrise. So what? I'll just sleep later. So I won't see the sunset. I'll go to bed earlier. So I won't hear the birds singing or the children laughing. So I won't see the flowers growing on the hill. So what? I'm happy here. I'm at peace.

"Yeah, I'll miss some people. . . . My sisters. I'd come home from work at night and Mary would always give me a great foot massage. And Martha would bake the best bread and she'd always have a great casserole on the stove.[15]

"But the people that I wanted to be with . . . You know, when I was sick, we sent them a telegram. I thought he'd come back. He said "I'll always be there for you." Well, he didn't even reply to the telegram. And I just couldn't hold out any longer. I think that's what did it – what broke my heart."

[Cue: Lazarus raises hand to ear.]

People: "Lazarus, Come Forth."

"Did you hear something? [pause] Ah, it's probably a rock slide up the hill. I'm just going to take a look though.

---

15. These remarks allude to another story about Lazarus and his sisters in Luke 10:38-42.

There's this little crack in the rock where it didn't . . . Hah. Now he comes! [As if calling out from the grave to Jesus:] You're four days too late. I'm dead."

[All during the following section, Lazarus speaks directly out to the congregation as if he's looking at Jesus among them.]

"God, look at him. Is he . . . angry? He's shaking his fist at the tomb. I think he wants you to come out. I think he wants to go about twelve rounds with you. Or wrestle you. I used to see that look in his eyes. I'd be with him at a sickbed – when some little girl or an old woman would be sick and in pain. And I'd see that rage and that fury come up in him. And I used to admire anyone who could care so much about anything. And oh! he'd used to get furious at the soldiers and the politicians and the lawyers and the priests and the leaders. Every one of them who put down people, who condemned and judged people. He would just shake there with white fury because he knew how much life was in people and how it was being crushed."

[The next few lines are spoken over the shoulder as if to Death.]

"Oh, no, don't worry, I'm not going to leave you. No siree. I told you I'm staying here with you because you're my friend. He wasn't there four days ago. He stood me up. [As if calling out these next words to Jesus:] It's too late. Go away. Sorry.

"What a relief! I don't have to care about him or anybody else anymore. But there were times when he would look in my eyes. He would look right down to where the stench and the filth and the darkness was and somehow he found a way down to the very place I didn't want him or anyone else to find. And suddenly I knew it was okay . . . that he loved me . . . even though I stank to high heaven. He loved me."

[Cue: Lazarus raises hand to ear.]

People: "Lazarus, Come Forth."

[Lazarus now abruptly turns his attention to Death:] "What do you mean? What do you mean I'm not telling you the truth? Yeah, I told you I'm going to stay here. I'm not going. . . I don't care about him anymore. No. [Long pause.] I forgot. I can't fool you, can I, Death? All right. I'll tell you the truth. The reason why I'm not going to leave this tomb is because I know there are people out there just waiting to kill him. And if I walked out, I'd be his death warrant. They're just waiting to nail him to a tree. And a risen Lazarus would be the hammer in their hands. And I won't do that.

"I mean, that man cares about everything. I mean, if a bird falls out of the sky, he cares about it. Or a bruised flower falls over at sunset, he feels it. Or if a child skins his knee or a mother is abandoned by a husband, he cares. No, I deserve to be here with you because I don't care about anyone or anything, but, as much as he's broken my heart and let me down and double-crossed me, I still wouldn't do anything to harm him. That's why I'm staying here."

[Looking out into the congregation] "Huh . . . I wonder if he heard me. He's . . . crying now."

[Back to Death:] "What? What do you mean I *can't* stay here? What do you mean I'm not dead. I've been dead for four days. I stink. You know that. You mean I still do care about him. And as long as I care that much, I can't be dead. Well, thanks a lot. . . . So you're going to double-cross me too, huh? You mean I'm still alive because I still love him?

"All right. All right. I'll leave your tomb, but I'm going to take these with me, these winding cloths . . . To remind me that I'm going to have to die again. And again and again. But I'm going to come back, Death, and when I do, I'm coming back with him. And when we come back, we're going to swallow you up. And then where will your victory be?

[Begins to move to side as if to exit. Stops and turns to Death:] "The sofa still should go here. But it should be red. . . a brilliant glorious red!"

Additional Reflections

This homily turns the traditional Lazarus story literally inside out. It approaches the familiar gospel story from the perspective of what is going on *inside* the tomb. Through interactive visual and oral-aural storytelling techniques, it casts the people in the congregation as Jesus. This is accomplished by giving them the words of Jesus to speak and by having Lazarus visually place Jesus in their midst. Thus, it reverses the usual axis of sacred and profane space in church architecture, placing the person of Jesus in the nave among the congregation rather than in the sanctuary with the presbyter.

The traditional presuppositions of the Johannine narrative is also reversed in the story. In the beginning, Lazarus seems quite content, even relieved, to be dead. In fact, he resists Jesus's initial attempts to call him back to life and tells Jesus to go away. The power of Jesus that calls Lazarus back to life is not some divine intercessory ability or supernatural strength, but rather his human ability to care for people so passionately as to inspire devotion, attachment, and loyalty among others. As the story unfolds, what it means to be "alive" or "dead" thus takes on a very different meaning.

MARTHA AND MARY

Liturgical Occasion: Sixteenth Sunday of the Year – C Cycle
First Reading: Genesis 18:1-10
Second Reading: Colossians 1:24-28
Gospel: Luke 10:38-42

Background

The church where this homily was preached was famous for its liturgies and especially for its music and choir. Its main Sunday liturgy would often be so crowded that people would arrive thirty minutes early just to get a seat. It was not unusual for overflow crowds to be standing several deep in the aisles and vestibule area.

When I am asked to preach in a new or unfamiliar setting, I always like to attend the liturgy there beforehand to get a sense of the congregation, the style of worship, the design of the space and other environmental factors that might influence storytelling. When I visited this parish, I was shocked. The main liturgy had no music or choir to speak of and the church itself was practically empty. When I inquired, I learned that there had been a dispute going on that had split the community with many of the regular parishioners going elsewhere to worship. Given that context, this story of Martha and Mary developed.

Scripture of the Day

First Reading: Genesis 18:1-10. Abraham is visited by the Lord when three men appear nearby. Abraham runs to invite them to stay and rest with him. They agree and are welcomed with lavish hospitality, refreshment, and food. One of the men asks where Sarah is and, when told she is in the tent (turning 21 quarts of flour into cakes and rolls for them), he replies that he will return in a year's time and Sarah will have a son.

Second Reading: Colossians 1:24-28. Paul announces that his mission is to preach the glory beyond price, the mystery of Christ, our hope of glory. There is suffering in that mission but it is a joy when done for Christ's body, the church.

Gospel: Luke 10:38-42. Martha welcomes Jesus to her home. As she busies herself with all the details of hospitality, her sister, Mary, sits by the Lord's feet listening to his words. Finally, Martha asks Jesus to get Mary to help her. Jesus refuses and instead tells Martha that she is too anxious and that Mary has made the better choice and won't be deprived of it.

Martha and Mary

Everything had been going so well.

I mean, one minute they were all eating and drinking and laughing and listening to Jesus tell some stories – Jesus, Mary, Lazarus, the Twelve, and Martha going back and forth from the kitchen with the hors d'oeuvres.

The next minute all pandemonium had broken loose: Martha had come roaring out of the kitchen yelling at Mary; Mary started to cry; Jesus yelled at Martha who dropped the cheese and crackers on the floor; Lazarus leaped to his feet knocking over a table and chair, telling Jesus that he had no right to talk to his sister that way; while James and John tried to calm Lazarus down.

And the only sensible response in this whole mess was Peter who had been sitting in the corner with the rest of the disciples: he leaned over to Andrew and in a stage whisper said: "Start putting the hors d'oeuvres in your pockets! I bet they throw us out any minute like they did last month. You know, I keep telling him, 'Jesus, if you're going to insult your hosts, couldn't you at least wait until after dessert?'"

[Spoken as aside to congregation:] I wonder. Does that scene remind you of anything that might happen when your family gets together? Naaahhhhh, I didn't think so. Mine neither, except every Christmas, Easter, Thanksgiving, and birthdays in between!

Well, Martha had stormed into the kitchen, angry, hurt, fighting back the tears, holding onto the sink trying to catch her breath, when there came a knock on the door. And who do you think it should be? You got it! Jesus. Ole how-to-win-friends-and-influence-people himself!

[As Jesus:] "Martha, is it safe to come in here? Can we talk? Would you mind putting that rolling pin down. Thank you. You're not going to throw anything at me, are you? Are you? Truce?

"Well, I have some good news and bad news. The bad news is the living room's really a mess, Martha. There's salsa on the ceiling, goat cheese in the sofa, and figs ground into the carpet. Mary's still sobbing and James and John have taken Lazarus for a walk around the block to calm him down. Peter? Oh, he's still shovelling down the hors d'oeuvres.

"But the good news, Martha, is that you showed me something, something I didn't know. You showed me that that mess in there is the kingdom too, isn't it? You showed me that, Martha, you really did – by daring to bring your hurt and pain and anger right out into the open like that. You just blurted it out. You were so honest! So human and down to earth. You felt slighted and overlooked and left out, didn't you? So you said what was in your heart. My God! That took guts, Martha.

"You know sometimes I think this kingdom of God thing is so easy, so simple: Feed the hungry, love your enemies, welcome the strangers, right? You know, just do it. But I forget. Sometimes loving your own sister and brother is so much harder! Especially when your sister or your brother has become a stranger.

"Sometimes when I'm preaching, I get carried away. And suddenly I'm soaring way over everybody's head, telling everybody else what to do – hate your mother, hate your father, follow me, do good, avoid evil. Soon I'm flying high above the earth in Elijah's chariot of fire, heading straight into the heart of God – until someone like you comes along, Martha, and points out that my wheels are stuck in the mud. I look down and, sure enough, you're right. There's my chariot of fire all aflame with the love of God and the kingdom, stuck in the mud, hissing and sputtering and coughing and smoking. I haven't moved an inch, haven't left the ground. In fact, if anything, I've sunk a couple of inches deeper into the whole muck and mire and mess of everything. Oh sometimes, I get so discouraged and disappointed. And I think: Oh God! When will this thing ever fly? But then, I remember and I say, 'Wait a minute: that mud is blessed and holy, that mud is what our weak flawed hurting humanity is made from, that mud is what God created and loves so much in us and which the poor angels envy!'

"I don't know about you, Martha, but no one can hurt me like my own family at times. Or disappoint me like the disciples. I know they've left everything to follow me but sometimes I just have no patience for them. I keep forgetting. I keep thinking it's all so easy, so simple. You know, how I can go on and on about how important it is to love the poor and the hungry, the blind and the lame, but when Peter and James and John and all the rest are poor and hungry and blind and lame and dumb, I can blow up at them and completely lose it. I turn on them and snap at them and dress them down in public.

"You know, when they ask me who is the greatest in the kingdom, I put a child in their midst and say: behold! The kingdom of God. And yet when they act like children – fighting and bickering among themselves or are hurt or needy or frightened or jealous, then I have absolutely no patience for any of them. Then I want them all to be perfectly grown-up and adult and mature. I keep forgetting just how weak and human they are.

"Maybe if I want them to be the best possible servants, I need to stop taking them for granted and start treating them like you treated me, Martha, as an honored guest and friend, and not a stranger!

"Well, Martha, there's the news, good and bad. What do you say? The kingdom's waiting for us in the next room – and it's quite a mess, with overturned furniture, hurt feelings, and a meal in shambles. Maybe if we go in together,

you and I, and just keep talking and listening and sharing
the pain and forgiving one another over and over and over
again, maybe we can do something. What do you say,
Martha? Shall we give it a try?"

Additional Reflections

In the Catholic tradition, this set of readings is usually
associated with homilies about contemplation versus action
in the spiritual life. But, from what I observed at the parish
and from the people I spoke with there, it was obvious to me
that the pain, hurt, and anger caused by the ongoing dispute
was so raw and pervasive that it had to be addressed somehow.

As we have seen, it is precisely because story refrains
from making truth claims about the factual nature of reality
that allows it to be heard where other forms of discourse would
only aggravate and polarize. As a guest preacher, someone
who was not a regular member of the parish nor had any
understanding of the dispute in the community, I could not
address this issue directly without making matters worse.
What I could do as storyteller, however, was to craft a midrash
that might allow the members of the community to enter into
the gospel story and find themselves and their own pain there.

Thanks to a midrashic sense of textual play (and "interplay") observed in the rabbis, I recalled that the very next two
verses of the Genesis story after the selection read (Genesis
18:11-12) contained the warm and humorous details of Sarah's
laughing at the news of her impending fertility. Sarah's laughter suggested the tone of my story. In laughter and humor, a
divided community could find common ground.

Also, playing with the "glory" of Christ mentioned in
the selection from Colossians, I thought it important to
portray Jesus as someone who could make mistakes, who
could apologize, could learn from another, ask for help,
experience the pain of falling short of one's ideals, and find
God in the "mess" of human relationships. The "glory" of
Jesus then takes on another possible meaning.

The story ends with an invitation to possible collaboration, not any sure conclusion or happy ending. How Martha
responds is left open to the imagination of the listeners. They
must complete the story and begin a new one.

Conclusion

EPISTEMOLOGIES PRODUCE PARADIGMS, PARADIGMS SHAPE theory, and theory influences practice. In the previous chapters, we have examined how the recovery of story as a way of knowing is helping create a new emerging paradigm or worldview called the postmodern. That worldview, in turn, is forcing a reevaluation of the assumption that "modern," scientific methods of theory and practice are "intrinsically superior,"[1] timeless, "objective," and normative. The recovery of story as an epistemology in postmodern thinking also calls into question the categorization of all "premodern" modalities of knowing as inherently "backward"[2] or inferior and asks us to reimagine how these "nonmodern" modalities may be rehabilitated and their values rediscovered by us today.

In the Introduction, after a brief treatment of the shift from modern to postmodern "systems of mind,"[3] I proposed that story is not just an art form or literary genre but an epistemology, a way of structuring thought. I then turned in Part I to an exploration of how the modalities and techniques of our knowing shape and structure thought. How we know affects not only the content of our knowledge but the quality of our relationship to that knowledge as well. With story as the focus of our attention, we proceeded in Chapter One to study the psychodynamic differences between storying as oral-aural interplay and story as literature in the structuring of thought. Each modality of knowing, oral-aural and literate, yielded very different encounters with reality. Storying demanded face-to-face, cocreative, interactive rela-

---

1. Berger, "Toward a Critique of Modernity," 335.
2. Ibid.
3. Kitazawa, "Myth, Performance, and Politics," 160.

tionships of personal presence in the here-and-now. Reading and writing emphasized the permanence, exactness, and repeatability of the text and fostered distance and separation between the knower and the known. With literate modes of knowing, the primary relationship was no longer among people but with the impersonal text as material object. The invention of the printing press accelerated the shift from oral-aural modes of knowing to literate ones and promoted different configurations of power in society.

Chapter Two explored the story of how Thomas Kuhn broke with his own training in "modern" assumptions about the history of science and discovered for himself a way of reinterpreting "premodern" opinions dismissed by his colleagues as "absurd"[4] and ridiculous. By seeking to understand Aristotle's theory of motion, Kuhn learned the chief hermeneutic principle of a narrative epistemology: what is known depends wholly on the perspective of the knower and the contexts of the knowing. By pursuing Kuhn's hints of how he came to this insight from his study of Gestalt psychology,[5] we considered how recent studies in perception, sensation, and cognition suggest that what we know and call reality is actually created or constructed through the fictive participation and interaction of brain, mind, and world. Kuhn's insight led to his rejection of a hierarchical or accumulative view of knowledge in which only one truth at a time could sit perched, king-of-the-hill style, atop a junkheap of discarded, discredited opinions as it waited to be replaced by the next one sure truth. Kuhn's reading of the history of science allowed him to value the contributions and insights of *both* Aristotle *and* Newton simultaneously within their respective historical and cultural contexts and perspectives.

In Part II, we examined the interrelationships among epistemologies, paradigms, theory, and technique in the history of psychotherapy. In Chapter Three, we examined how Kuhn's discovery of an alternate way of reading the history of science led him to his concept of paradigms. After commenting on the advantages and limitations of paradigms, we considered how changes in the techniques and modalities of knowing led to a shift from a medieval world-

---

4. Kuhn, *The Essential Tension*, xi.
5. Ibid., xiii.

view to a "modern" one. This "modern" worldview valued the empirical, quantifiable, and measurable in its search for objective scientific knowledge. Then we looked at how the mechanistic assumptions, expectations, and presuppositions of the modern paradigm affected theory and practice in the field of psychotherapy from Freud to the family therapists of the 1950s.

In Chapter Four, we considered how psychotherapists trained in systems theory and cybernetic approaches to operational functioning have recently begun to question some of their own premises in their practice of family therapy. In different ways, these therapists have turned their attention to considering the narrative epistemology of the postmodern critique as the basis for developing new approaches to the theory and practice of psychotherapy. We examined just some of the elements shaping postmodern thought: quantum physics and Heisenberg's principle of uncertainty, Bertalanffy's perspectivism with its emphasis on context, Bruner's and Watzlawick's constructivist psychology. Attitudes to the relationship between language and knowledge, however, emerged as our main focus, since postmodernism rejects the representational claims of language and prefers to favor fictive forms of language instead, primarily story. This is because story makes no truth claims about "representing" an external objective reality. Story proposes one possible interpretation of one possible perspective on the world. Story does not offer truth, so much as an analogous truthfulness based on a very personal, subjective, particularized, and, therefore, limited experience of reality. Chapter Four concluded with a consideration of the evolving therapeutic theory and techniques of Michael White and David Epston based on their interpretation of narrative epistemology.

In Part III, we explored postmodern approaches in the study and proclamation of the Hebrew and Christian scriptures that derive from the recovery of Israel's long tradition of storying and narrative epistemology. Chapter Five examined Walter Brueggemann's work in biblical theology over the past twenty years together with his more recent analysis of the major differences between modern and postmodern approaches to scripture studies. Throughout his career, Brueggemann has focused on the importance of story in Israel's development of a narrative epistemology. By nurturing an alternative imagination through her storying, Israel found that she could survive the systematic oppression and institutional disconfirmation of the dominant culture and ideology. By hoping in the imagined future of her stories, Israel could marshal her powers to act in her own interest in the present while finding new meanings in her past. Through this process of storying, Israel also found a new identity – as the story partner of YHWH. For Brueggemann, the Exodus event is primarily an epistemological transformation in which Israel withdrew forever from all official narratives or ideologies that attempted to define and control her. Instead, Israel chose to find her own story and identity and the power that telling her own story conferred upon her, no matter the consequences. The Exodus event provided Israel with a new way of thinking, imagining, and relating – namely, in and through her storying – to herself, her God, and the world.

Chapter Six examined how Israel's tradition of a narrative epistemology did not end with the destruction of temple and cult after the fall of Jerusalem in 70 C.E. or with the close of the biblical canon. Instead Israel developed a new form of storying called midrash in which she told stories about her stories. What was especially significant for the purposes of this study was how Israel continued to rely primarily on narrative modes of thinking, knowing, and relating in the transmission of her truth. By deriving the tradition of one – but dual! – Torah (written and oral), Israel insisted on the integral nature of written text *and* oral commentary. (Israel even insisted that the latter include not only all minority opinions but rejected ones as well, in case they prove true at some future time in the history of the community.) From her experience in Egypt, Israel knew that any single truth, if unchallenged, can turn tyrant; any single text become an ideology, if no alternative interpretation is permitted.

Midrash preserved Israel's suspicion of all absolute arrangements of power or *a priori* structures of thought by insisting that every text, utterance, and pronouncement, including Torah, was not self-evident or obvious but demanded a process of interpretation, discussion, dialogue, and debate. Midrash and postmodernism both share an aversion to representational language and the closure of thought,

preferring instead to play with the multiple meanings, paradoxes, contradictions, ambiguities, and irrational complexi-
ties of story and narrative knowing.

Finally, in Chapter Seven, we looked at how the recovery of story as an epistemology in a postmodern world might
shape the theory and practice of preaching. I presented six
story-homilies as examples of "Christian midrash" together
with brief descriptions of the pastoral contexts of each homily. By trusting what Brueggemann calls the "scandalous
particularity"[6] of "the little story . . . free of systematic
perspective, and especially of systematic theology,"[7] I have
tried to recover story as a way of knowing among the people
and congregations that have welcomed me as a minister of
the Word among them.

I conclude this study by tracing the trajectory between
two stories from the scriptures, Hebrew and Christian. Let
me offer brief summaries of both stories before commenting
on them.

The first is the story of the Tower of Babel (Genesis
11:1-9). After the chaos of the flood (6:9-9:29) and the utter
destruction of humankind come the great lists of descendants of Noah and his sons, Shem, Ham, and Japheth (10:1-
32), detailing their *separation* "into their own countries, each
with their own language, family by family, nation by nation"
(10:5). The chapter concludes with the verse: "and from them
came the *separate* nations on earth after the flood" (10:32).
Immediately following this verse comes the opening of the
story of the Tower of Babel: "Once upon a time all the world
spoke a single language and used the same words" (11:1).

The second story is the Christian account of the giving
of the Holy Spirit to the followers of Jesus following his
death, resurrection, and ascent into the heavens (Acts 2:1-
13). The event occurs during the Jewish feast of Pentecost
and is marked by strange signs: "a strong driving wind,"
"tongues of flame," and "talking in other tongues" (2:2-4).
Those gathered in Jerusalem for the feast come "from every
nation under heaven;" yet "each one heard his own language
spoken" and proclaimed "How is it that we hear them, each
of us in his own native language?" (2:5-8).

---

6. Brueggemann, *Texts,* 59.
7. Ibid., 58.

The movement from union to exquisite differentiation seems to lie at the heart of the mystery of all creation and life – from the Big Bang to the division of cells, from symbiosis to individuation. In a sense, the above two stories express that same theme by tracing the contradictory human impulse for linguistic unity and differentiation which storying as a way of knowing and relating seems better able to tolerate and embrace than any other modality of thought or communication. For from one story told, many are heard; and each in the listener's "native language" because "it depends on your listening with your heart." I believe that only a narrative epistemology can transmit and engender knowledge with "tremendous admiration, affection, respect, and love."[8] This is finally what this book has been about.

When I began considering the problem of story and knowing, I thought of story as a technique for change as one might use psychodrama, sandplay, dream analysis, paradox, or genograms in therapy. Coming from a background in drama and ritual, I had seen evidence of the psycho-physical changes in consciousness that can occur when those assembled in theaters and churches become caught up in a kairotic moment of communion, be that through the poetry of Shakespeare, the chanting of Kol Nidre, the singing of a gospel choir, or the breaking of bread. When I began telling stories, I experienced that same transformation of consciousness in myself and the listeners. I wished to learn more about how story could be used to affect change.

In the process of finding out, I wrote and reflected extensively. I found myself looking at story very differently than I had when I first began. I concluded that story was not just one more therapeutic device or change agent but a way of knowing that challenged many of my own assumptions about science and modern culture.

The human experience of anxiety often leads us, individually and collectively, to seek comfort and consolation in a language of union, be that the preverbal embrace and soft

---

8. John Mohawk, Seneca Indian and editor of *Akwesasne Notes*, largest Indian newspaper in North America, quoted in Jerry Mander, *In the Absence of the Sacred: The Failure of Technology and the Survival of the Indian Nations* (San Francisco: Sierra Club Books, 1991), 113.

cooing sounds of our mothers when we were frightened as infants; a single uniform language of the "same words" after the destruction of humankind in the flood narrative of Genesis; or one categorical system of clear and distinct ideas, such as Cartesian rationalism or Newtonian physics following the collapse of the medieval synthesis. This impulse for security via the unity and conformity of thought, language, ideas, custom, religion, and so forth is normal, natural, and very human. But it can also be very dangerous and destructive as the Tower of Babel story suggests and can lead to even greater confusion, misunderstanding, alienation, and division among those who would seek to bridge the distance between themselves as they would between the heavens and earth – by a single structure, language, or ideology.

Perhaps, as the account of Pentecost above suggests, a better way to realize union in the midst of radical diversity is to seek ways of speaking and understanding the many disparate tongues, dialects, and regional accents we hear around us. This is hard work, and often frustrating, in which one learns by mistakes, misunderstandings, correction, new attempts, and new mistakes. This is infinitely more difficult and time-consuming than building Babel-high skyscraper towers complete with satellite dishes toward the heavens or threading fiber optic cables beneath the ground. There is no single technology, no super interactive multimedia computer system, not even the "information superhighway," that can do that hard work for us.[9] Each of us must do that ourselves, one sound, syllable, and silence at a time as we assemble a multicultural community of tents in our hearts where storying strangers, telling and listening to each other, can sojourn together with our eavesdropping God in the wilderness of existence and find communion and understanding. For, if God learned one thing from his encounters with the rabbis

---

9. I refer the reader to the heartbreaking account of the impact of satellite television on the native Dene and Inuit peoples in the Northwest Territories of Canada in Mander, *In the Absence of the Sacred,* 97-119. Similar accounts of sudden and rapid cultural disintegration, suicide, elder abuse, and alcoholism have been reported in the island cultures of Micronesia following the import of videorecording machines and videotapes there. (Personal communication between the author and Rev. Fran Hezel, S.J., Superior, Jesuit Missions, Micronesia.)

debating Ochnai's oven, it is this: if the Holy One wants people to listen, he'd be better off keeping his opinions to himself and speaking in story instead!

Bibliography

Anderson, Bernhard W. *Understanding the Old Testament.* Englewood Cliffs, NJ: Prentice-Hall, 1975.

Anderson, Harlene and Harold Goolishian. "Supervision as Collaborative Conversation: Questions and Reflections." In *Von der Supervision zur systemischen Vision,* ed. H. Brandau. Salzburg: Otto Muller Verlag, 1990.

Anderson, W. T. *Reality Isn't What It Used To Be: Theatrical Politics, Ready-to-Wear Religion, Global Myths, Primitive Chic, and Other Wonders of the Postmodern World.* San Francisco: HarperCollins, 1990.

Avis, J. M. "Deepening Awareness: A Private Study Guide to Feminism and Family Therapy." In *Women, Feminism, and Family Therapy,* ed. L. Braverman. New York: Haworth Press, 1988.

Barbour, Ian. *Myths, Models, and Paradigms: A Comparative Study in Science and Religion.* New York: Harper, 1974.

_____. *Religion in an Age of Science: The Gifford Lectures 1989-1991.* Vol. 1. San Francisco, Harper, 1990.

Barnet, Richard. *The Rockets' Red Glare: When America Goes to War – The Presidents and the People.* New York: Simon and Schuster, 1990.

Berger, Peter. "Toward a Critique of Modernity." In *Religion and the Sociology of Knowledge: Modernization and Pluralism in Christian Thought and Structure,* ed. Barbara Hargrove. New York: Edward Mellen Press, 1984.

Berman, Marshall. *All That is Solid Melts Into Air.* New York: Penguin Books, 1988.

Berman, Morris. *The Reenchantment of the World.* New York: Bantam Books, 1984.

Bialik, Chaim N. "Revealment and Concealment in Language." Quoted in Samuel C. Heilman. *The People of the Book:*

Drama, Fellowship, and Religion. Chicago: University of Chicago Press, 1983.

Bloom, Floyd and Arlyne Lazerson. *Brain, Mind and Behavior.* 2d ed. New York: W. H. Freeman and Company, 1988.

Bloomer, Carolyn. *Principles of Visual Perception.* 2d ed. New York: Design Press, 1990.

Bolman, Lee G. and Terrence E. Deal. *Reframing Organizations: Artistry, Choice, and Leadership.* San Francisco: Jossey-Bass Publishers, 1991.

Borges, Jorge Luis. "Tlon, Uqbar, Orbis, Tertius." In *Labyrinths.* New York: New Directions, 1964.

Boyarin, Daniel. *Intertextuality and the Reading of Midrash.* Bloomington, IN: Indiana University Press, 1990.

Brazelton, T. Berry and Bertrand Cramer. *The Earliest Relationship: Parents, Infants, and the Drama of Early Attachment.* Reading, MA: Addison-Wesley Publishing Company, 1990.

Brueggemann, Walter. *Abiding Astonishment: Psalms, Modernity, and the Making of History.* Louisville, KY: Westminister/John Knox Press, 1991.

_____. *The Creative Word: Canon as a Model for Biblical Education.* Philadelphia: Fortress Press, 1982.

_____. *David's Truth in Israel's Imagination and Memory.* Philadelphia: Fortress Press, 1985.

_____. *Finally Comes the Poet: Daring Speech for Proclamation.* Minneapolis: Fortress Press, 1989.

_____. *Hopeful Imagination: Prophetic Voices in Exile.* Minneapolis: Fortress Press, 1986.

_____. *Hope within History.* Atlanta: John Knox Press, 1987.

_____. *In Man We Trust: The Neglected Side of Biblical Faith.* Atlanta: John Knox Press, 1973.

_____. *Israel's Praise: Doxology against Idolatry and Ideology.* Philadelphia: Fortress Press, 1988.

_____. *The Land: Place as Gift, Promise, and Challenge in Biblical Faith.* Philadelphia: Fortress Press, 1977.

_____. *The Prophetic Imagination.* Philadelphia, Fortress Press, 1978.

_____. *Texts Under Negotiation: The Bible and Postmodern Imagination.* Minneapolis: Fortress Press, 1993.

Brueggemann, Walter and John Donahue. Foreword to *The Land: Place as Gift, Promise, and Challenge in Biblical Faith* by Walter Brueggemann. Philadelphia: Fortress Press, 1977.

Bruner, Jerome. *Acts of Meaning*. Cambridge, MA: Harvard University Press, 1990.

_____. *Actual Minds, Possible Worlds*. Cambridge, MA: Harvard University Press, 1986.

_____. Foreword to *Freudian Metaphor*, by Donald Spence. New York: W. W. Norton & Company, 1987.

Buber, Martin. "Distance and Relation." *Psychiatry* 20 (1957).

_____. *Moses*. Atlantic Highlands, NJ: Humanities Press International, 1946.

_____. *Tales of the Hasidim: The Early Masters*. New York: Schocken Books, 1978.

Burke, James. *The Day the Universe Changed*. Boston: Little, Brown and Company, 1985.

Burtt, E. A. *The Metaphysical Foundations of Modern Science*. Garden City: Doubleday Anchor, 1955.

Capra, Fritjof. *The Turning Point*. New York: Simon and Schuster, 1982.

Cassidy, David. *Uncertainty: The Life and Science of Werner Heisenberg*. New York: W. H. Freeman and Company, 1992.

Cohen, Gershon. "The Talmudic Age." In *Great Ages and Ideas of the Jewish People*, ed. Leo Schwartz. New York: Modern Library, 1956.

Coomaraswamy, Ananda. *The Transformation of Nature in Art*. New York: Dover Publications, 1934.

Crick, Francis and C. Koch. "The Problem of Consciousness." *Scientific American* 267 (September 1992).

Davidson, Mark. *Uncommon Sense: The Life and Thought of Ludwig von Bertalanffy*. Los Angeles: Jeremy P. Tarcher, 1983.

de Gramont, Patrick. *Language and the Distortion of Meaning*. New York: New York University Press, 1990.

de Mello, Anthony. Lecture at Christ the King Retreat House, Syracuse, NY (August, 1983).

Dickinson, Emily. *The Complete Poems of Emily Dickinson*. Edited by Thomas H. Johnson. Boston: Little, Brown, and Company, 1960.

Donahue, John. *The Gospel in Parable: Metaphor, Narrative, and Theology in the Synoptic Gospels*. Philadelphia: Fortress Press, 1988.

Dorfman, Ariel. *The Empire's Old Clothes: What the Lone Ranger, Babar, and Other Innocent Heroes Do to Our Minds*. New York: Pantheon Books, 1983.

Edwards, Viv and Thomas Sienkewicz. *Oral Cultures Past and Present: Rappin' and Homer*. Oxford: Basil Blackwell, 1990.

Efran, Jay, Michael Lukens, and Robert Lukens. *Language, Structure, and Change: Frameworks of Meaning in Psychotherapy*. New York: W. W. Norton & Company, 1990.

Ellul, Jacques. *The Technological Society*. New York: Vintage Books, 1964.

Ferris, Timothy. *Coming of Age in the Milky Way*. New York: Doubleday, 1988.

Fisch, Richard. Review of *Problem-solving Therapy*, by Jay Haley. In *Family Process* 17 (1978).

Foucault, Michel. *Power/Knowledge: Selected Interviews and Other Writings*. New York: Pantheon Books, 1980.

_____. "Technologies of the Self." In *Technologies of the Self*, ed. L. Martin, H. Gutman, and P. Hutton. Amherst: University of Massachusetts Press, 1988.

Fraade, Steven. *From Tradition to Commentary: Torah and Its Interpretation in the Midrash Sifre to Deuteronomy*. Albany, NY: State University of New York, 1991.

Gardner, Howard. *Frames of Mind: The Theory of Multiple Intelligences*. New York: Basic Books, 1983.

Gaventa, John. *Power and Powerlessness: Quiescence and Rebellion in an Appalachian Valley*. Urbana, IL: University of Illinois, 1980.

Gay, Peter. *Freud: A Life for Our Time*. New York: W. W. Norton & Company, 1988.

Genovese, Eugene. *Roll, Jordan, Roll*. New York: Pantheon, 1974.

Glatzer, Nahum N., ed. *Hammer on the Rock: A Short Midrash Reader*. New York: Schocken Books, 1962.

Goffman, Erving. *Asylums: Essays in the Social Situation of Mental Patients and Other Inmates*. New York: Doubleday, 1961.

Goldberg, Michael. *Jews and Christians, Getting Our Stories Straight: The Exodus and the Passion-Resurrection*. Philadelphia, Trinity Press International, 1991.

Goldin, Judah. "The Freedom and Restraint of Haggadah." In *Midrash and Literature*, ed. Geoffrey Hartman and Sanford Budick. New Haven: Yale University Press, 1986.

_____. "Midrash and Aggadah." In *Judaism: A People and Its History*, ed. Robert Seltzer. New York: Macmillan, 1989.

Goody, Jack. *The Domestication of the Savage Mind*. Cambridge: Cambridge University Press, 1977.

_____. *The Logic of Writing and the Organization of Society*. Cambridge: Cambridge University Press, 1986.

Gordon, Thomas. *Teaching Children Self-Discipline*. New York: Times Books, 1989.

Graff, Harvey. *The Legacies of Literacy: Continuities and Contradictions in Western Culture and Society*. Bloomington, IN: Indiana University Press, 1987.

Guttman, H. A. "Systems Theory, Cybernetics, and Epistemology." In *Handbook of Family Therapy*, ed. A. S. Gurman and D. P. Kniskern. New York: Brunner/Mazel, 1991.

Haley, Jay, ed. *Changing Families: A Family Therapy Reader*. New York: Gruen and Stratton, 1971.

Handelman, Susan. *Slayers of Moses: The Emergence of Rabbinic Interpretation in Modern Literary Theory*. Albany: State University of New York Press, 1982.

Havelock, Eric. "The Linguistic Task of the Presocratics, Part One: Ionian Science in Search of an Abstract Vocabulary." In *Language and Thought in Early Greek Philosophy*, ed. K. Robb. La Salle, IL: Hegeler Institute, Monist Library of Philosophy, 1983.

_____. *The Muse Learns to Write: Reflections on Orality and Literacy from Antiquity to the Present*. New Haven: Yale University Press, 1986.

Hedges, Lawrence. *Interpreting the Countertransference*. Northvale, NJ: Jason Aronson, 1992.

Heilman, Samuel C. *The People of the Book: Drama, Fellowship, and Religion*. Chicago: University of Chicago Press, 1983.

Heinemann, Joseph. "The Nature of the Aggadah." In *Midrash and Literature*, ed. Geoffrey Hartman and Sanford Budick. New Haven: Yale University Press, 1986.

Herzstein, Robert Edwin. *The War that Hitler Won: Goebbels and the Nazi Media Campaign*. New York: Paragon House, 1987.

Heschel, Abraham. *Between God and Man*. New York: Free Press, 1965.

_____. *God in Search of Man: A Philosophy of Religion*. New York: Noonday Press, 1992.

_____. *The Sabbath: Its Meaning for Modern Man*. New York: Farrar, Strauss, and Giroux, 1987.

Hoffman, John. *Law, Freedom, and Story: The Role of Narrative in Therapy, Society, and Faith*. Ontario: Wilfred Laurier University Press, 1986.

Hoffman, Lynn. "Constructing Realities: An Art of Lenses." *Family Process 29,* no. 1 (1990).

Holtz, Barry, ed. *Back to the Sources*. New York: Summit, 1984.

Hopkins, Gerard Manley. *The Poems of Gerard Manley Hopkins*. 4th ed. revised and enlarged. Edited by W. H. Gardner and N. H. Mackenzie. London: Oxford University Press, 1970.

Horsley, Richard. *The Liberation of Christmas: The Infancy Narratives in Social Context*. New York: Continuum, 1989.

Illich, Ivan. *In the Vineyard of the Text: A Commentary on Hugh's "Didascalicon."* Chicago: University of Chicago Press, 1993.

Illich, Ivan and Barry Sanders. *The Alphabetization of the Popular Mind*. San Francisco: North Point Press, 1988.

Imber-Black, Evan and Janine Roberts. *Rituals for Our Times: Celebrating, Healing, and Changing Our Lives and Our Relationships*. New York, HarperCollins Publishers, 1992.

Jackson, Don. "The Myth of Normality." *Medical Opinion and Review* 3 (1967).

Jensen, Richard. *Thinking in Story: Preaching in a Post-literate Age*. Lima, OH: C.S.S. Publishing Co., 1993.

Kaschak, Ellyn. *Engendered Lives: A New Psychology of Women's Experience*. New York: Basic Books, 1992.

Kelber, Werner. *The Oral and Written Gospel: The Hermeneutics of Speaking and Writing in the Synoptic Tradition, Mark, Paul, and Q*. Philadelphia: Fortress Press, 1983.

Kirk, Martha Ann. *Celebrations of Biblical Women's Stories: Tears, Milk, and Honey*. Kansas City: Sheed & Ward, 1987.

Kitazawa, Masakuni. "Myth, Performance, and Politics." *The Drama Review 36* no. 3 (Fall 1992).

Kuhn, Thomas. *The Copernican Revolution: Planetary Astronomy in the Development of Western Thought*. Cambridge, MA: Harvard University Press, 1957.

_____. *The Essential Tension: Selected Studies in Scientific Tradition and Change*. Chicago: University of Chicago Press, 1977.

_____. *The Structure of Scientific Revolutions*. Chicago: University of Chicago Press, 1962.

Küng, Hans and David Tracy, ed. *Paradigm Change in Theology: A Symposium for the Future*. New York: Crossroad, 1989.

Kurtz, Stephen. *The Art of Unknowing: Dimensions of Openness in Analytic Therapy*. Northvale, NJ: Jason Aronson, 1989.

Laing, R. D. *Self and Others*. London: Penguin Books, 1990.

Langford, Jerome. *Galileo, Science, and the Church*. 3rd ed. Ann Arbor, MI: The University of Michigan Press, 1992.

Lerner, Michael. *Surplus Powerlessness: The Psychodynamics of Everyday Life and the Psychology of Individual and Social Transformation*. Oakland, CA: The Institute for Labor and Mental Health, 1986.

Lifton, Robert J. *The Nazi Doctors: Medical Killing and the Psychology of Genocide*. New York: Basic Books, 1986.

_____. *Thought Reform and the Psychology of Totalism: A Study of "Brainwashing" in China*. New York: W. W. Norton & Company, 1961.

Lindberg, David. *The Beginnings of Western Science: The European Scientific Tradition in Philosophical, Religious, and Institutional Context, 600 B.C. to A.D. 1450*. Chicago: University of Chicago Press, 1992.

Lord, Albert. *Epic Singers and Oral Tradition*. Ithaca, NY: Cornell University Press, 1991.

_____. "Homer and Other Epic Poetry." In *A Companion to Homer*, ed. A. J. Wace and F. H. Stubbings. New York: Macmillan, 1963.

_____. *The Singer of Tales*. Harvard Studies in Comparative Literature, 24. Cambridge, MA: Harvard University Press, 1960.

Lovejoy, Arthur. *The Great Chain of Being: A Study of the History of an Idea*. The William James Lectures 1933. Cambridge, MA: Harvard University Press, 1936.

Lowe, Roger. "Postmodern Themes and Therapeutic Practices: Notes Towards the Definition of 'Family Therapy': Part 2." *Dulwich Centre Newsletter* 3 (1991).

Lukas, J. Anthony. *Common Ground*. New York: Alfred A. Knopf, 1985.

Luria, Alexander. *Cognitive Development: Its Cultural and Social Foundations*. Edited by Michael Cole. Trans. by Martin Lopez-Morillas and Lynn Solotaroff. Cambridge, MA: Harvard University Press, 1976.

Mander, Jerry. *In the Absence of the Sacred: The Failure of Technology and the Survival of the Indian Nations*. San Francisco: Sierra Club Books, 1991.

McLuhan, Marshall. *The Gutenberg Galaxy: The Making of Typographic Man*. Toronto: University of Toronto Press, 1962.

McNamee, Sheila and Kenneth Gergen, ed. *Therapy as Social Construction*. London: Sage Publications, 1992.

Medawar, P. B. *Limits of Science*. New York: Oxford University Press, 1987.

Milgrom, Jo. *Handmade Midrash*. Philadelphia: The Jewish Publication Society, 1992.

Miller, Alice. *Thou Shall Not Be Aware*. New York: New American Library, 1986.

Miller, Arthur. *Death of a Salesman: Certain Private Conversations in Two Acts and a Requiem*. New York: Viking Press, 1949.

Miller, J. Hillis. "The Fiction of Realism." In *Dickens Centennial Essays*, ed. Ada Nisbet and Blake Nevius. Berkeley: University of California Press, 1971.

Moustakas, C. *Rhythms, Rituals and Relationships*. Detroit, MI: Center for Humanistic Studies, 1981.

Neusner, Jacob. *Invitation to Midrash: The Workings of Rabbinic Bible Interpretation*. San Francisco: Harper & Row, 1989.

Nichols, Michael. *The Self in the System: Expanding the Limits of Family Therapy*. New York: Brunner/Mazel, 1987.

Nichols, Michael and Richard Schwartz. *Family Therapy: Concepts and Methods*. 2d ed. Boston: Allyn and Bacon, 1991.

Ong, Walter. *Interfaces of the Word: Studies in the Evolution of Consciousness and Culture*. Ithaca, NY: Cornell University Press, 1977.

_____. *Orality and Literacy: The Technologizing of the Word*. London: Methuen, 1982.

_____. *Presence of the Word: Some Prolegomena for Cultural and Religious History*. Minneapolis: University of Minnesota Press, 1981.

_____. "Writing is a Technology That Restructures Thought." In *The Written Word: Literacy in Transition*, ed. Gerd Baumann. Wolfson College Lectures 1985. Oxford: Clarendon Press, 1986.

Ornstein, Robert. *The Psychology of Consciousness*. 2d rev. ed. New York: Penguin Books, 1986.

Osborne, Richard. *Philosophy for Beginners*. New York: Writers and Readers Publishing, 1991.

Packer, Martin J. "Hermeneutic Inquiry in the Study of Human Conduct." *American Psychologist 40* (10).

Parry, Milman. *The Making of Homeric Verse: The Collected Papers of Milman Parry*. Edited by Adam Parry. Oxford: Clarendon Press, 1977.

Paulsen, Gary. *Nightjohn*. New York: Delacorte Press, 1993.

Polkinghorne, Donald. *Narrative Knowing and the Human Sciences*. Albany: State University of New York Press, 1988.

Richie, Donald, ed. *Rashomon*. New Brunswick, NJ: Rutgers University Press, 1987.

Rosenau, Pauline. *Post-modernism and the Social Sciences: Insights, Inroads, and Intrusions*. Princeton: Princeton University Press, 1992.

Rossoff, Don. "The Midrashic Process." Master's Thesis, Hebrew Union College-Jewish Institute of Religion, 1979.

Rotenberg, Mordechai. *Re-Biographing and Deviance: Psychotherapeutic Narrativism and the Midrash*. New York: Praeger, 1987.

Scarry, Elaine. *The Body in Pain: The Making and Unmaking of the World*. New York: Oxford University Press, 1985.

Schaefer, Charles. *The Therapeutic Powers of Play*. Northvale, NJ: Jason Aronson, 1993.

Scholem, Gershom. *Major Trends in Jewish Mysticism*. New York: Schocken Books, 1961.

Schon, Donald. *The Reflective Practitioner: How Professionals Think in Action*. New York: Basic Books, 1983.

Shakespeare, William. *The Complete Works of Shakespeare*. Edited by Hardin Craig. Glenview, IL: Scott, Foresman and Company, 1961.

Shengold, Leonard. *Soul Murder: The Effects of Childhood Abuse and Deprivation*. New York: Fawcett Columbine, 1989.

Shlain, Leonard. *Art and Physics: Parallel Visions in Space, Time, and Light*. New York: William Morrow and Company, 1991.

Shweder, Richard. *Thinking Through Cultures: Expeditions in Cultural Psychology*. Cambridge, MA: Harvard University Press, 1991.

Smith, Huston. *Beyond the Post-Modern Mind*. 2d ed. Wheaton, IL: The Theosophical Publishing House, 1989.

Spence, Donald. *The Freudian Metaphor*. New York: W. W. Norton & Company, 1987.

Stern, David. "Midrash." In *Contemporary Jewish Religious Thought*, ed. Arthur Cohen and Paul Mendes-Flohr. New York: Scribners, 1987.

Sue, Derald and David Sue. *Counseling the Culturally Different: Theory and Practice*. 2d ed. New York: John Wiley & Sons, 1990.

Tarnas, Richard. *The Passion of the Western Mind: Understanding the Ideas that Have Shaped Our World View*. New York: Ballantine, 1991.

Tartar, Maria. *The Hard Facts of the Grimms' Fairy Tales*. Princeton: Princeton University Press, 1987.

Tower, Cynthia Crosson. *Understanding Child Abuse and Neglect*. Boston: Allyn and Bacon, 1989.

Tracy, David. *Plurality and Ambiguity*. San Francisco: Harper & Row, 1987.

Van Doren, Charles. *A History of Knowledge: Past, Present, and Future*. New York: Ballantine Books, 1991.

Visotzky, Burton. *Reading the Book: Making the Bible a Timeless Text*. New York: Doubleday, 1991.

Waskow, Arthur. "God's Body, the Midrashic Process, and the Embodiment of Torah." In *Body and Bible: Interpreting and Experiencing Biblical Narratives*, ed. Bjorn Krondorfer. Philadelphia: Trinity Press International, 1992.

Watzlawick, Paul. *The Language of Change: Elements of Therapeutic Communication*. New York: Basic Books, 1978.

Watzlawick, Paul, Janet Beavin Bavelas, and Don Jackson. *Pragmatics of Human Communication: A Study of Interactional Patterns, Pathologies, and Paradoxes*. New York: W. W. Norton & Company, 1967.

Watzlawick, Paul and John Weakland, ed. *The Interactional View: Studies at the Mental Research Institute, Palo Alto, 1965-1974*. New York: W. W. Norton & Company, 1977.

Watzlawick, Paul, John Weakland, and Richard Fisch. *Change: Principles of Problem Formation and Problem Resolution*. New York: W. W. Norton & Company, 1974.

White, Michael. "Deconstruction and Therapy." *Dulwich Centre Newsletter* 3 (1991): 30.

_____. "Pseudo-encopresis: From Avalanche to Victory, From Vicious to Virtuous Cycles." In *Selected Papers*. Adelaide: Dulwich Centre Publications, 1989.

White, Michael and David Epston. *Narrative Means to Thera-peutic Ends.* New York: W. W. Norton & Company, 1990.

Wolf, Fred Alan. *Taking the Quantum Leap: The New Physics for Nonscientists.* San Francisco: Harper & Row, 1981.

Wolpe, David. *The Healer of Shattered Hearts: A Jewish View of God.* New York: Henry Holt and Co., 1990.

Woodham-Smith, Cecil. *The Great Hunger: Ireland 1845-1849.* New York: Old Town Books, 1962.

Zeki, Semir. "The Visual Image in Mind and Brain." *Scientific American 267,* no. 3 (September 1992).

Zipes, Jack. *The Brothers Grimm: From Enchanted Forests to the Modern World.* New York: Routledge, Chapman, and Hall, 1988.

_____. *Fairy Tales and the Art of Subversion: The Classical Genre for Children and the Process of Civilization.* New York: Methuen, 1988.

Index